Surviving Becky(s)

Race and Education in the Twenty-First Century

Series Editors

Kenneth J. Fasching-Varner, Louisiana State University;
Roland Mitchell, Louisiana State University; and
Lori Latrice Martin, Louisiana State University

This series asks authors and editors to consider the role of race and education, addressing questions such as "how do communities and educators alike take on issues of race in meaningful and authentic ways?" and "how can education work to disrupt, resolve, and otherwise transform current racial realities?" The series pays close attention to the intersections of difference, recognizing that isolated conversations about race eclipse the dynamic nature of identity development that play out for race as it intersects with gender, sexuality, socioeconomic class, and ability. It welcomes perspectives from across the entire spectrum of education from Pre-K through advanced graduate studies, and it invites work from a variety of disciplines, including counseling, psychology, higher education, curriculum theory, curriculum and instruction, and special education.

Recent Titles in Series

Surviving Becky(s)

Pedagogies for Deconstructing Whiteness and Gender

Edited by
Cheryl E. Matias

LEXINGTON BOOKS
Lanham • Boulder • New York • London

Published by Lexington Books
An imprint of The Rowman & Littlefield Publishing Group, Inc.
4501 Forbes Boulevard, Suite 200, Lanham, Maryland 20706
www.rowman.com

6 Tinworth Street, London SE11 5AL, United Kingdom

British Library Cataloguing in Publication Information Available

Library of Congress Cataloging-in-Publication Data Available

ISBN 978-1-4985-8762-4 (cloth)
ISBN 978-1-4985-8763-1 (electronic)

This book is dedicated to gramellie.

Your activism for equity in education will never be forgotten.

Contents

Acknowledgments

No book is ever a project solely mused upon by the self. Indeed, it takes a village. As such, I first want to acknowledge the many contributors to this project beyond what was published. I hear your pain. I see your soul. With over 100 initial submissions to this project, I honor all those courageous authors who took the time and effort to write their truths. I hope and pray healing extends to you and your family, and that we remain connected throughout the years.

Without my *pamilya*, I am nowhere. They are my rock. They are my reason for being. They are my motivation. It took a devastating experience professionally to realize where my true loyalties reside. Thank you for always standing by my side and for having my back when I needed it most. I am so proud of how we stood strong after the storm, and I look forward to basking in the rainbows later.

To my scholar homies, you know who you are. The countless drinks, text ventings, and critical dialogues were not only personally healing; they were the single driving force that helped me complete this book. I could not have done this without you. Thank you for always having my back and pushing me to do better. You give me strength even when you all think I need none.

To Dra. Aurora Chang, thank you for lending your eye, heart, and expertise on this manuscript. I felt safe with you. That, in and of itself, is most telling.

To my "gramma," Elisa Maun Matias, though you departed from this earth before I could share these written words, the ideas have always been with you. I miss you dearly, but you will live on. I promise. I want it to be clear and written in stone that you were my inspiration for becoming a teacher.

To my mom, you are my life, and thank you for giving it to me.

Introduction

The term "Becky" is gaining popular parlance both in the informal critiques of the academy, specifically in the field of education, which is replete with white females, (see Matias & Nishi, 2017) and in the general public from BBQ Becky (see https://www.youtube.com/watch?v=Fh9D_PUe7QI) to security Becky (see https://www.youtube.com/watch?v=faI8kacPGbQ). Popular press articles, for example, characterize the different archetypes and behaviors of a Becky (see Harriot, 2017; Kelly, 2016), whereas scholars are critically examining the deleterious impact of how whiteness entangled with dynamics of gender, femininity, and innocence embodied in the white woman negatively impacts folks of color. In fact, as Accapadi (2007) asserts, white women occupy an interesting social echelon because as they are privileged in whiteness, they are oppressed in patriarchy. Yet, it is this precise understanding of her "one up-one down" social positioning where she draws from her whiteness even more so to gain some semblance of power. Therefore, the dynamics of race and gender are ever-present in the behaviors, rhetoric, and societal response of the popularized typology of a Becky. And, more deeply, because whiteness is her claim to fame, for lack of a better word, white women who embody the Becky will not only cling onto their whiteness in more nuanced, covert ways, they will also express whiteness as such, as well.

But who exactly embodies the Becky? Are all white women Beckys? Why study this archetype? That Becky is just another white woman who enacts her white privilege at the expense of people of color is popularly accepted. In fact, even Merriam-Webster Online Dictionary acknowledges the term and defines it as "a white woman who is ignorant of both her privilege and her prejudice" (see https://www.merriam-webster.com/words-at-play/words -were-watching-becky). That part is understood. Yet to leave the understanding of what constitutes a Becky to that simple reductive definition leaves

1

society no answer as to how to address her behaviors. Better yet, even before addressing it, one must be able to identify the behaviors of a Becky and how they operate as a way to further the racial oppression of people of color, particularly of Black people. Essentially, further exploration must be done to investigate how her privilege in whiteness connects to the racial oppression of people of color. For in the end, those enactments of her white privilege are at times deadly to people of color. Meaning, she need only to cry out and society falls to its knees, so to speak. One need not look any further than the murder of a fourteen-year-old African American boy, Emmett Till, to realize this murderous reality. Therefore, there is something very complex, very dangerous behind the façade of innocence so employed by Becky(s). And that, in and of itself, necessitates the study of the Becky.

However, before I dive more psychoanalytically into the portrait of a Becky, I offer my own desires to study Becky. Having explored and opened the field of the emotionality of whiteness in my first book, *Feeling White*, earning several distinct recognitions for my work in whiteness, and dedicating my professional life to the pursuit of a more racially humane society, I am preoccupied in finding ways to both understand the context of race while finding ways to elevate society toward a better coexistence. Throughout my tenure as a university professor, I have been bombarded with a plethora of stories, literature, and studies that explicate over and over again the atrocities groups of color experience under whiteness, white supremacy, and racism. As a scholar, such findings solidify my research trajectory. As a woman of faith, bearing witness to such stories and studies both disheartens me and serves as a determinant to continue the work. In soliciting chapters for this book alone, I bore witness to many people's struggles with surviving these dehumanizing behaviors. Some called to cry on my shoulder; others needed a space to vent out their rage. With over 100 submissions to the book itself, there clearly was a lot of pain out there. And, as I vulnerably accept the pains of how people survive racism, white supremacy, and whiteness, I am renewed in my dedication to alleviate that pain. Plainly, I do not do this work simply because it is fabulous to do so. Indeed, the real work of racial justice is rife with constant hate mail, threats, and ostracism, all of which my family and I have, and still, endured. Therefore, like most racially just scholar activists, I do this work as a forever commitment to do what I was first hired to do—bring racial justice to education and society.

As one Black woman critical race theorist once said to me, the prevalence of racial atrocities goes on and on and on and on. No doubt, this speaks to critical race theorist Derrick Bell's notion of the permanence of race. However, beyond nihilism, there is something prophetic in knowing that the issues of race have a permanence. In fact, I reframe this idea by acknowledging that race is a constant, a common denominator, a proven theorem. And, in reframing it this way, I recognize that there is something oddly familiar, predictable almost, about how the operations of race ensue, which then can be applied in how we, as a society, respond to them. Meaning, if we know that what goes up must come down as a constant, then we can manipulate variables in ways to play with this constant. For example, in this case, we can build aircraft or de/anti-gravitational chambers. With respect to race, manipulating variables means developing an arsenal of tools to disarm. In fact, my mentor, Danny Solórzano, one of the leading professors of Critical Race Theory in education at UCLA, always reminds his students of this fact: that research for research's sake is not worth doing if we cannot find tools we can use to make a better society. Abiding by his teachings, I, too, am always finding an arsenal of tools that we can engage with to disarm whiteness and protect our humanity.

Finally, as a former K–12 classroom teacher in both Los Angeles and New York City and having been a public school student in the greater Los Angeles area, the dynamics of race inside K–12 classrooms are near and dear to my heart. From watching my own Black and Brown friends drop out of school due to the lack of authentic care, love, and respect from their teachers to witnessing my own K–12 students, and their families, disrespected, uncared for, and unloved in a white educational system, my commitment to improving teaching and education writ large is unwavering. Now, as a university professor teaching and researching in the field of education, too often do I see this cyclic pattern of lovelessness. Though couched in en vogue terminologies of social justice or culturally responsiveness, I still see through their deception. In fact, what annoys me most is how radical concepts like multicultural education, culturally responsive teaching, or social justice, first conceptualized by scholars of color who directly addressed white supremacy and racism in education, get watered down by the ocular of whiteness that permeates the field of education. Since 2001, scholars like Christine Sleeter have announced the overwhelming presence of whiteness particularly in the field of teacher education; a field that prepares U.S. K–12 teachers. Although there have been great strides in hiring more professors of color with expertise on race, those same professors are still writing about not being accepted in the same field proclaiming itself to be a welcoming space. Some contributed to this book! Clearly, whiteness is still enacting. Now, in 2019, what are we doing about whiteness if we are still too afraid to discuss it within our own field? In fact, whiteness is not even a research category inside the largest, most premier professional educational organization, yet after each racial atrocity like the Charleston massacre, they issue a statement demanding more studies on racism be undertaken. Beyond saying the word race, are we too afraid to deal with the real issues of whiteness and white supremacy, especially during a time period when white national marches are publicly on the rise? I, for one, cannot turn a blind eye to harsh reality. As a racially just educator, I am forced to see. Beyond that, I am compelled to do something.

With understanding how I arrived at this work, I can now address my readers. I strategically offered up my personal stake to remind my readers, even if some are themselves white women, that I do not do this work simply to defame white women. No. To be clear, I do this work precisely because the behaviors need to stop. As such, for my white women readers, I ask that they engage with this book in a more personal manner. That is, if you believe yourself to be against racism, then use this book as a reflection of the behaviors of Becky and how might you be complicit. For my readers who have survived these kinds of behaviors, my hope for them is that they learn that: 1) they are not alone, 2) their humanity is recognized in these stories, 3) they understand more deeply how whiteness operates in their daily lives, 4) by understanding whiteness more deeply, they are better able to find tools to disarm whiteness, and 5) they can laugh a bit about the absurdity of it all.

In short, there must be a thorough, exhaustive portraiture of the Becky. Not only does she populate most of K–12 classrooms across the U.S., but she also occupies most of the positions inside departments of educations in higher education. And although there have been social, literary, and historical ruminations of the characterization of white women as Miss Ann,[1] the modern characterization of Becky is different and has no academic literature that explores: 1) the characterization of Becky, 2) why such characterization is relevant to education, and 3) how that characterization impacts the hope for racial justice in education. Plainly, to date, there exists no formal literature that formally explores the theoretical and practical implications of the Becky.

Yet, although there is no literature studying Becky(s) per se, the relevance of studying white women has been established. Frankenburg (1993), for example, explores the social construction of whiteness in white women and how that construction impacts race relations and racial identity. Vera & Gordan (2003), as another example, use Hollywood films to investigate depictions of whiteness. In fact, one chapter draws upon the film *Gone with the Wind* to illustrate the typology of white females in juxtaposition to Black mammies. Such a depiction then reinforces white female standards of beauty, purity, and innocence while juxtaposing that with the servitude of women of color to white women, particularly of Black women to white women. Furthermore, acknowledging that white women make up the majority of U.S. teachers, Hancock and Warren (2017) dedicate a whole book on the work white women must engage in to ensure a more nurturing and equitable education for the nation's majority of students of color. Finally, Godfrey (2003) further interrogates the oft association of innocence and sweetness to white women in her critical historical analysis of the "sweet little white girls" who vehemently reacted to the Little Rock Nine in 1957 post–*Brown v. Board of Education*. In her analysis she shows how the characterization of "sweet little white girls" left the vitriol, violence, and aggressive behaviors of white women during that time intact and uncovered. Clearly, the study of white women is nothing new, yet the particularities of the modern conceptualization of Becky are in order.

Therefore, this edited book is the first to survey the increasing phenomenon of *Beckyism*; the behaviors and rhetoric that Becky(s) engage in which uphold whiteness at the expense of people of color's humanity, dignity, and expertise. And since there is much confusion on who embodies the Becky, this book identifies characteristics that embody the Becky, why such an embodiment is a relevant phenomenon to explore, and how can utilizing this characterization help scholars, educators, students, and staff who are committed to diversity and inclusion understand how might racial and gender dynamics impact students, faculty, and staff of color working in predominantly white institutions (e.g., schools, universities, etc.).

However, because revealing racial and gender microaggressions are, at times, retaliatory, the book encouraged contributors to write their experiences with Becky(s) in fan fiction style. Fan fictions, as Preston (2013) suggests, are "those types of narrative writing that take existing fictional setting as the basis for further speculative fiction" (p. 9). Meaning, within each section are a few short stories that connect together via a theme. These themes explore how Becky(s) behave. Though these short stories have no citations, they are nonetheless pedagogical tools to teach about a particular behavior and how it impacts survivors. Therefore, this book is about learning pedagogies toward deconstructing whiteness and gender within Becky(s).

There were other reasons as to why this book utilizes stories instead of expository essays. First, stories are less threatening. As a woman faculty of color myself, I am not blinded by how whiteness operates. For example, in doing the work, I have often found that some whites, particularly Becky(s) themselves, negatively react to my scholarship. Instead of entertaining the argument, they refuse to simply hear the message altogether. They find ways to discredit the work by engaging in the century-old "belittling" maneuver. "This is just your story; just autobiographical," as if my story, as one of the few women of color in a predominantly white department, does not count. This is why I focus on the emotionalities of whiteness. It is precisely those very emotionalities that shut down the potential for racial understanding. I understand that it may seem tough to understand one was born into a system wrought with racial power and privilege, but the discomfort in learning just how that power and privilege impacts people of color does not parallel how people of color must survive under it. Therefore, writing these in fan fiction stories is, admittedly, a form of placating whiteness simply because the message will not be heard if the receiver refuses to listen. As such, a simple story will do.

Another reason for why I opted for collecting stories is that I want to return to the basics in Critical Race Theory (CRT): storytelling and parables (see Bell, 1992). In fact, one of my own tenure letters claimed that I needed to do more "traditional" race and whiteness work. As such, I return to the purpose of CRT counterstorytelling. Fortuitous is this approach, but in that I not only counter majoritarian stories (see Solórzano & Yosso, 2001), in doing so, I also shed light onto the mechanisms of whiteness and gender and their impact on people of color. The purpose here is not to vilify all white women. Instead, the goal is to highlight how behaviors, attitudes, emotions, rhetoric, and epistemological stances can, at times, mimic Becky(s) who, beyond their intention to do good and be liberal, engage in ways that ultimately exert whiteness. These exertions in turn are traumatic, passive aggressive, violent, or simply counterintuitive to the goals of racial justice, antiracism, or educational equity.

Finally, the use of stories and anecdotal records is the common practice in the field of teaching. Meaning, teachers learn from other teachers through the use of stories. As such, this book draws from this informal process and utilizes it as a way to teach a lesson, moral, or principle of how Becky(s) behave. In fact, these stories do not stem from nowhere. Indeed, they are in much respect anecdotal. When asked if their stories related to their lived experiences with white women, 81.3 percent of the authors who responded to the post survey responded in affirmative. The remaining 18.8 percent claim their stories were a composite or amalgamation of the racial microaggressions they felt throughout their lives by white women. One author writes, "I see this story as connected to my personal experience working with white women in education."

Another writes, "While most of the incidences are based on my experiences, they are steeped within the context of this fictitious story, so I feel that the original instances are masked." Therefore, inasmuch as the stories were in some way based on their personal experiences with white women, the creative form of writing a story offered them some protection.

Though the stories did offer protection to some, it also offered an avenue for authors to create a moral to their story or engage in a topic creatively, which in the end, gave them more freedom and impact. One author writes, "It is interesting to use some of my own lived experiences in fiction form to express meaning in the educational space pertaining to racial issues." One author writes how she loved the return to traditional CRT parable and counterstorytelling. When asked why she even considered contributing, she writes the following:

I was very much attracted to the call because it was allowing for 1) a creative expression of how to talk about racism through a fictional story and 2) it was centering understanding/making sense of white women and the roles that they play in perpetuating white supremacy. I felt that as a contributor to the book, I would be able to use my creativity to talk about racism and white supremacy in ways that I felt would be useful as teaching tools and a means of spurring critical and needed discussions in the classroom. It allowed me to use popular culture to infuse a story of white supremacy within a story of science fiction. Furthermore, the call reminded me of Bell's parables such as Space Traders, which presents the reader with an ethical and moral dilemma based on racism and the realism of racism, and in recalling how I made sense of Bell's work, I felt that a creative story would have more impact than a traditional academic journal article or book chapter.

Another writer echoes this sentiment when she writes about how fan fiction allows for more freedom. She writes the following:

I submitted to "Surviving Becky" as I was struck by the possibility of scholarly freedom the project entailed. That is to say, using fiction as a medium to articulate the blunt realities of white supremacy and dominance, moves beyond the limitations and rigidity of Western forms of scholarship and knowledge production. Relatedly, I was excited as such a project aligns well with the intellectual and political projects of Critical Race Theorists such as Derrick Bell and Richard Delgado.

Other authors write about how by engaging in stories we can be more creative with our pedagogical impact. One writes, "I thought it was a creative way to provide a social and educational commentary on a phenomenon that women of color experience pretty much daily" while another writes, "We thought this was a creative way to critique white supremacy from an intersectionality lens." Clearly, writing stories are not just for story's sake. As my mentor stated above, the stories in and of themselves become the tools that can help people learn; they become the pedagogical strategy.

As aforementioned, in my own experiences, writing has been both traumatizing and cathartic. This sentiment was shared by most of my authors, as well. One author writes, "The process was more difficult and also cathartic than I had originally imagined." Another writes, "It was cathartic. Sometimes things that happen in your department feel like a big secret that you can't tell anyone because you're not always sure who has your back. But it was nice to be able to just be honest." Still another writes, "I found the experience cathartic and freeing. While most of the incidences are based on my experiences, they are steeped within the context of this fictitious story, so I feel that the original instances are masked. Thus, unless you know the truth of my experience, I do not believe one will be able to readily see me within my real life context. So, it will be liberating to see my survival for all to see from the safety afforded by the cover of the story and further enclosed by the creative genre. Kudos to the editor for coming up with this idea." Finally, another author shares this sentiment and writes, "It was definitely cathartic being able to have some distance from the feelings of the real experience but also taking those feelings and inserting them into the characters in a way that I wish I was understood in that moment. I appreciate the opportunity to be able to control the narrative because often that feels like a space where there is little or no control."

Two authors discussed how writing the story was therapeutic. One writes, "It is therapeutic to share experiences that can be frustrating or burdensome. Writing this chapter allowed me to creatively share some of those experiences and hopefully help someone else in the process." Another writes, "Creating this story was therapeutic! Developing this story was absolutely liberating as it made me imagine a world that occupy people of African Diaspora that rejected the notion of being 'simply happy or content' with a presence with mediocrity of a White man or woman. As a person who is of African descent, we do not entertain this from people who share our cultural background." Clearly, both found the process as a way to heal from their past transgressions with white women.

Another author describes how therapeutic *and* traumatizing it was for her. She writes the following:

> In many ways this process was both traumatic and therapeutic. It was traumatic because it brought up some suppressed memories of oppressive incidents involving Becky's. It was therapeutic because we had an opportunity to process those painful memories. Additionally, because this was science fiction we had the ability to take control of our story and write our own conclusions.

However, in the end 100 percent of the authors who contributed to this book claimed that they are happy with their short story. One author writes, "I'm just grateful this book finally exists in the world and I'm honored to get to be a part of it." Another writes the following:

> Thank you, for giving me the opportunity to participate in this scholarly and highly creative activity. This project is a critical moment for me in my career because it allowed me to experience the intersection of scholarship, creativity, and personal self. How often, if ever, do scholars in the academy experience anything like this?

This project then was not simply to share stories of white women behaving badly. Instead the book is a project of the heart; for though the stories are wrought with pain and trauma of my authors, they are also written with courage and hope for the better. And to honor their survival, I do their courage justice by writing an introduction for each section that delves deeply into one of the characteristics of a Becky. After each section there are guiding questions readers can ask others or of themselves to more deeply understand the behaviors of Becky(s). Of the 19 stories in this book, there were 8 major categories. These categories should not be read as independent of each other, but rather as a continuum of each, for one informs the other. These categories include the following: Becky(s) as Colonizers, Becky(s) as Weaponized Emotionalities, Becky(s) as Entitlement and Privilege, Becky(s) as Terrors, Becky(s) as Presume Experts/Authority, Becky(s) as Allies/Victims?, Becky(s) as Violent, and Becky(s) as Manipulators and Gaslighters.

The portraiture of a Becky is of grave importance because the process of her characterization is connected to the dehumanization of people of color. She is more than just a term. Indeed, she embodies a phenomenon. Admittedly, I first playfully engaged the terminology with scholars like Michael Dumas on social media as a way to vent out the behaviors of white women in a field that is replete with them. But to be clear, I do not in any way support studies like critical Becky studies, for the term Becky itself is simply a characterization of a white woman who engages in privilege and power in deleterious ways. If there are to be more formal studies on white women, I hope this exploration of what characterizes a Becky motivates more formal studies of white women and not become the presumed theory that drives the study itself. As a cautious scholar, I understand characterizations can make light of a more serious situation. Sensitive to that, I take every precaution to say that these stories are based on lived experiences and are thus noteworthy of telling but are not in and of themselves units of analysis unless more formally applied.

In the end, I am a teacher, a mother, and a racially just activist. In these roles, my primary goal in life then becomes to educate for racial justice with love and humanity. My hope for this book is that it allows people of color a moment to laugh, cry, and shiver knowing they are not alone in experiencing the brutalities that Becky(s) engage in. Simultaneously, I truly hope that those white women who embody some of these characteristics realize they do so and instead of further relying on the inhumane condition of whiteness, they turn around and say, "I'm sorry. How can I do better?" a seemingly simple task that nonetheless acknowledges the humanity of those they hurt most. Though such a task seems nearly impossible especially since many of us are still waiting for that apology, I continue to hold out for hope, because without it, there is no reason for this book.

NOTE

1. See https://en.wikipedia.org/wiki/Miss_Ann, https://www.theroot.com/miss
-ann-s-revenge-1790857709, http://www.northendagents.com/miss-anns-seduction
-black-men-problematic-white-women-champion-tiffani-jones/, https://www.npr
.org/2013/09/16/221452333/introducing-miss-anne-the-white-women-of-a-black
-renaissance.

REFERENCES

Frankenberg. R. (1993). *The Social Construction of White Women, Whiteness Mat-ters*. Minneapolis: University of Minnesota Press.

Godfrey, P. (2004). "Sweet little (white) girls"? Sex and fantasy across the color line and the contestation of patriarchal white supremacy. *Equity & Excellence in Education, 37*(3), 204–18.

Harriot, M. (2017, August 29). "The 5 Types of Becky." *The Root.* Retrieved from https://www.theroot.com/the-five-types-of-becky-1798543210.

Hancock, S. & Warren, C. (2016). *White women's work: Examining the intersectionality of teaching, identity, and race*. North Carolina: Information Age Publishing.

Kelly, C. (2016, April 27). "What does Becky mean? Here's the history behind Beyoncé's 'Lemonade' lyric that sparked a firestorm." USA Today. Retrieved from https://www.usatoday.com/story/life/entertainthis/2016/04/27/what-does-becky
-mean-heres-history-behind-beyoncs-lemonade-lyric-sparked-firestorm/83555996/.

Matias, C. E. (2016). *Feeling White: Whiteness, Emotionality, and Education.* The Netherlands: Sense Publishers.

Matias, C. E. & Nishi, N. (2017) "Becky Please" in S.Hancock & C. Warren (Eds.). (2016). *White women's work: Examining the intersectionality of teaching, identity, and race*. North Carolina: Information Age Publishing.

Preston, J. (2014). *Whiteness in academia: Counter-stories of betrayal and resistance*. Cambridge, UK: Cambridge Scholars Publishing.

Sleeter, C. E. (2001). Preparing teachers for culturally diverse schools: Research and the overwhelming presence of whiteness. *Journal of teacher education, 52*(2), 94–106.

Vera, H. & Gordon, A. (2003). *Screen Saviors: Hollywood Fictions of Whiteness.* Lanham, MA: Rowman & Littlefield Publishers, Inc.

Section One

Becky(s) as Colonizers

A foreigner, having come to a land by the accidents of history, he has succeeded not merely in creating a space for himself but in also taking away that of the inhabitant, granting himself astounding privileges to the detriment of those rightfully entitled to them. And this is not by virtue of local laws, which in a certain way legitimize this inequality by tradition, but by upsetting the established rules and substituting his own. He thus appears doubly unjust. He is a privileged being and an illegitimately privileged one; that is, a usurper . . . he knows, in his own eyes as well as those of the his victim, that he is a usurper" (Memmi, 1965, p. 9).

Albert Memmi's (1965) portraiture of a colonizer as "illegitimately privileged," "a usurper" astutely describes the ill-fated, moreover, manipulative relationship between colonizer and colonized under a state of racist colonization. Yet, when picturing a usurper as one who wields power, one is quick to think of a man. In fact, Memmi further describes this colonizer in masculine ways. In his assertions, he states, "*He* enjoys the preference and respect of the colonized themselves . . . " (emphasis added, p. 12), "should *he* ask for or have need of anything, *he* need only show *his* face to be prejudged favorably by those in the colony who count" (emphasis added, p.12), or "The colonizer partakes of an elevated world from which *he* automatically reaps the privileges" (emphasis added, p. 13). In all these assertions and ruminations, the state of colonization and the colonizer himself are masculinized, as if men are the only usurpers of this world. But, what of she? What is the role of white women in enterprises of colonization? For far too long, white women have been depicted as innocent, so innocent that their mere honor was historically defended in unjust, inhumane ways. In fact, their honor has been the bastion of white supremacy and Black oppression. The lives (and death) of Emmett Till or the Central Park Five are just a few cases whereby justice, legality, and human rights were violated upon the false claims of Black men threatening white women's chastity. Clearly, this innocence inscribed onto white women has real racial ramifications for people of color, particularly for Black men. In fact, the authors of one of the chapters in this section point out, "We want readers to realize how damaging Becky[s] can be even though they appear to be harmless. Further, we would like people to realize how Black men are negatively impacted by Becky[s] in academia and beyond."

The so-called innocence of white women must continue to be interrogated. Jones-Rogers (2019), for example, describes how past journalists oftentimes depicted southern white women as unaware of the atrocities embedded in slavery, claiming that white women were shielded from the nasty business of slavery, leaving white women ignorant and blameless. Yet, in analyzing legal and financial documents, military and government correspondences, and narrative accounts, Jones-Roger proves that white women "not only witnessed the most brutal features of slavery, they took part in them, profited from them, and defended them" (p. X). As such the colonial project of slavery was sustained not only by the master, but also by the mistress as well. For how can hundreds of years of colonial slavery, anti-Black racism, and human genocide happen with almost half the population claiming blindness to it? This sentiment eerily echoes Bonilla-Silva's (2006) question of how there have been hundreds of years of racism without racists? The answer is there haven't. Active players were required to keep the colonial enterprise alive. Therefore, claiming innocence becomes a strategic maneuver to relinquish, worse yet, mask one's culpability in the trade.

That white women can be, at times, colonizers is oftentimes such a far-fetched concept that to even utter it produces cognitive dissonance. In my own experiences in the field of teacher education, for example, merely positing that perhaps white teachers in urban schools are not actually saving their students of color brought so much cognitive dissonance we had to end class. Yet it is precisely this dissonance that causes me to wonder, why is this so foreign to accept? What is the pre-existing condition that makes this notion of complicit white women so difficult to accept? The assumption of white women's innocence is a proxy for feigning innocence based on an epistemology of racial ignorance (per Mills, 2007) and, in actuality is a weaponized strategy to uphold the colonial enterprise under the guise of benevolence. In fact, similarly, President McKinley delivered the "Benevolent Assimilation" speech to convince the public and colonized Filipinos that U.S. colonization of the Philippines was not only for the best interest of the colonized, but also a moral and benevolent endeavor for the U.S. Re-appropriating colonization as a moral, benevolent engagement masks the true strategic maneuver of what colonization does to a country: extraction of natural resources, forced labor, and historical pillage. Colonization is sold as a benefit to the colonized when, in fact, it is always at the expense of the colonized.

The stories in this section explore how white women engage in colonizer-like behaviors, oftentimes suppressing the humanity of people of color and white supporters (allies) alike. Although the behaviors in the stories are aggrandized as hyperboles whether depicted as a futuristic alien invasion or a fantastical queen with superpowers, they nonetheless are reminiscent of the behaviors commonly experienced by people of color in our current society. To note, regardless of white women's intentionality—though intentions indeed matter—these colonizing behaviors are weapons used to harm or control the actions, beliefs, and free will of people of color. Furthermore, oftentimes these Beckys will also gaslight their victims forcing them to believe that they do this because of love. Seemingly a twisted sadomasochistic relationship (see Matias & Allen, 2013), these Becky(s) nonetheless hold on to these unhealthy, manipulative connections to people of color because in the end, it gives her some of the power that is already inscribed in a colonial white supremacist society.

Becky(s) as colonizer is then nothing more than, as Memmi (1965) suggests above, a usurper, who participates in an enterprise that racially stratifies society to her own benefit. Specifically, to compensate for her gender oppression in a patriarchal system, she aligns herself (whether consciously or subconsciously) with whiteness, knowing that her participation in racial supremacy grants her a piece of the American apple pie. Unlike the depictions of male colonizers who boldly and forcefully demand subjection of the colonized, Becky(s) engages the colonized in emotionally and psychologically manipulative ways, gaslighting them to question whether Becky is truly helping or actually harming; much like the sly elderly witch convincing a potential victim to satiate their burning appetite with a bite of the shiny red apple. Meaning, Becky(s) as Colonizers come in pretending to save or help out when in the end, the apple still kills. Though the behaviors may not be as intentional as those of the witch who is willfully trying to dominate, they are nonetheless damaging. Over and over again, Becky(s) reiterates her innocence in victimhood. Like white females who teach in urban schools, make false claims of sexual harassment against Black boys, or characterize themselves as victims of "aggressive" women of color, Becky(s) as Colonizers engages in tactics that usurp power and control over folks of color, and sadly, more precisely over women of color.

REFERENCES

Bonilla-Silva, E. (2010). *Racism Without Racists: Color-Blind Racism & Racial Inequality in Contemporary America.* Lanham, MD: Rowman & Littlefield.

Jones-Rogers, S. (2019). *They Were Her Property: White Women as Slave Owners in the American South.* New Haven, CT: Yale University Press.

Matias, C. E, & Allen, R. L. (2013). Loving Whiteness to Death: Sadomasochism, Emotionality, and the Possibility of Humanizing Love. *Berkeley Review of Education,* 4(2). http://dx.doi.org/10.5070/B84110066.

Memmi, Albert. (1965). *The colonizer and the colonized.* New York :Orion Press.

Mills, C. (2007). "White ignorance." Sullivan, S., & Tuana, N. (Eds.). *Race and epistemologies of ignorance.* New York: SUNY Press.

Chapter One

The Makeover not the Takeover

Surviving the Becky Coup D'Etat

Darryl A. Brice and Derrick R. Brooms

It is a cold fall night in the Pacific Northwest as Professor Baldwin sits in his office at his desk grading sociology deviance assignments. He has been grading for the past two hours and is starting to experience the law of diminishing returns. The first paper only took 15 minutes to grade, but now he has been staring at this last paper for 45 minutes. "Darn, I'm so tired," he thought, "but I got to get this done. Students are waiting for their grades." As his mind flirts with the hope of sleep, he notices his office light flickers, his desk lamp cuts off, and he hears a knocking sound on the wall in his office behind a stack of books. Startled, he quickly gets up and removes the books off from his shelf. "What is that knocking?" he wonders aloud. Running his hand on the back of the bookcase, he finds a loose panel in the dated wood-grained wall. As he removes the panel, a box made out of some kind of black metal shoots out and lands in front of him. "What the?!" He reaches out, touches the box, and immediately starts to hear the voice of W. E. B. DuBois relaying this message.

"If you are hearing this message then you are successfully receiving my message from the future. Though I am not DuBois, I know he is the most influential figure in your career as a sociologist. Therefore, I chose his voice to pay homage to a Black scholar who is too often denied. This message is a warning of what is to come if humanity doesn't recognize the destructive nature of a particular character. Who I am is not important. But you must hear my story. There are visitors on this earth who are trying to erase all memory of their existence. They first arrived around the year 2085. The planet was in shambles because global leaders ignored the threats posed by global warming. Structures that had stood for centuries were falling apart, roads were barely traversable, and most of the population was struggling to find enough food to eat. As this was happening, astronomical amounts of CO_2 in the atmosphere started attracting illegal aliens to earth. At first our humanity hoped that these new visitors would help because they had advanced technologies that could remove CO_2 from the atmosphere, thus lowering the core temperature of the earth and making it habitable for all life forms again. These visitors met with a few global leaders, who all happened to be white men. These leaders kept the visitors' first contact with earth secretive because they didn't want to incite global panic. These leaders claimed they discovered the new technology that not only restored the planet but also created jobs and eventually returned the planet into a fully functioning white supremacist society. What these white men didn't know was that the visitors were not interested in keeping these white men in power long term. Instead of white men running the world, the visitors placed white women in these hallowed leadership positions."

At this point, Professor Baldwin was starting to feel overwhelmed and a bit dizzy, but despite this he could not release the black box. The voice continued. "I know that you have a lot of questions, but this is a one-way communication. I did not have access to the more advanced technology that would allow us to have a conversation across time periods. But, I can see and feel your emotions. I chose you to receive this message for several reasons. One, I, too, am a Black male that has had a lot of contact with problematic white women. I believe you refer to them as 'Beckys.' This moniker stuck and they are called Beckys in my era also. What you don't know yet is how powerful these Beckys will become in the future. They seem innocent now, but they have in the past and will in the future wreak havoc. Think of Emmett Till. Second, as a Black sociologist you are trained to question everything, especially how past events impact the present. I am now asking you to think about how present events impact the future."

"But why favor white women?" pondered Professor Baldwin. But once he utters this question aloud, Professor Baldwin realized he already knew the answer. White women possessed both insider and outsider status among the people of earth. On the one hand, their whiteness granted them many privileges that People of Color did not have in society. On the other hand, they had to deal with oppression and marginalization because of institutionalized sexism and patriarchy. This made white women the perfect subjects for the visitors' colonization training program.

The voice continued, "These women had access to both white men and People of Color, which allowed them the ability to gain the trust of and spy on both groups. The visitors' entire plan was to set up a colonial model so they could extract and use the CO_2 produced by the excessive burning of fossil fuels. They had been studying humans since the beginning of time, and they were aware that white men could not be trusted because of the years of lies, broken treaties, and wars that created savage inequalities throughout the entire world. Also, People of Color couldn't be trusted in a leadership role in this colonial model because too many of us had been directly involved in anticolonial movements. Therefore, white women were perfect candidates for the visitors. White women started getting recruited to training centers based on their political in-betweenness to everything. No one really knows what happened in these training centers, but they were set up as paid internships for white women who wanted to take leadership positions in the government, academia, and many other vital institutions in the United States. The process was known as Becky Educational Training or B.E.T. My research showed that B.E.T. in your time period used to be about and for Black people. Interesting development. What I do know is that the white women that made it through the training process were given genetic enhancement. For example, the ones that were sent to colonize Communities of Color were even given curvier body types so they could blend in and attract mates from these communities and infiltrate the family structure."

The voice from the future could feel that Professor Baldwin was having problems believing this could happen at all, so he approached the topic another way. "As a sociologist you are well aware of the Thomas Theorem which suggests that if you perceive something as real, then it is real in its consequences." Professor Baldwin nodded in agreement. "Well, imagine these Beckys with genetically enhanced abilities coupled with their insider status slowly supplanting white male leaders over a period of 50 years. People in the future genuinely believed that these women were worthy of their positions and that they would look out for marginalized and oppressed people because some of them had similar experiences." The voice stopped and there was a long awkward pause. Then he started again, "Oh, you are not having problems believing that Beckys run the world in the future?! You are struggling with the whole alien/visitor concept?!"

The voice knew certain facts about Professor Baldwin's life and decided to pull some memories from the depths of the Professor's mind as evidence. All of a sudden Professor Baldwin started remembering a time where he was sitting in his high school religion class and one of his classmates asked the teacher, a priest named Father Mike, if he believed in aliens. The class would regularly try to get Father Mike off topic so they could waste time and never get to the lesson. However, this day Father Mike was sharp and surprised everyone with his answer. Father Mike went on to explain that he did believe in aliens because he believed in God. He said that humans who didn't believe in aliens were egocentric because they thought they were the only intelligent beings that God created in the entire universe. He added that there are species of animals on earth that we hadn't discovered and yet many believe that in the whole universe we are the only intelligent beings. Remembering this, Professor Baldwin was really feeling disoriented. He had buried that memory in the deep recesses of his brain, almost forgetting it happened. The voice apologized. "Sorry for accessing your memories like that, but you need to believe what I am telling you." The voice could feel that Professor Baldwin was starting to understand.

"Now that you believe what I am saying, you need to know how to identify the most dangerous forms of Beckys that you encounter on a regular basis. Beckys can be hard to identify. All Beckys are white women but not all white women are Beckys. I am going to access your memories again to show you that you work with some of the most volatile types of Beckys. You have to think about them as land mines because they appear innocuous, but they are very dangerous. You are dealing with figurative land mines, but in the future these Beckys are literally volatile. The first type you have to be on the look-out for is the RDLB. I'll explain what that means in a bit." At this moment the voice stopped, and Professor Baldwin was suddenly in a trance-like state where he was remembering his interactions with a white woman co-worker. Except the memory was more like he was reliving multiple interactions with this colleague. The woman named Denise liked to talk about hip-hop and she even taught Black history classes at the college. When he first met her, she asked Professor Baldwin if he liked Tupac or Biggie. He dismissed this as a white woman trying hard to fit in. She had a Black boyfriend that she liked to parade around campus in efforts to "prove" that she wasn't like other white people. She appeared harmless on the surface, but Professor Baldwin was starting to realize that she was the best code switcher he had ever witnessed. He couldn't believe he didn't recognize this before. When she was around white counterparts she sounded and behaved just like they did. She flipped her hair and would insert the word "like" into sentences where it didn't belong. When she was around Black colleagues she knew and correctly used African American Vernacular English better than some Black people, and seamlessly drew from a range of Black cultural references. He was starting to realize how dangerous these types of Beckys can be in a professional setting. Professor Baldwin remembered how many People of Color trusted and looked out for Denise, but Denise never reciprocated. Instead, she advanced her own career while many of her colleagues of color remained stuck in their positions. The voice started to speak again. "If you haven't figured it out yet, RDLB stands for Rachel Dolezal Landmine Becky." The Professor started laughing, but the voice became very stern. "The reason we call this type of Becky RDLB is because the visitors patterned all of the future Beckys of this type off of Rachel Dolezal. In my time period, this type of Becky land mine can physically transform herself into a Black woman. She can change her straight hair into an afro; her thin lips become fuller; her body becomes full figured; and she can vary the shade of her skin to match the complexion that is most desirable for the occasion. There are people married to these RDLBs that have no idea their wives are white women. More importantly, they hold top decision-making positions in society as Black women, but in reality these women are RDLBs."

Professor Baldwin gasped. He was starting to understand how insidious the Becky problem was in his time period. The voice went on to the next type of Becky the professor needed to keep an eye out for. "You must be on the lookout for Waterworks Landmine Becky (WLB). This Becky uses crying as her weapon of choice." At this point the professor was having another one those experiential memories. This time he was in a meeting geared toward professors of color when a white woman named Sharon showed up. This was not a problem until many of her colleagues of color started talking about the racial microaggressions they dealt with in and out of the classroom. At this point Sharon interjected and started to tear up as she went off on a diatribe about how no one realizes her hardships at work because she grew up poor and was a single parent. Of course, she refused to consider the benefits of whiteness in her life. This diatribe derailed a productive conversation about race in a meeting designed to talk about race. Many of the attendees tried to comfort Sharon, which caused the focus of the meeting to be about the WLB. The DuBoisian voice snatched the Professor back from his memory and said, "If you think this is bad, in the future WLB is enhanced to shoot lasers out her eyes instead of tears. If you try to expose issues of race, the visitors' existence, or anything deemed unworthy of discussion they will shoot lasers from their eyes that completely evaporate whatever they hit. This was one of the genetic enhancements that Beckys received in B.E.T.

"Another type of Becky you will encounter is Confrontational Landmine Becky. Confrontational Becky always interacts with you as if everything you do is a problem, as though you were always in need of accommodation and are the main problem to everything. This aggressiveness will baffle most because these Beckys usually have lower-ranked positions within institutions and yet they are responsible for policing your movements. I know you don't like this feeling but hold on because you need to see it for yourself." Professor Baldwin was thrusted back into his first year of teaching at the college. He remembered coming into work feeling proud about earning a job as a college professor because he was a first-generation college student that now held an esteemed faculty position. He was feeling great about this accomplishment until the administrative assistant, who was a CLB, asked him who he was looking for when he entered his office building. More importantly, she asked this and followed up with informing him that she was calling security. For some reason, she could not understand that he was a professor and he was just trying to get to his office. He explained that he was a new faculty member. Upon hearing this she demanded to see his ID. As a new faculty member who wasn't sure if this was standard practice or not, he showed her his ID and kept walking. He knew that this didn't seem right and that this interaction really pissed him off, but he wasn't sure anything could be done about it. This was another painful memory that he had suppressed. The voice brought him back, "In the future, CLB's can literally bite your head off—similar to the movie 'Venom.' Their mouth can extend open like a snake, and they can consume a head that is five times the size of their mouths. After they do this, the visitors collect the remaining pieces of the body. I am not sure what they are used for. The small portion of us that know about the visitors think they use the bodies for fuel or food.

"The fourth type of Becky that you must be aware of is Interrupting Landmine Becky. Interrupting Landmine Becky may operate in ways similar to CLB and WLB and, in fact, may use confrontation or waterworks in order to interrupt. Sometimes a verbal confrontation undermines a conversation or decreases the likelihood of advancing a point. These confrontations are mostly subtleties and infrequently overt and loud confrontations. Instead, they are to operate in a stealth-like fashion, often leaving those impacted unsure of how they were interrupted. Similarly, ILB can use tears as an interruption. Beyond intent, the impact of tears is that they have the power to extract and draw attention away from the issue at hand and instead move the focus of attention to Beckys. But, the interruptions are still even more than this. Sometimes the interruptions are offered in forms that seem like alignment—at least verbalized that way, but they still operate in incongruent ways. The interruptions are filtered through a particular perspective where ILB may ask questions about clarity, she may offer that she doesn't see the situation based on her perspective, or might even suggest that your viewpoint is off and you're reading into the situation 'too much.' In each of these ways, Becky acts as both an interrupter and a supporter. This weaving in and out of conversations and seemingly supporting multiple angles—that of the system and sometimes your own—can be difficult to decipher. Essentially, you begin to doubt your own reality because her constant interruptions lead to gaslighting. And to make matters worse, the future Beckys are genetically enhanced to engage in mind bending whereby they can infiltrate your mind and bend some of the ideas so much so that you cannot even remember your truth anymore."

"The final type of Becky that you have to navigate is the 'But . . . ' Landmine Becky. BLB operates in ways that play on interruptions and often can subvert conversations, discussions, and even progress. BLB engages in conversations well beyond areas of their own professed expertise, yet positions themselves as central figures in the conversation and focus. In classic style, BLB sometimes enter conversations by acknowledging their lack of knowledge about a particular subject, issue or phenomenon and yet still feels compelled to assert themselves, their viewpoints, and their perceptions into the conversation." As the voice continued talking, Professor Baldwin's mind drifted off as he recalled a recurring instance used consistently as an entrée into conversations: "This is not my area of expertise, but . . . " He seemed stunned in the frequency of these occurrences. The voice got his attention again. "While Becky might acknowledge shortcomings and lack of insight, BLB still has the confidence, sense of power, and entitlement to assert herself in the conversation. As mentioned, BLB interrupts the discussion, often shifts the focus, and at the same time repositions herself as simultaneously lacking knowledge and possessing knowledge as if she has critical insights to offer." As Professor Baldwin thought about his own experiences, BLB claimed to be an ally in a number of instances; however, he recalled her undermining of his (and other people's) knowledge really contradicted such sentiments. The voice forewarned the professor, "While BLB often uses words in covert and double-meaning ways that may seem like Interrupting Landmine Becky, it is most important that you watch how BLBs moves. Oftentimes their use of 'but' is intended to reposition them for a better attack because what they do is always aligned with their own best interest at heart."

As he listened to the different typologies of Beckys, Professor Baldwin was able to move again while still being linked to the voice so he began composing an email detailing strategies to employ to protect himself and others from Becky landmines. He wrote that these strategies should be used with caution. The first strategy he jotted down was WWBD, an acronym for What Would Becky Do. This was akin to the What Would Jesus Do phenomenon (WWJD) that was popular in the 1990s. The point of this WWJD trend was to remind Christians to behave in a Christ-like manner. WWJD was regularly found printed on rubber wristbands and was a visual reminder of how one should behave. Similarly, Professor Baldwin wrote a note to have wristbands printed with WWBD on it to remind people to be on the lookout for Beckys. The professor considered that taking the moral high ground with Beckys was largely a waste of time because they were not concerned with acting equitably with People of Color. He wrote, "If you are encountered by a Becky, just remember that there are some instances where it is appropriate to fight fire with fire. Therefore, when Beckys ask or rather demand that you do something, all you need to do is ask, What Would Becky Do. If Becky would respond to that same request she makes of you, then that is how you should respond. If Becky likes to CC a bunch of people on an email that was initially between the two of you, then that is how you should respond too."

Professor Baldwin also realized the WWBD wristband can be effective for one more reason. The wristband also can be a good distraction tool. The voice chimed in and added, "One characteristic that all types of Beckys share is that they are meddlesome. So, there is a good chance a Becky will ask you what WWBD means and you can tell them it stands for What Would Bunnies Do. The benefit of using the bunny acronym is that many Beckys have a lot of concern for environmental issues. This concern doesn't usually extend to Colleagues of Color, but they will engage you in hours-long conversations about recycling and composting." While Professor B reflected on these points, the voice said, "You could tell them What Would Bunnies Do reminds you of how you need to act to preserve the environment. One mention of the environment will usually send Beckys off on a tangent and they will forget what they were going to bother you about. You have to be careful using this tactic because it could lead to Beckys talking to you about environmental problems every time they see you. You might even end up on a listserv about the environment. So, you can't appear too enthusiastic when they start down this path. Say what you need to say and GET OUT! If you don't you may find yourself on a weekend trip in the middle of the woods with white people bidding on who gets to control your body while you remain in the sunken place."

At this point, the psychic connection was starting to weaken. The voice said, "Our time is running short, but I have a few final pieces of advice. You need to connect with other People of Color and form maroon societies throughout the world. This way you can disseminate necessary strategies. You also need to use different forms of communication that are not easily detected. Think about how our ancestors sang Negro spirituals and sorrow songs that had messages embedded in the lyrics. Lastly, you have one added advantage over Beckys, the melanin in your skin has the ability to disorient them. In your time period many Beckys have confusing and conflicting feelings about People of Color in general and Black people specifically. Beckys despise, fear, and yet, are oddly still attracted to you. They don't understand this attraction, but it is a built-in protective mechanism that you can use to your advantage. In the future melanin weakens Beckys like kryptonite weakens Superman. This is our most effective weapon in the future. It is up to you to use this new knowledge about how Beckys operate. It is also vital to strategize with others about how to best protect your communities. If you can expose Beckys as potential land mines, then the visitors will have to come up with a more equity-minded solution. I know this is lot to take in, but I will reach out to you again as soon as possible. I have been trying to connect with you for years. You may have noticed that lights go out sometimes as you approach them, and you also suffer from sleep paralysis—where you are awake but can't move. These were all failed attempts at making a psychic connection with you. In the future, when a light goes out listen for the knock or if you are 'stuck' in your sleep, relax and listen for the knock. The black box will appear and all you have to do is touch it."

Professor Baldwin always thought these occurrences were odd, but he dismissed them. He didn't realize the voice was gone and the connection had ended until he heard a knocking sound that brought him out of his trance-like state. It took three more knocks for him to realize that someone was knocking on his office door. He wiped his eye and looked at the clock on his computer. He felt like he was talking to the voice for hours, but surprisingly only five minutes had passed. The black box was gone, and all of the books were restacked. Professor Baldwin looked around his office and at the pictures of DuBois, Harriett Tubman, Malcolm X, Assata Shakur, Dr. King, and Muhammad Ali that hung on the walls. Filled with emotion, he pulled *Souls of Black Folk* off the shelf, held it in his hand, and went to answer the knock at his door.

Chapter Two

The Battle of the Elders

Queen Becky and the Table of Elders

Eligio Martinez Jr.

THE TABLE OF ELDERS

Since the beginning of time, the Five Kingdoms have ruled the planet. After centuries of war for dominance, the leaders of the Five Kingdoms gathered to sign a peace treaty. Before the treaty could be signed, King Alexandre of the Snow Dwellers stopped a rebellion led by his brother Malachi, who had become a powerful warlord and terrorized the other kingdoms. King Alexandre did this by driving a dagger into Malachi's heart. While the treaty was intended to bring all the kingdoms into a peaceful coexistence, there were concerns within some of the kingdoms given the history of war and conquest mainly by two of the Five Kingdoms: the Snow Dwellers and Dragon Masters. Despite the turmoil, the peace treaty was signed by the rulers of all Five Kingdoms. The peace treaty called for the creation of a Table of Elders which would ensure that peace, power, and prosperity would be shared amongst the Five Kingdoms.

With the establishment of the Table of Elders, each Kingdom was allowed to select its own Elder without interference from the other tribes. Each tribe selected its Elder based on communal respect for the Elder's training and knowledge about their tribe's culture, history, and traditions. While some kings and queens would serve on the table, the appointment of the Elder was a decision made by the entire kingdom and not simply the ruling elite. The only exception was the Snow Dwellers, who initially kept the seat in the ruling family to keep the peace within the Kingdom. Elders would serve a term no longer than 20 turns around the sun. Most Elders stayed on the table for no more than 12 turns to encourage the generation of new ideas and knowledge and to limit the corrupting influences of power. On the table, the Elders were responsible for ensuring the maintenance of balance and peace across the Five Kingdoms. Elders also protected and updated the codices, which included the history of the Kingdoms, determined what was right and just, through a process of knowledge sharing and collective uplift.

When Queen Becky joined the Table of Elders as the representative of the Snow Dwellers, other elders were worried the dynamics would change. Being a direct descendent of Malachi and King Alexandre, Queen Becky believed that her seat on the Table was rightfully hers through her ancestral blood. As she expressed "This seat, is my direct inheritance, everyone will pay for what they have done to us." Queen Becky's uncle who was the outgoing Elder felt that Becky's beliefs about the superiority of the Snow Dwellers over other tribes and her hunger for power too strongly resembled those of Malachi. Upon her arrival on the table, Becky immediately clashed with other elders. She constantly dismissed their perspectives and questioned the validity of their claims. Queen Becky made it clear that the dynamics of the Table of Elders were about to change. A young elder named, Tecun, would face the wrath of Queen Becky in her quest to control the Kingdoms.

The Beginning

Amongst the Five Kingdoms, the River Warriors and Volcano Explorers had always maintained a strong relationship. For most of their existence, the River Warriors had lived within the depths of the Magical Jungle. In earlier times, they had battled off and defeated the evil warlord Malachi during one of his invasions by hiding in the depths of the jungle and using guerilla tactics to catch Malachi's troops off guard. Despite living far away on the Volcano Islands, the king of the Volcano people sent his troops to attack Malachi's army through the sea and help drive him back to the Snow Dwellings. The Volcano Explorers and River Warriors formed a strong partnership between the two tribes that stood until this day.

The Sand Snakes lived in the harsh desert climate but over time had adapted to survive and flourish under the heat. The Sand Snakes were peaceful and always welcomed traders and travelers through their kingdom. Although peaceful, they maintained a strong army led by fierce female warriors.

The Dragon Masters lived high above in the Sky Mountains. Their name came from the location of their home above the clouds and the legends that came from their ancestors of living amongst the dragons during mythical times. While peaceful, the Dragon Masters have long felt that they were very similar to the Snow Dwellers and superior to the other tribes because of the elevated location of their home.

The Snow Dwellers lived up high in the frozen mountains. Their elevated homeland often gave Snow Dwellers a sense of superiority that caused some

Snow Dwellers, like Queen Becky, to "look down" upon the other tribes. Throughout their history, they had tried to invade the Five Kingdoms and enslave the other tribes. It wasn't until King Alexandre's reign when the idea of a peace treaty was discussed, which caused internal turmoil within the Snow Dwellers. It was during this time that Malachi attempted to form an alliance with the Dragon Masters and overthrow King Alexandre.

Malachi had convinced the Dragon Masters that an alliance with him would bring them a higher status than the other tribes and together they would conquer the other kingdoms. "Join forces with me and together we can control the kingdoms." Malachi pleaded to the Dragon Masters. "Together the Snow Dwellers and Dragon Masters will be unstoppable!"

After this failed attempt, the Dragon Masters were sent back to the Sky Mountains. When a peace treaty was brought to the table, the Dragon Masters were hesitant to join as they resented the lack of respect that other tribes showed toward them after their failed alliance with Malachi. Over time, the Dragon Masters became more peaceful and open to collaborating with the other tribes. This was a result of the Elders believing that their predecessors had made a mistake in siding with Malachi. Maeda, the current Elder from the Dragon Masters, worked hard to build relationships with the Volcano Conquerors and the River Warriors, in order to move past the bad history between the tribes. "I know that my ancestors were guided by greed for wealth and power," Maeda expressed, "but we have recognized our mistakes and know that we are more powerful when all the kingdoms are united."

Queen Becky and Tecun

Queen Becky was the descendant of King Alexandre and Malachi. As a child, she quickly felt a sense of elitism, given her family's historical legacy to the Snow Dwellers Kingdom. She also grew up with little exposure to people and places outside of the Snow Dwellers and her Kingdom, because her parents wanted to keep her protected from the outside world. Despite her father being the second oldest child of her grandfather, Becky manipulated her family members with her magical tears from a young age to ensure that she would eventually become the Queen. When young Becky did not get her way, she would begin to cry and scream "Why does everyone hate me?!" Her tears were like a toxin that manipulated others to do as she requested. As Becky grew older, the power of her tears increased.

When her uncle lost his only son, she knew all she had to do was eliminate her cousin Camelia so that she would then become the heir to the throne. As such, she began to cast doubt upon Camelia, spreading rumors about her character, intellectual abilities, and overall ability to lead the Snow Dwellers.

Becky was known for controlling the narrative about Camelia, presenting her as not collaborative, aggressive, and always in need of some form of special accommodation. Plainly stated, Becky ruined Camelia's reputation so much that Camelia often found herself too tired to fight back the rumors and ended up becoming reclusive. She internalized all the negative things Becky had said and done to her to a point where she became suicidal. When Camelia's father was ready to pass down the crown to her, Camelia mysteriously disappeared. With no other heir, Becky assumed the crown, as she was the oldest child in her family. Queen Becky, used her magical tears to manipulate the Snow Dwellers and cast a spell over them, ensuring that they would do as she pleased. From the moment Queen Becky sat on the throne, she made it clear that she had no intentions of giving up her seat. "This seat belongs to me, and nobody will ever take it away," she retorted.

While Queen Becky was preparing to take her seat at the Table of Elders, a young prodigy named Tecun from the Magical Jungle was unaware that his life would soon change. Tecun's great grandfather was the emperor of the River Warrior who defeated Malachi and formed an alliance with the Volcano Conquerors. Tecun had shown great promise to be a leader from a young age, constantly leading his peers on expeditions through the jungles. Tecun had also excelled as a student and understood the Codices better than anyone else in the jungles. Despite his age, he had shown great promise to eventually become an Elder. However, Tecun's life quickly changed when the Elder from the River Warriors became ill and Tecun was forced to join the Table of Elders at a very young age.

Queen Becky's Terror Reign

When Queen Becky joined the Table of Elders, she immediately pushed the others around and strategically used her magical tears to her advantage. When someone disagreed with her, she would cry, "I just want to contribute but you won't let me." Her tears would drive others crazy and force them to give in. Believing that Elder Maeda of the Dragon Masters was too old to continue serving, she vocally questioned his ability to make rational decisions.

Knocking on Maeda's head, she stated "'Knock! Knock!' Hello, is someone still in there?" Whenever Elder Maeda spoke, she interrupted him by saying "Here we go again, another crazy idea," never allowing him to finish a thought. When others would challenge her, she would feign innocence and cry, saying, "I'm sorry, I didn't hear what he said." Queen Becky would deliberately mispronounce or "forget" names of other Elders, a behavior she continued when new Elders joined the table. When Maeda grew tired of Queen Becky's treatment, he decided to step down, and told the Elders, "I'm sorry I must leave you at such a difficult time, but I can no longer tolerate her crude behavior." Queen Becky laughed and replied, "I didn't realize you were still with us! Don't worry, you won't be missed."

As the Dragon Master's prepared to find Maeda's replacement, Becky found her opportunity to strike and set up a meeting with a young Dragon Master, Ferdinand. "I can help you become the next Elder, you just need to side with me and trust me," Queen Becky said. "Promise me that you'll be my ally and I will make you powerful." Maeda had found out about this secret meeting and hid in a secret closet to listen to the conversation. Becky told Ferdinand, "I will give you gold to pay off others and ensure you become the next Elder." When Ferdinand was appointed to the Table of Elders, Maeda expressed his concerns to the Dragon Masters and other Elders.

"I do not feel comfortable with this selection. Queen Becky has corrupted Ferdinand, and I believe that he will put his own personal interests before that of our tribe!"

To deflect the accusations, Queen Becky used her magic tears to distract the others from Maeda's concerns. Crying loudly, Queen Becky pleaded, "I don't understand why Maeda hates me so much. I only wanted what was best for him and thought I was offering my support to him, but he always attacks me. I am the one who is innocent here!" She drew the power of her magical tears to cause tension between Maeda and other Dragon Masters, and take away the attention from Ferdinand's appointment.

As Queen Becky's influence began to grow, she began to change the traditions and practices of the Table of Elders. Under Queen Becky, the Table agreed to a tribal hierarchy, which served to destabilize the Table and create tensions amongst the Five Kingdoms. Ferdinand and the Dragon Masters formed an alliance with Queen Becky and supported her push to consolidate power. In exchange for loyalty, Queen Becky assured Ferdinand power, as she expressed, "Follow me and I will give you an honorary Snow Dweller status. Together, we'll control these inferior tribes and make them do as we please." The remaining tribes would be subjugated to a second-class status and denied the same privileges as the Snow Dwellers and Dragon Masters. Restrictions were put on the other tribes that reduced their ability to travel and trade freely amongst the Kingdoms.

While the Elders had collectively written the Codices, Queen Becky began to re-write stories and history of the tribes in which the Snow Dwellers were portrayed as possessing superior intelligence and knowledge. "I can't believe that these savages think they are equal to us!" she demanded, "I order you to change these Codices, and show the kingdoms how inferior these tribes are to the Snow Dwellers and Dragon Masters!" When the other elders protested claiming, "You cannot just change the protocols and codes based on your interests," Queen Becky grew angrier. Using her manipulative powers of tears she began to cry and her magical tears hypnotized them, making them chant in unison, "Yes, our beloved queen. So innocent, beautiful, pure, and moral."

Queen Becky rewrote the Codices erroneously portraying the River Warriors as savages who had attempted to invade the Snow Dwellings but were subdued by the intelligence and strength of the Snow Dwellers. The Sand Snakes were dismissed as nomads who did not have the capacity to form a civilization, wandering through the desert in search for food. Queen Becky rewrote the history to show how often the Snow Dwellers had saved the Sand Snakes from starvation and provided them with resources to survive during the intense summer months. When Huanani, the female Elder with a dark face from the Volcano Explorers, attempted to challenge Queen Becky, Ferdinand silenced her by yelling, "How dare you speak to our Queen like that. Did your parents not teach you any manners?" Queen Becky threated to remove Huanani from the Table of Elders if she did not cooperate and replace her with someone who understood what was "best" for the Kingdoms. In her manipulative sly way, Queen Becky preached, "Huanani, don't be so aggressive. I'm doing this for your own good. I'm saving you and your people." Upon these manipulative, ahistorical words, Huanani stood up with great confidence. "Queen Becky what are you talking about? How is this helping us? When in the past have you ever helped us?" Upon hearing these words, Queen Becky darted toward Huanani's brown body. While creating circles on Huanani's shoulders, Queen Becky stated, "Wow, you are so unapologetic. How dare you speak to me that way. Do you know who I am and what I can do to people who look like you?" Queen Becky began to cry manipulative tears trying to force Huanani to forget historical reality, but Huanani resisted. She was not going to fall for this white woman's tricks. Noticing her resistance to her tears, Queen Becky screamed, "You all are good for nothing. I allow you to have some power because you, too, are women, but you never know your place. You can never outrank me. Know your place, Brown girl." At this, Huanani fell. Her face froze and her eyes went blank. Queen Becky went in, "Who is the best standard of beauty?" Huanani replied, "You are, ma'am. Your pure white skin and blonde hair is what I admire." Queen Becky continued, "Who is the indolent, lazy person not intelligent enough to rule on their own?" Huanani turned fully entranced and said, "I am my queen." Queen Becky belted a cackling laugh and signaled with her hand to remove Huanani from her sight.

Without telling the rest of the Elders, Queen Becky sent messengers to deliver the updated Codices to all the tribes. Queen Becky ordered her army, "Make sure that every child from all the kingdoms is taught to respect the superiority of the Snow Dwellers!" The Snow Dwellers began teaching Queen Becky's ideas of Snow Dweller superiority over others to young children across the Five Kingdoms. This created confusion in all the Kingdoms, as the messengers stated that the Codices were sent from the Table of Elders. Tribal leadership began to question what was going on and requested that the Table meet with the Kingdoms to discuss the changes. Queen Becky and Ferdinand denied this request by saying "This decision did not come easy, but all of the Elders felt this was the right thing to do and voted unanimously in favor. There is no need to discuss this again."

Very concerned with how history was being recreated, the Leaders of the Volcano Conquerors summoned Huanani and asked her to explain the action of the Table of Elders. At first Huanani was still hypnotized by the evil power of Queen Becky, she began whispering, "I am the problem. I should just behave." When one of the leaders heard this he screamed, "Huanani, snap out of it. You are not the problem! You are made to feel as if you are the problem." At this moment Huanani woke up. "What happened?" she asked. The tribe began to question whether or not she was able to represent and fight for the tribe. Sensing that her tribe was upset with Huanani, Amanirenas, the Elder from the Sand Snakes, came to the Volcano Conquerors Kingdom and stated "Queen Becky betrayed us all. She did this without consulting the Table of Elders!"

The Sand Snakes and Volcano Conquerors began to prepare for what they felt would be an inevitable war with the Snow Dwellers and Dragon Masters. Unsure of where the River Warriors stood, the Volcano Conqueror King sent out a messenger to visit the emperor of the River Warriors. However, Queen Becky's army intercepted and captured the messenger, who was taken back to the Snow Dwellings. Queen Becky ordered a soldier from the Dragon Master to dress up as a River Warrior and instructed him to "Make sure those peasants get my message loud and clear!" The imposter returned the message to the Volcano Conqueror king threatening that a strike against Queen Becky would result in retaliation from the River Warriors. Queen Becky was using manipulation in all kingdoms to develop fear and retaliation amongst all!

Sensing the opportunity to strike with a weakened Table and confusion amongst the Five Kingdoms, Queen Becky proposed to disband the Table of Elders and consolidate the power of the Five Kingdoms in her hands. "These are tough times for the Kingdoms," she proclaimed. "There are too many new Elders and I think it's best that one person take control of the Table of Elders." Queen Becky proposed that the longest serving Elder would serve as sole Elder and the remaining elders would serve as her advisory council. "All of you will be my 'advisors' and help me rule, I mean run the Kingdoms. You can trust me on this."

Believing that Tecun was too weak to fight against her given his youthfulness, Queen Becky attempted to persuade him into joining her side. "I have my eye on you, little Indian boy, come here and talk to your queen."

The Conflict

As the youngest member of the Table of Elders, Tecun was approached by Queen Becky, who asked for his support to disband the Table of Elders. "Support my proposal and I will make sure that you and your family are taken care of for a long time." Tecun was promised that he and his family would be moved from the Magical Jungle and be given a place within the Snow Dwellers, where they would be granted great wealth. Queen Becky told Tecun "Be a good River Warrior and allow me to rule over the Elders. Do this and everyone will see that you are not a stupid youngin." Surprised at her comment, Tecun responded "Stupid?"

"Oh, I'm sorry. I shouldn't have said that, but the other Elders think you're too young and don't know what you're doing. I'm the only one who believes in you and stood up to their attacks on you. Help me and I will validate your appointment to the Table of Elders."

Tecun, however, feared that if Queen Becky disbanded the Table of Elders, it would also give her the power to continue to rewrite the Codices the way that she wished. He feared that this would put some of the tribes at risk, as Queen Becky believed the River Warriors and Sand Snakes to be inferior to the other tribes.

Queen Becky warned Tecun to not go against her, "If you do not cooperate, there will be consequences and I will make sure that you never set foot on the Table of Elders again! I will make sure that everyone becomes ashamed of you." Becky also threatened to discredit his accomplishments and ensure that he was not viewed as possessing legitimate knowledge.

Tecun felt like he was up against a wall. On one hand, he feared for the overall well-being of his family and he knew that if he sided with Queen Becky, his family would perhaps be better off. However, he knew this was a risk because he could not trust that Queen Becky would do right by him. On the other hand, Tecun felt that he would betray his family and ancestors who entrusted him with the responsibility of representing the River Warriors. Tecun also felt the burden of being the great grandchild of the greatest River Warrior emperor who united the smaller tribes in the jungle and formed a strong kingdom.

Unsure about what to do, Tecun ran away and decided to take a journey alone in the deepest part of the jungle and search for answers. In solitude, he attempted to find the answer to his dilemma. One night, Tecun was awakened by the spirt of his great grandfather, who like him, had also served on the Table of Elders. As he awakened, his great grandfather's spirit said, "I know why you are here, my child. Rest assured that things will be okay." Tecun confessed that he didn't know what to do, "I don't know what to do, Papa . . . I'm afraid that if I don't do what Queen Becky wants, she'll go after our family and attack them."

As his great-grandfather's sprit walked with Tecun, he told him the story of how before the Table of Elders was formed, Malachi had approached him and asked him to form an alliance with him and overthrow King Alexandre. His great grandfather was not yet emperor and was awaiting for his father to pass down the throne to him. Malachi offered his great grandfather his allegiance and made him a false promise that he would ensure that his great grandfather became Emperor, even though this was about to happen anyway. Similar to Queen Becky, Malachi had threatened his family if he did not cooperate and told him that once he overthrew King Alexandre, he would banish the River Warriors. His great grandfather knew that Malachi had also approached the Volcano Conquerors King with the same offer. Recognizing that both of their statuses as rulers over their kingdoms would be in jeopardy, the two kings became allies in resistance and rejected Malachi's offer.

His great grandfather told Tecun, "Don't let fear rule your life. Instead, turn that fear into your driving force to keep fighting for our tribe. No matter what trinkets are offered to you by Queen Becky or Ferdinand in exchange for your loyalty, do what you believe is right." Tecun responded by asking, "What if she wins, will she validate our history, culture and people, or will she discredit us and our accomplishments?" His great grandfather's spirit hugged Tecun and slowly started to walk away.

"Validation," his great grandfather said, "should not come from those that are at the table, especially not Becky and the Snow Dwellers. Validation comes from within the tribe, from our people, not some white demon. The most important form of validation is knowing that our people entrusted you with the honor of representing the River Warriors. You need no greater validation than that." As the spirit faded away into the sunrise, he told Tecun, "Be proud of who you are and where you come from." As the conversation ended, Tecun realized that he was in a part of the jungle that possessed magical plants to help his fight. Tecun knew that he was ready to return from his journey and challenge Queen Becky.

The Showdown

With Tecun's absence, Queen Becky tried to take advantage of the situation and set up a meeting to disband the Table. "It's time to get rid of these savages," Queen Becky told Ferdinand. Knowing that she would only have two votes against her, Becky knew it was the perfect time. As the meeting began, Queen Becky proclaimed to the others, "As the longest serving Elder, I have the authority to vote on behalf of Tecun. Since he joined the Table of Elders, I have taken him under my wings and supported him to ensure he succeeds as an Elder."

Ferdinand seconded Queen Becky's stance, "Yes my Queen, I believe that you have done what the others have not been willing to do. I second your proposal to disband the Table of Elders."

Amanirenas quickly jumped and challenged Queen Becky and Ferdinand, "You cannot disband the Table. That is a violation of the peace treaty that was signed by all the Five Kingdoms!" Before Huanani could stand and challenge her, Queen Becky raged in anger, "SILENCE CHILD!" and released her magical tears onto Amanirenas and Huanani. The tears paralyzed them and controlled their brown female bodies; just the way she liked them.

Surrounded by her army of Snow Dwellers, Queen Becky forced the others to sit at the Table of Elders and turned to Amanirenas and Huanani and said, "Soon, none of this will matter. This is my destiny and how things should have been a long time ago." As Becky attempted to continue, Tecun emerged from the outside riding a golden jaguar. As the River Warrior army stormed in, he turned to the other elders and said, "It's time for justice and time to reclaim our table."

Becky turned to Tecun and said, "Son, let me do what's best for everyone. Come sit at the table and join the others." Queen Becky released her magical tears in order to control Tecun, but her tears had no effect on him. Surprised, she yelled, "No, what's happening?!" and began to cry even harder to no avail.

Tecun dismounted his golden jaguar and walked to the Table. He looked at Queen Becky square in the eyes and said, "When your great uncle King Alexandre defeated Malachi, he went to Magical Jungle to see my great grandfather and gave him a Ceiba tree." As Tecun pulled something from a bag he was wearing, Queen Becky recognized that something was wrong.

"You see, your great uncle predicted that this day would come and he trusted my great grandfather with the Ceiba tree and it's magical healing powers that could counter the spell that the magical tears of Snow Dwellers could have."

Tecun opened the bag and released a potion into the air that broke the spell that Queen Becky had on Amanirenas and Huanani. Queen Becky began to scream in fear, "No! No! No! What are you doing? Stop what you are doing, I'm begging you!" She ordered Ferdinand to do something, but he stood still. As Tecun approached Becky, he pulled something from underneath his belt. "Your great uncle also gave my tribe the dagger that he drove into Malachi's heart to end his terror reign and now it is time to end your terror reign as well!"

Queen Becky pleaded with Tecun to stop, "Please stop I'm begging you! I only wanted what was best for you. Give me another chance and I can show you that there's another way." Tecun leaped into the air and as he came down, he drove the dagger into Queen Becky's heart. The Snow Dweller soldiers put their weapons down and appeared to break out of Queen Becky's spell. As Tecun stood over Queen Becky's body, he proclaimed, "Today is the start of a new beginning for the Table of Elders, let our differences be our strength for generations to come! And never again be swayed by the manipulations of Beckys."

Section One

Guiding Questions

1. How are some of the behaviors from the five types of Becky(s) described in one of the stories found in your own work and personal environment? How do they serve to colonize people of color?
2. When thinking about colonization as usurping power, how does the Queen usurp power in the second story and how is that maneuver similar to situations that have played out in your environment?
3. When witnessing colonizing behaviors of Becky(s), what are some strategies you can employ to de-escalate her usurped power?
4. If you exhibit some of these behaviors, what are some tools that can be applied to ensure that one is not usurping power in ways that colonize others?

Section Two

Becky(s) as Weaponized Emotionalities

From mugs stating "collecting white tears" to open call outs of white fragility (see DiAngelo, 2018), the operating mechanisms of white women's tears are noteworthy; for they are not merely popular parlance used to convey distaste of them (see Donnella, 2018), rather they are strategic maneuvers of whiteness. In an opinion piece, Hamad (2018) describes white women's tears as "the tactic many white women employ to muster sympathy and avoid accountability, by turning the tables and accusing their accuser."

In my own book, *Feeling White*, I assert that white tears are a "seemingly invisible state of emotionality [that] intoxicates us all" (Matias, 2016, p. 2). This intoxication is traumatic for folks of color (per Hamad, 2018; Matias, 2016). In fact, it can be deadly in that, simply put, "Black people got killed when a white woman cried" (Kemp, 2019). Again, we needn't look further than how these tears have been strategically and historically employed to convey a damsel in distress in need of protecting. And, it is precisely this false need for protection that can be brutal, violent, and deadly.

For example, note the false tears of Carolyn Bryant Donham who lied about being sexually assaulted by a young Black boy, Emmett Till. These seemingly innocent "white" lies about Till's sexually groping and menacing, which included allegations of him making wolf whistles at her, led to Till's brutal murder and death by Donham's husband, Roy Bryant, and brother, J.W. Milam. Actual evidence was unnecessary; the only requisite was a white woman's allegation coupled with her performance of distress. At the young age of 14, Till was kidnapped, tortured, murdered, and left in a river that severely disfigured his face and body. His mother, wanting others to recognize the atrocities that Till underwent, left the funeral casket open to forever remind everyone that the trauma and violence of white supremacy is real.

This repugnant murder was precipitated by the expressed tears of a white woman, a woman who later divorced her husband, Roy Bryant, claiming he was physically abusive. Though sensitive to issues of domestic abuse and its impact on victims, this state of mind begs me to psychoanalytically question her motives of pretending to be sexually assaulted by Till. Herman (1997), the author of *Trauma and Recovery*, states, "Chronic abuse causes serious psychological harm" (p. 116). Some of these psychological resultants are developing "characteristic personality changes, including deformations of relatedness and identity" that make them "particularly vulnerable to repeated harm, both self-inflicted and in the hands of others" (p. 119). I do not want to travel down a path that blames the victim; however, I question the likelihood of how psychological damage leads one to victimize another, for the worst type of victim is one who makes a victim of another. And, with respect to the overarching analysis of white women and tears, one must critically question the un-evidential presumption that they are, indeed, victims. This presumption is the undergirding context for which only an allegation justifies the reactive behavior of protecting, even if this so-called "protection" comes at the expense of the humanity of the person of color who is allegedly the culprit. For anyone who elicits the tears of a white woman, the notion of innocent until proven guilty need not apply. The mere production of these tears is enough for an indictment and, in the case of Emmett Till, enough to justify his murder.

Returning to Hamad's (2018) definition of white tears as "the tactic many white women employ to muster sympathy and avoid accountability, by turning the tables and accusing their accuser," I employ another example.

In my experiences, white tears have diverted attention away from the unethical and unprofessional behaviors of white women only to be redirected to the accused. For example, a white woman cried to my white administrators, claiming she *felt* threatened by me (a five-foot, barely 100-pound woman of color) without ever having made physical contact with me. Though she did take my course a semester before, the only interaction I had with her during the semester in question was giving her cyber feedback on her work so that her work can get published (and it did get published), providing close to a dozen recommendations for her, and virtually helping her in conference presentations. All of this I did during the semester I was on maternity leave because she claimed it was urgent. In fact, I feared that to deny these requests would mean another accusatory email to my white administrators about how I am not serving students. For women of color, it is a damned if you do and a damned if you don't situation. This damned if I don't was confirmed when my student evaluations came back one semester noting that one white female deemed me inaccessible to students because "she's not even available on the weekends." Entrenched in this evaluation is the mentality that women of color need to be available to the needs of white women at all times, including weekends. Just as hooks (1994) claims that the servant/served paradigm continues to exist between white and Black feminists (whereby white feminists expect Black feminists to serve their causes and never are expected to serve the interests of Black feminists), I was just another Filipina woman expected to *nurse* the needs of white women at their beck and call.

Though I am sensitive to the dynamics of power between a professor and student, this does not negate the fact that those who seemingly have less power in a traditional power structure can still engage in manipulative behaviors, via white tears, that subvert the positional power in lieu of racial power and privilege. Meaning, one can have professorial power in their positional standing, but will ultimately lose power when intersectional dynamics of race, gender, and sexuality are at play. Plainly, I cannot out power whiteness because a white woman's tears are more powerful than my humanity. Or, to extend Hamad's (2018) definition of white tears as simply avoiding accountability and mustering sympathy, it is about reifying white women and whiteness in general as innocent and thus, in their innocence, can never be questioned. Just as Donham's integrity was not questioned, neither was this particular white woman. Their mere discomfort (which at times have no basis) is all that is needed to begin an autopilot process of protecting her feelings.

In this instance, this particular white woman cried tears, claiming she *felt* threatened without me actually ever threatening. In fact, she did what Becky(s) do. That is, she extracted what she needed from me (the labor of women of color), when she needed it, despite the burdens it placed on me only to then turn around and cry tears to all my white supervisors, claiming my request to meet with her upon my return from maternity leave to discuss her scholarly work was in and of itself a threat. Indeed, she engaged unprofessionally, but that was unquestioned because as a Becky she reeks innocence. Though she felt fine while controlling my labor, when I asked about meeting with her to discuss her work (a situation that would respect my role as a professor), she reneged, and then approached the university's legal counsel and my white administrators to cry about feeling intimidated by me: an unwarranted feeling. She did this without ever recognizing how her feelings of intimidation were an emotional projection of her not wanting a woman of color to be her equal, let alone her professor. Not only was her behavior so unprofessional and unethical, it was also emotionally manipulative and ridden with white racial privilege. And sadly, since whiteness is so predictable when it comes to white women's tears, these white supervisors did what whiteness does: refuse to listen to folks of color or honor her truths by simply siding with the white tears.

As such, the weaponizing of white emotionalities such as white tears, defensiveness, guilt, or shame, to name a few, engages whiteness in a very uniquely gendered way, which ultimately reinforces white supremacy (see Matias, 2016). If white supremacy is about upholding the interests of whites at the expense of the humanity of people of color, then white women's tears and emotionalities, which have historically caused the violence, terror, and even death of people of color, are in and of themselves weapons used in defense of white supremacy. In fact, to feign innocence is just another operating mechanism of whiteness whereby white women are relieved from their culpability in the white enterprise. For, as historian Jones-Rodgers (2019) argues, white women were not "passive bystanders. They were co-conspirators" (p. 205). And, although they did not mirror the ways in which white men engaged in blatant acts of terror, like lynching, their emotions nonetheless continue to wreak havoc on the lives of people of color. Therefore, Becky(s) as weaponized emotionalities are white women who strategically (whether consciously or not) employ their emotions as a way to gain standing or privilege that is favorable to their sentiments and interests and is often used to garner sympathy for them. Meaning, they cry, knowing that this act will lead them to a more favorable situation; one that paints them as innocent and renders a swift guilty verdict to the alleged accused. The stories in this section are hyperboles of Becky(s) who engage their white emotionalities as weapons. Whereas one story depicts white tears as a Hulk-like response causing mayhem everywhere, the other exaggerates the power of white tears as a silencing mechanism, whereby the expression of tears literally has the metaphysical power of silencing the voice of women of color. In fact, the authors of one of the stories claim they wrote the piece because "white women's tears are often weaponized as a way to take power and visibility away from women of color and position them as dangerous in order to strip them of their voice, power, and agency." As such, writing this story then offered them "a creative way to provide a social and educational commentary on a phenomenon that women of color experience pretty much daily." Suffice it to say that these two such stories, though exaggerated; still convey how people of color, particularly women of color, survive when white women's tears and emotionalities are displayed.

REFERENCES

DiAngelo, R. (2018). White fragility: Why it's so hard for white people to talk about racism. Boston: Beacon Press.

Donnella, L. (2018, November 28). *When the White Tears just keep on coming.* Retrieved from https://www.npr.org/sections/codeswitch/2018/11/28/649537891/when-the-white-tears-just-keep-coming.

Hamad, R. (2018). How white women use strategic tears to silence women of colour. *The Guardian*. Retrieved from https://www.theguardian.com/commentisfree/2018/may/08/how-white-women-use-strategic-tears-to-avoid-accountability.

Herman, J. (1997). *Trauma and Recovery: The aftermath of violence from domestic abuse to political terror.* New York: Basic Books.

hooks, b. (1994). *Teaching to Transgress: Education as the Practice of Freedom.* New York: Routledge.

Jones-Rogers, S. (2019). *They Were Her Property: White Women as Slave Owners in the American South.* New Haven, CT: Yale University Press.

Kemp, A. (2019, May 7). *White Women's Tears and Racial Justice.* Retrieved from blog post https://www.dramandakemp.com/blog/2019/5/7/white-womens-tears-amp-racial-justice.

Matias, C. E. (2016). *Feeling White: Whiteness, Emotionality, and Education.* The Netherlands, Sense Publishers.

Chapter Three

The Ultimate Superpower

Surviving Becky's Tears

Erica R. Wallace and Rachel Kline

Nova Winters was in her final year of her student affairs graduate program at the Southern School of the Gifted & Extraordinary. Though it may sound like a school for students with high IQs, Southern students were gifted in quite different ways. Southern was a school for metahumans—human-like beings with superhuman powers and abilities. Metahumans of all ages could come to Southern to get an education like other humans did and learn how to use their special skills and abilities. Already somewhat ostracized from greater society, Southern was intended to be a place where all metahumans could feel included and empowered. However, that intent was not always realized.

At Southern (and in society at large), metahumans were classed into "Supers" and "Mutants." Growing up, Nova came to understand that "Mutant" was the term for the oppressed class of metahumans and "Supers" were the majority—the privileged class. She also understood that her brown skin made her a Mutant—one of the handful in her program and one of the few at Southern (6 percent to be exact).

Nova was born an empath with peak human strength. She could fully interpret and replicate the emotions and moods of others, and though she was average height and weight for her age, she had the ability to lift a car. The traits were easy for her to conceal. But when consumed with negative emotions, the intensity of her empathic powers and super strength are enhanced. Her eyes would flash with a purple glow, and her normally straightened hair would return to its naturally curly state and glow with streaks of purple and orange. Nova was taught to control that part of her. She couldn't be seen in that state, not in front of the Supers. As she approached the bus stop that morning, she did what she did every Monday morning—count the "Supers-to-Mutants" ratio, the SMR as she named it—on the way to campus. She finished counting the people at the bus stop just as her bus arrived. *Twelve Supers to Two*

Mutants. She boarded, found a seat, and leaned her head on the window, gazing out at the scenic route to campus and continuing her count along the way. *One more Mutant. Oh wow, another one over there!*

Suddenly a loud voice startled her. *What's the SMR today?* Nova nearly jumped out of her seat, which gained her the concerned looks of others on the bus. Only Nova was able to hear this voice. "I told you about scaring me like that, Kay," Nova forcefully mumbled under her breath. She turned and smiled nervously to those around her to signal that she was fine. *Sorrrry . . . if your mind wasn't so cluttered all the time, you could probably sense me in there.* Nova rolled her eyes. "*You're* the one that can pick up on thoughts, remember?"

Kadence McCall, a fellow Mutant, was Nova's best friend in the program and worked as a graduate community director on campus. Kadence had a hypersonic voice. Her whisper was so powerful that she could cause the ground to tremble around her. Because of this, Southern told her to communicate strictly through sign language. What Kadence hid from the Supers was that she was also a telepathic communicator. She was able to transmit information from one mind to another. She and Nova communicated this way often.

Meet me in front of Hodges, Kadence transmitted to Nova's mind. *I'm in my office, almost done submitting this work order, and I have a 9am meeting in your building. We can walk there together.*

The bus screeched to a stop. Nova gathered her things and began to move into the aisle. Before she could, a Super came from behind and bumped into her, pushing her back in her seat. Three more Supers followed behind, not acknowledging what just happened nor Nova's presence at all. She caught a glimpse of her flashing purple eyes in her reflection in the window and decided to wait and exit the bus last.

"I'm here," she mumbled under her breath to Kadence, "so I'll see you in like two." Her face showed her lack of enthusiasm to be there, when she heard, "Hey Supernova!" Immediately she broke out into a smile. Only her KINDRED students called her that. She turned around to see two of her favorites, Ty and Jess, and went over to talk to them. Nova's graduate assistantship was with the KINDRED Program, a peer mentor program for new Mutants on campus. KINDRED was one of the only good things about being at Southern. As ostracized as she felt daily on campus, she knew that they were the reason she did what she did.

Almost 10 minutes later, Nova walked up the steps to Hodges Hall where Kadence was impatiently waiting. Seeing that there were many people around, Kadence signed (while also projecting loudly into Nova's mind), *Where you been?!* "Chill out fam, I ran into Ty and Jess walking through the quad. Now if we don't want to be late we should go." Nova chatted about the interactions with her students as the pair started out toward the student union.

"Ty has gotten so good at his depictukinetics, and Jess's literary weapon proficiency has improved so much since her first year. Do you remember when she was so scared to use her powers in front of people? She asked me if I could come to her competition next week, so I told her to send me the details and . . . "

Kadence interrupted Nova's thought pattern. *Wait. Translation, please. Depictu-what?* Nova couldn't contain the excitement in her voice. "Depictukinetics. Art manipulation. You know Ty does graphic design. He's the one who designed the new logo for KINDRED. He's still trying to figure out which artist tool is best for him, but he's learning how he can actually create beings, objects, and powers with his art." She paused and without even looking at Kadence, said, "What's the grinning about?" Nova's empathic powers picked up on the swell of positive energy coming from her. *You just get so excited when you talk about them. As much as you hate it here, you're right where you're supposed to be. They need people like you in a place like this. You help them feel like they belong here.*

Nova half-smiled at Kadence's statement before her eyes briefly flashed with their purple glow. She did hate it there. She hated feeling invisible, being stereotyped as aggressive and dangerous, and that her students had to experience those things, too. The only thing that made her feel good was to be a support and an advocate for marginalized students who came from backgrounds similar to hers, but it infuriated her to no end when some of her cohorts couldn't see why it was important.

You're thinking about Becca and Reba, Kadence intuited.

Becca Van Buren and Reba Mason were fellow grad students who worked with Nova. They were both Supers. It was already bad enough that Nova had to exist on a campus that was predominantly Supers, have Supers as the majority of the faculty, and learn from a curriculum that barely acknowledged or included her lived experiences as a Mutant or those of her students. But when she, Kadence, or the few other Mutants in their program tried to challenge or add to that curriculum, they were always met with resistance. And although these sentiments were widespread throughout their program, Becca and Reba were definitely the worst offenders. They frequently dismissed their privilege as Supers and the oppression of the Mutant class by Supers by naming their oppression as women. In their history class, a few Mutants brought up the fact that the curriculum only talked about the good things that Supers had contributed to colleges but did not name the fact that colleges were on stolen Mutant land and used the labor from enslaved Mutants to build the schools.

Nova called out the fact that the building they had all of their classes in was named after a Super who worked to oppress and imprison Mutants. Reba rolled her eyes and asked why it mattered and why they kept having to bring up the past. She pointed out the plaque dedicated to the first Mutant who attended Southern and robotically recalled how "peaceful" of a time he had there. As if on cue, Becca added in, "There's not even a plaque for the first woman to attend Southern!" as if plaques were the epitome of a just society.

Nova and Kadence learned that calling them out only resulted in using up a lot of mental and emotional energy to explain their experiences which would only result in Becca and Reba crying to their professors and supervisors. After giving Reba and Becca a verbal dissertation about the problem with majoritarian stories and the importance of counternarratives, Nova was called to the dean's office the following day because of a complaint that she was "attacking" other students. She didn't say anything in class for the next week.

Your staff retreat was this weekend. Something happened. Kadence continued. Nova sighed. "So you know how someone called campus police on Ty for napping in the lounge in my building." *Yeah, I remember that. His best friend is one of my RAs. She told me that he wouldn't come out of his room for like three days after that.*

Nova painfully recalled the experience. "He got there super early to meet with me. He was up all night writing his paper on cosmic powers, so he was tired and I was running late. I didn't see how it happened but while walking to the building I felt it. I felt his fear so I ran to him. I don't know what would have happened if I hadn't got there when I did."

Yeah. We know there's a history of bad things that happen when police get called on us for no reason.

"So I thought it was important to bring it up at the staff retreat. We were discussing how we can create a more welcoming environment for students, particularly those from marginalized backgrounds. So I brought up the situation that happened to Ty. I talked about the long history of relations between Mutants and the police, long before any of us had the metagene that gave us our powers. I know we can't control what happens on other parts of campus, but I told everyone that we have a responsibility to make sure that in our building our students feel physically, emotionally, and mentally safe."

Yeah, makes perfect sense. What did they say?

"Before anyone could say anything, I started picking up on the strong emotions in the room. Guilt. Uncomfortability. Defensiveness. It felt like a cloud of smoke was in the room. It was so overwhelming it was hard for me to breathe. It was overpowering me."

And they were coming from Becca and Reba weren't they?

"They were coming from all over the room, but most strongly from Reba. And when she spoke, I almost lost it." Nova went on to tell Kadence how Reba felt like Nova was attacking the department, of course, with tears welling up in her blue eyes.

"She had the nerve to say, 'What are we supposed to do if *we* feel *unsafe* because there's a *suspicious*-looking person in our building? I don't want to feel threatened in a space where I should feel safe.' And do you know what I noticed? Literally the moment she started crying, everything I said and my entire presence ceased to exist."

You mean using her invisibility powers? I thought she could only make herself invisible.

"I thought so too, and I've definitely seen her use that to avoid accountability for her words and actions. But I think something happens when she cries that enhances that power. I couldn't even use my powers because she was so emotionally distraught that it overtook them. No one in the room could see me or hear me anymore. I kept trying to speak but it felt like all the air was being sucked out of my lungs. And they definitely forgot about Ty's ordeal. She became the priority in that space."

So they completely ignored all that coded language she used? Suspicious. Unsafe. We know she's not talking about the students who are Supers.

"Yes, we know that. And I couldn't believe no one called her on that. When her crying started to let up, I started to feel my powers coming back. But I was still so angry. I saw my reflection on my laptop and my eyes were glowing. Not the flicker that they normally do when I'm annoyed with this stuff, but glowing like a brand new light bulb. And my hair started to curl up, so I got up and left the room to get myself together before I completely transformed into one of those 'unsafe' and 'suspicious' Mutants she was talking about."

By the time Nova finished her story, she and Kadence had arrived outside her office space. The space was an open-layout with eight workstations contained by ceiling-to-floor glass walls. Most of the grads who worked in the space were already at their desks, including Becca and Reba. Becca looked up from her desk to see Nova and Kadence standing outside and flashed a big patronizing smile and waved at them both. Nova gave a half-smile in her direction.

Well, I have to go to this meeting, but see you at lunch? I'll swipe you into the dining hall.

"Sounds like a plan," whispered Nova. The two parted ways, as Nova took a deep breath, gathered her thoughts, and headed to her desk. Of course her desk was right in front of Reba's. Nova did not speak and avoided eye contact so as not to be emotionally triggered. She turned on her computer and typed into the search bar of the superpower research database: *Invisibility and tears.*

She had to know more about how these two worked together. She looked up at the clock. Three hours until lunch, five until class . . . .

Nova and Kadence were seated outside of the dining hall at a small table under a big orange umbrella. Nova sat quietly with her sunglasses on (although it was not very sunny) and was barely eating her food. Kadence, noticing the strange demeanor of her friend, tried using her powers to figure out what was going on inside Nova's mind, but there was too much interference for her to pick up anything.

Do you wanna tell me what's going on? Why are you wearing sunglasses? Nova tilted her sunglasses down on the bridge of her nose just enough so Kadence could see her glowing purple eyes. "They've been that way for the past hour."

So . . . what's happened in the past hour?

"Meeting with my supervisor. He told me that some of the staff are intimidated by me and that he wants me to work on being more friendly."

I'm sorry . . . WHAT?!

"Apparently, I've been referred to as angry, aggressive, emotional, and bossy."

Is this about the staff retreat?

"Of course it is. *Someone* reported me and I never had a chance to tell my side. But it's also about the time Reba tried to touch my hair and I told her she couldn't pet me. And about all the times you come visit me in my office and Becca feels left out of the conversation. And about the times I've corrected both of them for not getting my students' names correct—we all don't look alike. Who knew that they've both been complaining to their supervisors about me! Then their supervisors had a talk with mine and here we are."

What did you say to your supervisor?

"I asked him why are we valuing these Supers' tears more than actual Mutant lives? Why is it when I speak up about something that they have done that has negatively impacted me or one of my students that I get accused of hurting her because she starts to cry? My only options then are to back down and feel sorry for the person who ACTUALLY caused the harm or to get so upset that I'm not being heard that I end up embodying the same stereotypes they accuse me of. So what am I supposed to do?"

At this point Kadence began to get upset, too. She wanted to use her voice to speak out. She knew the power it has to shake the foundation of the campus, but she wasn't sure if she was ready to do that. If she did, they would start to see her just like they saw Nova—loud, aggressive, unsafe.

Do you ever get tired of always being strong? Kadence asked Nova. Nova lifted up her sunglasses, eyes still with their radiant purple glow, to look at

Kadence directly. "All the time. Do you get tired of being silenced?" Kadence paused then mouthed her response back to Nova: *All. The. Time.*

After lunch Kadence and Nova headed to class, a class they actually enjoyed since it was the only one with a Mutant professor. Today, their professor would be a little late to class due to an emergency meeting with the dean and decided to give them a bit of time at the beginning of class to meet as a group and work on their group project. They were assigned to complete an assessment project for a topic their group was interested in. The groups were preassigned to ensure that people were working with new folks in the classroom, which is how Nova and Kadence wound up working with Becca and Reba. Nova, aware of the SMR at all times, was thankful to have Kadence in the group with her since there had been many group projects and presentations where she was the only Mutant in the group. She would spend all semester having to jump through hoops to try to prove herself to the Supers in the group, having her (correct) answers questioned then double-checked, being assigned the grunt work rather than real work, and ensuring that she never showed her true feelings. During this project, whenever she would provide a suggestion, Reba would purse her lips, wrinkle her nose and give a long "Hmmm . . . I'm not quite sure how that would work, but good thinking, keep trying," which was incredibly patronizing. A few minutes later, Reba would come up with a suggestion that was almost exactly the same as Nova's and her and Becca would squeal with delight as they brainstormed a way to include the thought. Going through the motions of proving herself was exhausting and restarted each semester when she was assigned a new group and wound up having to prove herself all over again.

For this project, the group decided to explore living-learning communities, specifically the KINDRED, LLC. It hit on all of their interests: retention, residence life, multicultural programs, and admissions. Plus, it didn't hurt that Nova had spent the past three semesters working with the students and already had systems in place to interview the students. Becca, whose super power was super speed, had volunteered to transcribe all of their interviews. She cut the production time down by 75 percent by being able to listen and type quite fast. "What I found fascinating about these interviews was . . . " Nova didn't quite catch the end of the sentence because she had a voice in her head. *Typical Becca, always talking first. It's like she thinks she knows more about the Mutant student experience than we do since she transcribed the recordings.* Nova quickly shook her head to indicate to Kadence that, while she agreed, Kadence needed to get out of Nova's head and they both needed to fix their faces. Becca always jumped in quickly to talk first. Becca was used to people operating slower than she was used to, so she always spoke first. She did not mean anything by it, but speaking first and quickly just felt natural to her.

Nova asked Becca to repeat what she had said and Becca replied with, "I guess I was speaking too fast for you. Well, I was saying that as I was typing up the interviews, I noticed that there was a big theme of community being a factor for where people went to college, which is definitely different than I originally thought."

Reba interrupted in agreement "Same, I always thought that money would be the biggest factor for these kids to pick their college. Cause they come from these inner cities, you know they're poor. And I thought most of them would be athletes, but who knew they got academic scholarships, too! I figured a little charity would go a really long way, and we could help these poor Mutants get here. The biggest problem in college is access, right? So, wouldn't an increase in funds be more meaningful? We just have to support affirmative action. Those KINDRED kids need it."

Kadence sighed heavily at this suggestion which caused the desks to rattle a little. She had heard over and over that her students were told they did not belong on campus and were only there to meet a quota. Recently, someone posted a photo of the Mutant Engineering Organization meeting on social media with the caption "Affirmative Action Club" as if the collective GPA of that student organization wasn't 3.8. The gasp was one of the first audible noises she had made recently, but she felt a little pleasure at the confused looks that Reba and Becca had given her. Kadence looked over and saw the streaks of color entering into Nova's hair. Nova bowed her head, using her hands as a visor to hide her face. The ignorance and insensitivity toward the KINDRED students—*her* students—was triggering and Nova was doing her best to keep it together on her own. Kadence couldn't ask Nova to speak for her so she took a deep breath and did her best to speak in a low voice. "Do you think money, such as those scholarships you are suggesting, stop the isolation and alienation these students feel because they are in the minority? Without a strong community that cares about them and supports them, many of these students would leave. Mutants need community to be successful here," Kadence said, speaking as much about herself as she was her students.

Becca was clearly taken aback by Kadence speaking, which made a little sense. It was Kadence's first time saying anything out loud in a classroom setting since they started the program, and Becca was partly to blame for that. Not a fan of being corrected, Becca responded with "Okay, you didn't have to yell at me. I'm just being honest. Besides, isn't having a Mutant-only community basically self-segregation? Shouldn't we be about diversity and meeting new people? There are so many nice people here that if the Mutants only stay together, they won't get to know anyone else."

Nova knew her eyes were glowing purple again and took a few deep breaths to try to calm herself down. She closed her eyes and held onto the table to help ground herself before responding and could feel it collapsing in her hands. She had worked so hard for the past year and a half, helping the students in the KINDRED find a home here, confront the bias they received on a daily basis, and took on their emotions more than was probably healthy for her. She knew that the students in KINDRED needed that connection to each other and she knew the data would back her up. She was doing all she could to keep it together because she knew all too well the explosion that was about to happen next.

Kadence decided to speak up again, once more reminding herself to speak softly, "Niceness and civility doesn't equal justice. You don't understand what it's like to be a Mutant on this campus. Some of our Mutant students have things said to them in class, or walking around campus, or at the football games. Things that make it unsafe to be in the dining hall or in buildings. So until Southern can figure out how to make this place equitable for everyone, programs like KINDRED are important." The ground trembled as she spoke. Kadence, seeing Reba was about to speak, quickly added, "And no, it's not self-segregation. If anything, it's self-preservation." After Kadence gave her closing statement, Becca and Reba were silent. Then, with a puzzled look, Reba said, "But if they were good enough to be here to begin with, they shouldn't need extra things. Supers don't get their own living-learning community."

Nova had enough. She stood up with so much force that she made a crater in the floor and when she let go of the table it crumbled to pieces. And with glowing eyes and curls that looked like purple and orange flames, Nova looked directly at Reba and firmly said, "THIS ENTIRE CAMPUS IS YOUR LIVING-LEARNING COMMUNITY!"

The professor walked into class at that very moment, alarmed at the scene of what was happening without any context as to how they got there. Reba notices the professors presence and shouts, "I'm just trying my best!! Doesn't that count for anything?!" She bursts into tears and puts her head in her hands as she chokes back sobs. As Reba cried, Nova and Kadence felt themselves begin to fade. Once again, Reba's tears were causing them to go invisible. The entire classroom, including the professor, focused on Reba in a state of shock and disbelief. Becca handed Reba a tissue and whispered assurances that it was okay and that Reba was not a bad person. Reba continued "I'm just so tired. Anytime we're in class, it feels like I have to walk on eggshells! I always have to think very carefully before I speak because all you do is yell at us if we aren't 100 percent perfect. Nobody's perfect." Reba, who always touted the safety in going invisible, chose this moment to stay visible as if she knew her tears would gain her sympathy from her peers. Her tears were tiny trophies trailing down her face, a reassurance that she was still a good person because it was someone else's fault that she felt badly.

Becoming more confident in her voice, Kadence took a deep breath and composed herself before speaking again. All eyes still on Reba since Kadence and Nova had gone invisible, Kadence remembered the checklist her mother taught her to use before speaking in front of people:

Am I going to be too loud?

Am I going to seem angry?

Will I be doubted?

In that moment, a chuckle escapes Kadence's mouth. She shakes her head at the irony in Reba stating that she has to think before she speaks, as if thinking about what you're going to say is a bad thing. "Maybe Reba should have thought through that statement first" says Kadence. Becca gasps, "Is this funny to you? Reba is being completely vulnerable and you're laughing at her? Maybe if you weren't always so stoic and cold, people wouldn't be so afraid of you all the time." Kadence did not have time to respond to either statement since Becca continued with, "You don't know how hard it is for us. You're constantly making things so uncomfortable. It's so hard to hear people talk about the school that we love. We try so hard to be nice and all you do is point out our mistakes and call us bad people. We aren't bad, you're just mean. Whenever we speak, you get angry and yell at us. It isn't safe! We-"

At this point, Nova had no filter. "SO WHAT?! YOU HAVE TO BE UN-COMFORTABLE FOR THREE HOURS A WEEK. I FEEL UNCOMFORT-ABLE EVERY MOMENT OF EVERYDAY AND UNSAFE ALMOST AS OFTEN. BUT NO ONE SEES OUR PAIN. NO ONE CARES ABOUT OUR TRAUMA, ESPECIALLY WHEN IT'S CAUSED BY SUPERS LIKE YOU! YOU KNOW WHAT YOU DO? YOU USE YOUR WEAPONIZED TEARS TO MAKE US INVISIBLE. NO ONE SEES US! NO ONE HEARS US! OUR POWERS BECOME USELESS. YOU CALL US VIOLENT AND DANGEROUS YET, HISTORICALLY SPEAKING, SUPERS HAVE BEEN THE MOST VIOLENT PEOPLE. YOUR TEARS ATTEMPT TO CONCEAL OUR TRAUMA AND ALLOW YOU TO CLAIM IT AS YOUR OWN. YOUR TEARS ARE LIKE THE ULTIMATE SUPERPOWER. WHAT ARE WE SUPPOSED TO DO AGAINST THAT?!'"

The entire classroom went silent. Nova closed her eyes to fight back tears. She was no longer invisible. All eyes were locked on her. The scrutiny com-ing from all over the room made her feel watched but still not seen. She quickly exited the room. Nova knew that in order to care for herself and stop taking on the feelings of everyone in the room, she would need to head out-side and take a few deep breaths.

Back in the class, the Supers were shifting uncomfortably in their seats, unsure of how to respond. A few had already texted Reba notes of support and given knowingly and sympathetic looks in her direction. A few Supers who were tired of Reba's antics felt bad about the situation but decided it was better to stay silent; they were only a few weeks away from graduation. The Mutants were sharing glances among themselves, feeling relieved that someone had finally named what they had been feeling for a while but unsure of what would happen next. Becca let out a sigh and looked down at the crumbled table. It was clear that she was thinking and everyone braced for what she would possibly say next. "We really are just trying to be good people. I guess I never realized how my discomfort delegitimizes your pain."

Kadence thought she heard the sincerity in Becca's voice. "We've tried to tell you over and over and you've never listened, it's exhausting. But if you're finally willing to listen, we could grab a bite to eat one day and talk—like really talk—about what it's like to be a Mutant on this campus." The professor did not know what to do in that moment and thanked Kadence and Becca and decided to end class a little early to give students space to process what had happened. Kadence quickly gathered her things to go check on Nova. But before she could leave, the professor pulled her aside.

"Don't let their tears ever keep you from using your voice. Whether they are crying because they have come to the upsetting realization that Supers are not the saviors of the galaxy, the guilt they feel due to the actions of their ancestors, their eyes have been opened to how terrible this world can be, or to how terrible they have been themselves. Keep speaking truth to power. Just make sure you're ready with a box of tissues."

Kadence smiled and walked out of the classroom with her head held high. She and Nova didn't save the world today, but she at least hopes they saved someone some unnecessary tears.

Chapter Four

Attack of the 50-ft Becky

Kakali Bhattacharya & Paul Maxfield

At five-minutes-past-noon, a young blonde woman burst through the door, and strode quickly to the lectern at the front of the room. She carried a laptop and several loose cables. Thirty-five pairs of eyes followed her. Despite her neatly arranged blonde hair, impeccable makeup, and fashionably professional outfit, she exuded an air of panic.

"Sorry, sorry, sorry," she repeated nervously. She plugged in her wires and switched on her computer. "I lost track of the time."

"It's okay, Becky," Ruhi assured the perpetually unprepared new-hire. She recalled the stress of her own first year as an assistant professor, and tried to cut the junior faculty some slack. All the same, Ruhi doubted that she would ever have allowed herself to be late to her own talk. "Just take your time. Relax. Take a breath."

Ruhi was one of three women of color (and the only Indian) working in the College of Education at Dogwood State University, a predominantly white institution. She was in her early forties, and had recently gained tenure. The other two women were Kecia and Leilani. Kecia was Black, and in her sixties. Though she had experience, including a lot of institutional knowledge, she'd been stuck at the Associate Rank for over a decade, concerned that her academic accomplishments would not be given fair weight. Leilani was of Indonesian heritage, and the newest addition to the group. Ruhi and Kecia had been friends and mentors to Leilani, knowing that she'd be too isolated otherwise. The three women met weekly for drinks and to talk about work, family, and aspirations. Though Dogwood did little to support scholars of color, these three women did their best to support each other.

Becky had been another story. The three women were initially warm toward their new colleague. Leilani and Becky were the newest early-career faculty, hired at the same time. However, Becky aligned herself with power, smiling and flirting with the older white men within the college. She won their affection by acting like a little girl who needed constant saving. The men were eager to oblige. Becky's interaction with the three women of color were often superficial, layered with a demeanor of "niceness" which never felt sincere.

Disappointed but unsurprised at seeing how easily their older colleagues were getting played, the three women of color chose to focus on their own professional goals and steer clear of Becky. While Ruhi and Kecia were accomplished scholars, Leilani won an early-career award for her scholarship. Becky worried that the combination of her lack of publications and Leilani's success would earn her a negative merit evaluation from their department chair, Don. To shake off any negative attention on her mediocrity, Becky tried to sabotage the women of color, especially Leilani.

Becky told Ruhi's students that she could support them better in their research. However, the truth was that she needed the student labor for her own scholarly activities. She poached one of Kecia's brightest students, convincing him that Kecia did not have his best interest in mind when she was holding him to a high standard. When Kecia complained to Don, he made excuses, saying that it was ultimately the students' decision of whom they worked with. Besides, there were only so many students to go around, and Becky really needed the experience.

Meanwhile, Don made Becky the coordinator of a new program. She immediately began assigning new courses to Leilani, which not only required increased labor for preparation, but were also hosted at a satellite campus two hours away, significantly limiting Leilani's visibility on the main campus.

Ruhi, the most outspoken of the three, raised her concern with Don. However, he suggested that Becky's actions might stem from being poorly mentored. He suggested that Ruhi create a space for Becky at her Lunch-Hour lecture series. For three years, she had been organizing the series to showcase research in the college. Ruhi reluctantly agreed. While she had no desire to mentor Becky, she thought perhaps if Becky was focused on showing off her own work, she would have less time to sabotage others.

Yet, even with ample notice, multiple flyers across Dogwood campus and the College of Education building, massive email marketing, Becky could barely remember to get to her own talk on time, or seem somewhat prepared to deliver a lecture about her research expertise. Now, fifteen minutes past the scheduled start time, Becky nodded to Ruhi to let her know that she was finally ready to begin. Ruhi stepped to the microphone, and the room became silent.

"Hi everyone, thank you for joining us for the final lunch-hour lecture of the semester. I know many of you are busy, so I'm glad you could attend."

Ruhi proceeded to introduce Becky according to Becky's own prepared bio, which was light on academic achievements but heavy on name-dropping of various mentors and institutions. "Please join me in welcoming Dr. Becky Langford," Ruhi concluded to polite applause as she rejoined the audience.

Becky approached the front of the room, fumbling with a mobile microphone. "Eh, is this . . . can you hear me?" she asked. Finally, she began to speak. However, it was immediately clear that she was unprepared. She forgot the sequence of the ideas she wanted to share, several of her slides repeated, and at the end put up an erroneous table implying that minoritized people chose to take offense at the actions of white leaders and policymakers even when those actions were well-intentioned. She continued, "Policies like affirmative action were good, when they were needed. I mean, I voted for Barack Obama twice, but we have to look at who is being hurt by these policies. All lives matter, and all applications for various positions should matter, too."

"What do you mean, 'all lives matter'?" Kecia interrupted, her patience exhausted.

"I mean, as a white woman, I've experienced oppression too . . . from men. It's kinda like racism. It's everywhere. You know it but can't put your finger on it." Becky smiled.

"Are you saying we should do away with affirmative action?" Kecia followed up.

"Well, perhaps not. But we need to revise it."

"But the policymakers are mostly white. How do you expect a balanced perspective?" Ruhi inquired.

"I don't think that matters, as long as people mean well. There are good people on all sides." Becky shifted her stance, looking visibly uncomfortable.

"You believe all lives matter even when only some lives are represented, because all white people have good intentions?" Leilani asked.

"Whoa! No! I'm just saying that it's okay to be white. Sometimes we forget that when we do anti-racist work."

"You're arguing for preserving whiteness which denigrates people who are minoritized," Ruhi responded.

"Oh no, no. I'm a victim of whiteness, too. I have to fight the white man all the time. I am with you on this one." Becky nodded with a forced smile.

"You're not exempt from whiteness," Ruhi corrected. "You benefit from it. White men see you as one of them. They're always trying to protect and promote you. They always run to your rescue when you play damsel in distress."

Becky began to feel exposed. She couldn't respond to the critiques of her statements. Who the hell did they think they were? Didn't they know which university she came from? Didn't they realize how connected she was to all the big names in the field? It wasn't right! Becky started to panic. She could feel a tingle in her fingertips. "Oh no, it's happening again," she thought to herself. "Not in front of these people! I've got to get out of here."

Becky ran into the hallway, leaving behind a bewildered audience. Her neck and legs continued to extend as she ran down the hall. Her head began to butt against the ceiling, knocking the foam panels and light fixtures loose. By the time she reached the doors at the end of the hallway, her body had become too large to fit through them.

"What's happening?" shouted someone from the audience who had followed Becky into the hallway.

"Should we do something?" asked another voice.

"Get away!" Becky cried. "Leave me alone!"

She thrust her body repeatedly against the walls, causing the building to tremble. The audience panicked and began to run for the exits. Loose debris and dust began to rain down from the ceilings as Becky thrashed within the suddenly claustrophobic space.

Leilani grabbed Kecia's hand, pulling her toward an exit. Kecia screamed over her shoulder at Ruhi, "Call Don! Tell him what's happening."

Becky let out another shriek that was positively deafening in the confined space. Her head had broken through the floor above. Her arms flailed madly, blindly punching and tearing through the walls. "Let me out!" she roared over and over. "Let me out! Let me out!" Finally, with a kick that sent a violent shudder through the building's foundation, Becky broke through the brick side of the building, and escaped.

Ruhi finally got through to Don on the phone. "Don! It's Ruhi. Listen, Becky is out of control."

"Ruhi? Becky? What?" Don asked, drowsily.

"It was her presentation," Ruhi explained. "It wasn't good. People asked her questions she couldn't answer. She just went off. Now she's 20 . . . 30 feet tall! She's destroying the campus!"

"Are you sure it's *our* Becky?" Don asked.

"Of course, I'm sure."

"But she's so nice and sweet."

"It's an act. She is only nice to *some* people."

"I'm on my way," Don grumbled. "Probably just a misunderstanding. We'll sort it out."

"Okay," Ruhi said, unsure what Don had in mind to stop the 50-foot menace.

As Becky crossed the quad, Ruhi could feel the ground shake with each step. She followed through the gaping hole left behind in the wall, looking above the tree line to see her bobbing head. As her body had grown, her clothes had shredded and been replaced by an armor of thick green-gray scales.

By now, people were flowing from all the buildings on campus. Curious and terrified, they couldn't take their eyes off the massive creature turning this way and that. Too big and nowhere to hide, people were gazing up at Becky's hideous form in horror. Becky howled, and stomped on the ground, making the entire campus quake. Car windows shattered. Alarms blared simultaneously from several different directions. The chaos seemed only to enrage Becky further. She began to march away from the center of campus, crushing whatever got under her feet. Students, staff, and faculty, mobile phones aloft, recorded Becky's actions to post to social media.

"Leave me alone!" Becky shouted. The force of the sound waves blew out windows in the nearby buildings. She kicked at the crowd, sending several people flying, and then brought her foot down, flattening a Ford Ranger. "It's not fair!" Becky continued in her thunderous voice. Tears the size of a large pond welled in her eyes, overflowed, and splashed down on the people below, crushing those directly under the impact. Leilani fell on the pavement and was dragged by the sudden deluge of tears. She took in mouthfuls of the stream, stifling a surprised scream.

"Leilani!" Kecia shouted, racing to where their colleague's body lay unconscious. As Ruhi caught up, Kecia dove on top of Leilani, pressing her hands against her chest and breathing into her mouth with her nose pinched until Becky's salty tears gushed out of Leilani's lungs. Leilani sat up wide-eyed and gasping for air.

"We thought you were gone," Ruhi said, helping her friend to her feet.

"Ugh, me too," Leilani coughed.

News reporters had arrived on the scene. Scrolling banners along the bottom of television screens all across America had dubbed her "Beckzilla." Next came the Police, Fire, and Ambulance crews, all with flashing lights and sirens, but they were dwarfed and powerless to stop Becky's rampage. To Becky they were nothing but irritating gnats. A helicopter flew too close to her. She swatted it out of the sky, sending it crashing into the College of Business building where it exploded in a fireball. One foot came down, crushing a police car, while the other rolled a fire truck on its side. The SWAT team arrived in a heavily armored vehicle only to be immediately dispatched with a swift flick of a finger.

Ruhi finally found Don amidst all the turmoil. He stood on a pile of rubble that had once been the Gender and Women's Studies department. "Don, we've got to stop her!"

"She's just having a bad day," Don said. "Poor kid."

"Come on, man. Even you're not stupid enough to believe that." Ruhi said, gazing up as Becky unleashed a terrible roar.

"I'm sure she doesn't mean it," Don explained. "Just let me talk to her. She'll listen to me."

Ruhi followed Don to the overturned armored SWAT vehicle, where Kecia and Leilani were taking shelter as Becky was uprooting trees and tossing them this way and that. Don asked for a loudspeaker, and in his best authoritative voice said, "Becky, dear, I don't know what's going on with you, but I'm sure we can work this out. Go back to your original size, and stop all this crying. You're hurting innocent people. Do it now."

Becky glanced curiously in their direction. Face to face for the first time with monster-Becky, Don immediately regretted his decision. The three women fled, but Don stood transfixed as Becky bent over him. She reached down and picked up Don, closing her giant fist around his torso, so only his head poked out.

"Come on Becky, just calm down. We can talk about this," Don said in a small voice.

Becky raised him to eye-level. "You were supposed to protect me!" she accused. "Why did you let them hurt me? It's not fair!"

Before Don could answer, Becky, popped him into her mouth, chewed several times, and swallowed. Then she continued to trudge through campus demolishing everything in her way—Sociology, Political Science, Ethnic Studies, Anthropology . . . they all collapsed under her onslaught. She could not stop crying. Tears kept falling, creating sudden torrents in the walkways between the buildings that carried away debris and unsuspecting students. The three women followed at a cautious distance, until her path of devastation ended in a tangled web of power lines. The mob circled again, but Becky's flailing limbs and the risk of electrocution kept everyone at bay.

"What's that?" Ruhi asked.

"Huh?" Leilani responded, panicked and spinning around looking for yet another source of violence.

Ruhi suspected that after nearly drowning in the over-sized white-girl tears, Leilani would be dealing with Post-Becky Stress Disorder for some time. She had compassion for her but couldn't afford the time to comfort her with the 50-foot Becky still thrashing around.

"No, I hear it too!" Kecia shouted. "It's . . . it's coming from the sky!"

Above the tree line appeared first one, then several, and finally a whole fleet of helicopters. They landed quickly at a safe distance from Becky's grasping hands. The giant woman roared in fury and continued to struggle against the power lines. Men and women of color began to exit from the aircraft, each of them dressed like an Old-Navy catalog model—the men in khakis and polo shirts, the women in mom-jeans and tank-tops. A tall white man in a fitted black suit and tie stepped out of the lead helicopter and strode confidently toward Ruhi, Leilani, and Kecia.

"You!" he said in an authoritative voice, pointing directly at Ruhi. "I need a sit-rep[1] ASAP. What's going on here?"

"Becky was giving a lecture about her research, and then some people had some questions, and she freaked out, and then . . . this." Ruhi pointed at the fifty-foot menace.

"Did you at any point question Becky's motivations as a white ally or suggest that white privilege might blind her to the realities of people of color?"

"Um . . . maybe . . . a bit . . . " Ruhi admitted.

"All we were saying was that as a successful and educated white woman, she needed to investigate her positionality." Leilani blurted out.

The man in the suit listened and nodded. "Mhm. Mhm. We've seen this kind of thing before."

"Before?" Kecia asked. "I'm sorry, who are you?"

"We're the BEAST. I'm General Stanford."

"Beast?" Leilani asked.

"BEAST: Becky Emergency Action Security Team," Stanford explained. "Listen ladies, we don't have time for this. At any moment, this Becky can break free. If she comes into contact with another Becky, we could have a full-blown Beckydemic on our hands."

"Beckydemic?" Kecia asked. "You mean there could be more of them?"

"Yes, ma'am. I've seen . . . " Stanford paused and shook his head sadly. "Well, let's just say it wasn't pretty. I think we can nip this in the bud if we move quickly, though." With that, Stanford turned to his troops. "Ladies and gentlemen, what we have here is Beck-Con level 3 situation. Repeat, Beck-Con 3. Our goal is safety first, keep the target alive, contain the situation, and know that the target is NOT the enemy. Remember, this is what we've trained for. On my command, Mercury[2] maneuvers . . . Ready . . . Charge!"

The advanced guard moved forward in tight formation, opened their mouths and began to sing, "Is this the real life?" A second line of BEAST troops followed in the steps of the first. "Or is it just fantasy?" Becky paused in her struggles, watching the advancing casual clothes models with curiosity. "Caught in a landslide, no escape from reality." The force approached cautiously. "Open your eyes, look up to the skies, and seeeee."

Becky suddenly roared and struck out with her foot, sending half a dozen troops sailing backward to the waiting helicopters, their blades still spinning fast enough to decapitate one of the unintentionally airborne BEAST members.

"Oh no, it wasn't the helicopters," Kecia commented. "It was Becky that killed the BEAST."[3]

"Reinforcements," Stanford called. More singing Old-Navy models ran in to replace their fallen comrades.

"I'm just a poor boy, I need no sympathy," BEAST continued to sing.

Ruhi looked around and noticed that all of the white onlookers had fallen under the spell of the Bohemian Rhapsody[4], and were compelled to sing along. While Ruhi, Kecia, and Leilani had heard the song before, they didn't know the words and were somehow immune to its effects.

"Because I'm easy-come, easy-go, little high, little low."

"Noooo!!!" Becky cried. She stomped her feet, crushing more of the singing force, and pulled at the tangle of wires. There was a terrible creaking tearing sound as one of the towers bent and crumpled. Then Becky ripped her other arm free in a blaze of sparks.

"She's loose!" Ruhi shouted. "The BEAST lost!"

"We'd better get out of here," Leilani cried. Some of the BEAST troopers had already begun to retreat.

"No, wait," Kecia said. "Look!" Now that she was free, Becky began to perform air guitar in time with the song. "It worked." As the song moved into the operatic middle section Becky and the chorus of enraptured white onlookers began to clap rhythmically.

"We've got her! Everyone get back!" Stanford warned. "This next part is going to get a little bumpy."

"I think we'd better take cover," Kecia said.

"Why?" Ruhi asked.

In response, Becky's voice reached the crescendo of the song. "Beelzebub has a devil put aside for me! For meee! For MEEEEEEE!!!!!" As she hit the high note, windows all over campus blew out, sending glass showering down onto crowds of onlookers. Ruhi, Kecia, and Leilani dove for cover under one of the BEAST helicopters. In the next instant, Becky began head banging and jumping up and down in time with the hard rock passage. The ground shook violently. The concrete cracked and buckled. Buildings which had barely withstood Becky's onslaught finally crumbled. Many of the BEAST team struggled to keep their feet as well as their tune.

After fifty seconds of pure heavy-metal terror, the song entered the final movement, a soothing comedown. Becky concluded in a near whisper, which still sounded like a jet-engine, "Any way the wind blows . . . " she stood calm and looking wistfully into the distance.

"Good work, everyone," Stanford announced through a bullhorn. "Clear the wounded and proceed to phase two. Brady[5] tactics."

BEAST members who had fallen in the line of duty were carried away. The remaining troopers circled around the now-docile Becky. They began to chant in cadence: "Hoo HA! Hoo Hoo HA!"

"I don't know what I've been told," Stanford called through his bullhorn.

"I don't know what I've been told," the BEAST team echoed.

"Becky's heart is made of gold," Stanford continued. Each line was repeated and amplified by the troopers. "She only means the best. Her spirit is innocent. Becky, Becky you're so great. You, no one could ever hate."

Becky looked down at those around her with a bored expression.

"She's too strong," shouted one of the troopers, breaking away from the circle. He approached Ruhi, Leilani, and Kecia. "We need more power! Come on!"

"You expect me to kiss her ass after everything she's done?" Leilani blurted out.

"But we have to do something to stop her." Ruhi said.

"Why is it always us?" Leilani screamed.

"I don't know, Leilani. It just is," Kecia responded. "And if we don't act, we'll have a potential Beckydemic on our hands."

"There's gotta be another way," Leilani protested.

"Ma'am, there's no other way," another of the troopers explained, reaching out to grasp Leilani's shoulder. "Beckies need to be coddled to come down to their original size. Coddling from people of color is especially effective. Please, ma'am. Lives are at stake."

Begrudgingly Leilani took the trooper's hand. Ruhi and Kecia followed.

"Becky, Becky we love you," Stanford continued chanting. "Becky, Becky you're always true."

Ruhi noticed Leilani standing silently beside her, staring stonily up at Becky's nostril. She elbowed her in the ribs.

"Fine," Leilani huffed.

"In Becky we place our trust," Stanford called.

"In Becky we place our trust," Leilani joined in.

"What's good for Becky is good for us."

"What's good for Becky is good for us."

As the group continued to chant, Becky began to shrink. The scales melted back into her skin. Encouraged, the BEAST chanted louder and faster. As Becky became smaller, the circle closed around her. Finally, BEAST met in a big group hug with Becky at its heart. Stanford ordered a trooper to retrieve a blanket from the helicopters and wrapped it around the now normal-sized Becky.

"You're safe now," Stanford said, escorting her to one of the BEAST helicopters.

"Where are we going?" Becky asked.

"Somewhere where you'll be understood and protected," Stanford promised.

"They were so mean," Becky whined.

"I know, I know," Stanford assured her.

The helicopters lifted off and flew away into the sunset, leaving Ruhi, Kecia, and Leilani to limp back through the rubble heaps that used to form their campus.

"I don't know about y'all, but I could certainly use a drink," Kecia stated.

"Sudden Saloon?" Leilani suggested.

"You read my mind," Kecia agreed.

As they were leaving campus they passed a group of young blonde women. Ruhi lingered, listening to their conversation.

"Did you see what they did to her?" Ruhi heard one of the women sobbing. "It was like so unfair. I mean, it just makes me so angry."

"I know, right?" another woman agreed. "Hey, do you feel like a tingling in your body?"

"Betty, I think your hands are getting bigger."

Ruhi needed to hear no more. "Yeah, I think the Old Suds sounds like a great idea," she said, rushing to catch up to her colleagues. "Anywhere but here."

"Hope we can play Bohemian Rhapsody on the jukebox at the bar. We need to learn the words. It'll come in handy for next time." Kecia said.

"And there will be a next time," Ruhi added, as the three women walked away.

NOTES

1. Situation report.

2. In reference to Freddie Mercury, the lead vocalist of the rock band, Queen, who also sang the popular song "Bohemian Rhapsody."

3. Paraphrasing the final line from *King Kong*: "Oh no, it wasn't the airplanes, it was beauty that killed the beast."

4. https://www.youtube.com/watch?v=fJ9rUzIMcZQ.

5. In reference to the entertainer, Wayne Brady, who is well liked by white people in the U.S.

Section Two

Guiding Questions

1. Identify the behaviors that suppressed the powers of both Nova and Kadence. Why are these behaviors particularly oppressing?
2. In acknowledging how emotions are weaponized by Becky(s), consider other scenarios where this might occur. What strengthens their weaponizing? What weakens it?
3. In the 50-Foot Becky, they needed to call in a Becky Disaster Team to defuse the situation. How might this same disaster team be a way of protecting the emotionalities of Becky(s)? Do you see efforts similar to this team occurring in your environment? How might it impact race relations?
4. What are the risks in coddling the emotionalities of Becky(s)?
5. If you are a white woman, before weaponizing your own emotions, how can you self-identify how you feel? Why are you feeling that? Is it based on real substance or projected stereotypes? How can you take steps toward recognizing the need to have your feelings addressed above anyone else's? Do you need to feel comforted? By whom and why?

Becky(s) as Entitlement and Privilege

The term white privilege has become as fashionable as skinny jeans. Everyone is rocking it in some odd display of solidarity to a fashion norm. They dress it up with heels. They sport different colors. They know by virtue of wearing them they are making a fashion statement. The popularity of uttering or acknowledging white privilege, like fashion, is trendy. From white privilege workshops, conferences, and trainings to T-shirts sporting the phrase "got privilege?" (see McIntosh, 1988), stores even now carry different shades of skin colored Band-Aids in direct response to the now famous "invisible knapsack" essay by Peggy McIntosh (1988). And, more and more people are engaging the term itself. In fact, in my own experiences as a university professor, many white teacher candidates echo their acknowledgment of white privilege and how, by having it, they now want to "give back" to urban schools in communities of color. Yet, behind this seemingly liberal and just assertion, there are many dynamics at play. First, because of its popularity, it is almost as if simply uttering the words "white privilege" is tantamount to publically wearing a safety pin; one that immediately self-identifies a person as an ally and antiracist, and self-absolves them from ever being a racist. Similarly, with respect to the U.S. two-party system, white liberal Democrats quickly employ the phrase "I didn't vote for Trump" as a way to distance themselves from those who are deemed "true" racists. It is a ridiculous maneuver considering that people who engage in racist behaviors can be found anywhere and within all affiliations. As such, the quick employment of the term white privilege becomes a strategic maneuver to absolve one's own culpability in whiteness. Meaning, if one utters white privilege and professes any level of engagement with it, the presumption is that they could not possibly engage in racist acts. In fact, when asked what white privilege they have accrued, one of my teacher candidates discussed the privilege of having skin colored Band-Aids; as if the privilege of having skin colored Band-Aids were on par to the privilege of not fearing that your child might be shot by police! Clearly, there was a disconnect between pontificating one's loose admission of having white privilege to truly understanding the gravity of advantage that white privilege affords. The uttering of white privilege has the same effect as the wearing of safety pins in that it serves as a symbol of allyhood and antiracism without having to do the real work of racial justice. And that, in and of itself, exemplifies white privilege.

Second, for some to acknowledge that their lives have been structured by white privilege and then turn around and say they need to give back to urban communities of color makes me wonder as to what have they so wrongfully taken from communities of color that they now feel compelled to give back? This is an underlying quandary of white privilege. That some can say they need to give back because of the accrual of white privilege is in and of itself a slight recognition of how whiteness and white supremacy operate in society. Or, as Oliver & Shapiro (1997) so poignantly argues, "what is not often acknowledged is that the same social system the foster the accumulation of private wealth for many whites denies it to blacks, thus forging an intimate connection between white wealth accumulation and black poverty . . . in this sense we uncover a racial wealth tax" (pp. 5–6). Suffice it to say that white people who admit to having accrued white privilege, in some sense, acknowledge that they did so off the backs of people of color, and thus now feel compelled to give back to the communities they have stolen from. Yet white privilege becomes even more complex when applied to their qualifications of teaching in communities of color. In fact, many of my students divulged how they have had little to no contact with people of color in their lives because they lived in white communities. And yet, they feel confident enough to be a good racially just teacher in urban schools. Why would one feel qualified enough to even teach in a community where they have had limited to no interactions from people of that community? This is where white privilege alludes to entitlement. That is, to confidently presume oneself as qualified enough to teach in communities of color regardless of their lack of interaction with any people of color is a pompous endeavor. As of 2019, an overwhelming state of whiteness (Sleeter, 2001) persists in the field of teaching such that 80 percent of the teaching force racially identifies as white (NCES, 2019). Even more noticeable, yet not clearly reported, is that institutions of higher education where teacher education programs are housed are also predominantly white. Whiteness is not only embedded in the curriculum, teaching practices, and teacher beliefs of K–12 teachers; it is also embedded in the very programs that graduate these teachers. So left unchecked are the aforementioned commentaries made within teacher education. Simply put, because the whiteness in teacher education is intoxicating, white teacher (and teacher educators too) see no issue with how their predominantly white students confidently lay claim to teaching in urban schools in communities of color with little if any experience interacting with people of color. This is how entitlement gets institutionalized.

Clearly, white privilege has become an en vogue phrase. Gone are the old phraseologies of "I have a Black best friend" or "I voted for Obama" because all one needs to do is invoke some cursory understanding of white privilege to purchase a pass on racist behaviors. While the verbal articulation of white privilege is more prevalent, the real historical accrual of financial, educational, legal, political, racial, and emotional privilege is less understood. And, in this cursory understanding of that which is white privilege, white privilege continues to thrive in ways that negatively impact people of color.

In this section, the stories hyper-characterize Becky(s) as racially privileged and entitled to highlight how engagement in these behaviors does nothing but damage the hopes of racial justice despite all good intentions. Though written as fan fiction stories, the authors were quick to share that the stories are inspired by real life experiences they have had with well-meaning white women. Despite good intentions, these white women still behaved in ways that privileged her needs above anyone else while assuming that she was entitled to those privileges. Therefore, Becky(s) as Privileged and Entitled refers to white women who use their privilege and presume their entitlement to that privilege at the expense of the humanity, respect, and dignity of people of color and more specifically, of women of color.

In asking what one of the authors wanted their readers to come away with, one author writes, "Too often, Becky's behaviors and attitudes are excused, minimized, and obscured as she vies to maintain her position in a white supremacist cishetero capitalist patriarchy. I wanted to highlight these behaviors and attitudes so that they could no longer be discounted, because we cannot truly survive Becky until we know how she operates. Becky[s] gonna beck." Just as white teacher candidates' behaviors are overlooked in teacher education due to the overwhelming presence of whiteness, so, too are the everyday behaviors of Becky(s) as privileged and entitled. Another author writes, "I want readers to see the insidious, subtle ways that Becky[s] manipulate and the genre allows it to be shown without placing blame . . . " Within this response, the author divulges how the behaviors of Becky(s) as privileged and entitled are so manipulative and insidious that she was careful to not place blame for fear of retaliation. In fact, when asked about how it felt to write this story, one author writes, "I found the experience cathartic and freeing. While most of the incidences are based on my experiences, they are steeped within the context of this fictitious story, so I feel that the original instances are masked. Thus, unless you know the truth of my experience, I do not believe one will be able to readily see me within my real life context. So, it will be liberating to see my survival from the safety afforded by the cover of the story and further enclosed by the creative genre." Although the stories use humor to mock the behaviors of privilege and entitlement in Becky(s), they are not to be taken lightly. Drawing from this response, one can understand how the fear of retaliation from ostracism to job discrimination is very real. In fact, it is historical. Whistle blowers, for lack of a better term, have notoriously been castigated as troublemakers and disciplined via retaliatory and punitive measures to keep them silent about the atrocities within an organization. This is no different than the fear embedded in simply sharing these stories. The saddest part of all this bravery is that despite telling the story as a way to stop the inhumane behavior, white privilege and entitlement can rear their ugly heads simply by refusing to hear the moral of the stories turning its head on the message.

Therefore, although white privilege is like skinny jeans in that it is fashionably forward, one must realize that to wear them is also a commitment to discomfort. It is precisely this feeling of discomfort that will allow Becky(s) to learn that losing her privilege or revealing her entitled ways is not the same as being oppressed. Instead, in living with her discomfort, she is learning to live a more humane, racially just life where her feelings of discomfort bear her fair share of the racial burden.

REFERENCES

McIntosh, P. (1988). White privilege: Unpacking the invisible knapsack. *Race, class, and gender in the United States: An integrated study*, *4*, 165–69.

National Council of Educational Statistic, NCES. (2019). *Spotlight A: Characteristics of Public School Teachers by Race/Ethnicity*. Retrieved from https://nces.ed.gov/programs/raceindicators/spotlight_a.asp.

Oliver, M. & Shapiro, T. (1997). *Black Wealth/White Wealth: A New Perspective on Racial Inequality*. New York: Routledge.

Chapter Five

The World According to Becky

An Inverse Chronology of Humanity in a Teacher Preparation Program

Justin P. Jiménez

Because for me, they are special, and I believe I am special for them. Having spent several years developing her identity and acumen as a no-nonsense public defender in Chicago, Rebecca Crenshaw has struggled to connect to what she considers her true calling. As much as she enjoyed the grind of tirelessly advocating for others in and out of the courtroom, Rebecca also feels that a better work-life balance is necessary to bridge the gap between her aspirations and reality. Following her favorite feminist YouTuber, Laci Green, Rebecca begins her daily morning ritual of diary writing hoping to discover more about herself and her future. The sentiments are consistent as she anchors the eddying thoughts onto the page, "This is it. It is now or never. I have a singular responsibility to care for those who are less fortunate." Inspired by mainstream feminist treatises on empowerment, self-help manifestos to have it all, and icons such as Malala Yousafzai, Emma Watson, and Beyoncé, Rebecca believes she can make the most impact in education. She has even devoured a few books by Sheryl Sandberg and Megyn Kelly. She often ponders: "Why can't I have it all? What can we possibly accomplish if we all lean into what matters for a change?" Rebecca is captivated by the swell of women across the country who have political ambitions. Rebecca doesn't want to merely make a difference but to *be* the difference.

Motivated by the renewed charges for social transformation in daily life, especially in light of the 2016 presidential election, Rebecca moves back home to Whiteshore Lakes, Minnesota. She fills out an application for the elementary education licensure program at Eastcliff University, a large public institution. In her application, she proudly mentions the numerous accolades she received based on her participation in activities that defend the defenseless as an attorney. Not to mention, she lists her multiple certificates in equity, diversity, and interculturalism. Her acceptance letter arrives in late April.

71

JUNE 26, 2017

When Rebecca first steps foot on campus during a humid June morning, she takes in the grandeur of the campus. Although her hair starts to frizzle a little, the excitement of the hustle and bustle makes her forget her potential bad hairday. She is ecstatic for what's to come. She saunters down The Knoll, an area with manicured lawns where she'll spend most of her time. She feels like she belongs. Lawn signs abound with "everyone is welcome here" assuring Rebecca of her decision to attend this program. She catches a glance at a large bronze sculpture and marvels at its dignified stance: a striking woman grasping a school book and sporting academic regalia. At the foot of the sculpture is an informational plaque of Alma Mater. She mutters to herself, "Alma Mater depicts Athena. She is goddess of fortitude, grace, and power." Without any hesitation, Rebecca reaches for her phone and snaps a few pictures, throwing peace signs for her small yet strong following on Instagram. She includes the hashtags "blessed, nofilter, winning, womenarethefuture, forthem, and futureteacher."

Throngs of people are trying to figure out where they need to be for their orientation sessions and first classes, whereas Rebecca has already studied the campus map and knows that the education building is by the Mississippi. Proudly strolling past all the confused students, Rebecca enters the building and quickly finds her classes for the day. These sessions include professional dispositions and teaching for social justice. In her first class, she befriends Libby Whitaker, who like Rebecca, is also a twenty-something white woman who has decided to make the switch to teaching.

"Wow. There's a lot of people here. It's so great to see a bunch of us millennials wanting to do something noble." Libby smiles and tries to amplify her voice so as to make herself heard within the bellowing chorus of excited teacher candidates in the auditorium.

"Absolutely. Especially during these times, there are so many problems. I mean, Trump isn't going to help those who are disenfranchised, right? So, I guess we have to. And it's like that Gandhi quote, we need to be the change we wish to see in the world."

Both Rebecca and Libby chuckle and consult their schedules for the day. Rebecca is a little peeved about the requisite courses. "I still can't believe we need to take a class on race and diversity in education. It's 2018." Rebecca tells Libby in a scornful tone as she color-codes important dates in her passion planner. "I mean after all I've learned about this all before. Yes, there are different races. There's injustice everywhere. What else is there to know? It's common sense to me. I know all about race and diversity."

Libby nods her head and scoffs, "It's as if they think we don't know anything. We get it. I don't know about you, but I'm doing all that I can to show that black lives matter. Let's see . . . I voted for Obama . . . twice . . . and am rooting for all things Democrat. I always try to post all these things from HuffPost and Occupy Democrats on Facebook. There's always some good dialogue among my friends in Whiteshore Lakes."

"Quite frankly, I think it's a waste of time and money . . . the people that really need to have a course on race and diversity are those Trumpeters. We're the woke ones, right Libby?"

Rebecca and Libby finish their planning and commemorate their budding friendship with a gratuitous selfie. Rebecca immediately changes her Facebook profile picture, which includes Maya Angelou's enduring quote, "When people show you who they are, believe them." Rebecca also includes what she considers a felicitous hashtag, "woke," to capture their outlook on life. Libby and Rebecca admire their beguiling smiles and agree to embellish the picture with a trendy frame.

They try to stay focused on the themes in the orientation sessions. A keynote is delivered by a young black professor and the message couldn't be any more poignant. She poses, "How do we teach so we don't kill? Education is political. Where we are has been written by particular values, the types of things you are learning; in other words, the curriculum. How might we unlearn what we've been taught." While the message is riveting for Rebecca, she couldn't help but be turned off by the message. After the keynote, Rebecca and Libby discuss their reactions.

"Well, what did you think about that presentation, Libby?"

"I don't really get it. She is definitely passionate about what she's talking about, don't get me wrong. But what does she mean that education is political?"

"Yeah. It shouldn't be about Republicans and Democrats," Rebecca exclaimed. "We want to be teachers so that everyone can get a fair chance. Every child shouldn't be left behind."

Libby adds, "Yeah, this is what happens when we get all tribal. We can't make any progress. You know what, I think teaching in a way that doesn't kill actually means killing people with kindness. Why would I want to unlearn what I got from my progressive Midwestern upbringing? I mean, how is tolerance a bad thing? Way to make us feel good about being teachers!" Rebecca nods vigorously.

Libby assumes a power pose with arms in akimbo and overstates, "What I *really* want to learn is classroom management. You know some kids are rowdier than others. How am I going to control them without getting into trouble? Everything is so risky for us, and we might be called a racist for doing the right thing, even when what we do is what's best for these marginalized kids."

"Oh God forbid we get called racists! I get so stressed about the possibility of being called out. If people only knew what's in my heart and soul and all that I do to show I'm a bonafide social justice warrior . . . Anyway, I say we protest and scheme against people who are not like us over a skinny vanilla latte!"

JUNE 24, 2017

It has been about a week and Rebecca has her schedule down pat. It is frenetic as these courses often rotate frequently because of the compressed nature of her program. Her instructors for most of her courses are predominantly white women, and Rebecca believes she has gleaned so much from their expertise as well as their class activities. Sandy, a middle-aged white woman, is the instructor for her introduction to elementary school course. Sandy poses daily reflection prompts and has students record their thoughts in journals. For one class activity, Sandy breaks students up into small groups of 4 and assigns them a "diversity book" featuring children from different cultures that is appropriate for elementary students to discuss. As much as Rebecca doesn't like to harp on diversity, she feels enlightened about the many resources she can use to reach her "diverse students." When diversity is broached, Sandy has an uplifting attitude and recites, "We are all pirates. We all have differences. Remember that diversity is our strength and that it is our everyday work." Rebecca likes how she is learning about "different cultures" and believes these essentializing and "authentic" case studies help her to better relate to her future students. She understands that having different books in her classroom will go a long way in the fight for anti-racism.

Along with having these discussions of cultural groups and their representations in these books, Rebecca also takes seriously the notion of culturally sustaining pedagogy, and for her concerns mostly about securing academic achievement and finding ways to celebrate different cultures in discrete ways. Sandy facilitates the discussion with the class on relationship building with students, how there should be a certain level of intimacy to feel for what these students are going through.

She takes copious notes on how to implement some of these strategies in her own classroom. "I'm going to need a bigger binder for all these things I need to be doing. I need to get these methods right for my students!" Rebecca exclaims.

Libby laughs, "Look at you loving this diversity talk!"

Rebecca appreciates Sandy and the tangible ways that help her hone the moral practice of teaching. After several weeks of this seminar, Rebecca is elated about receiving an A on her final project intellectualizing the need for more empathetic relationships, building a "sentimental repertoire," and fostering soul-to-soul connections for anti-racist education, she realizes she must move on to a requisite course on race, school, and society. Rebecca is neither thrilled nor motivated for this course as she assumes that she is going to hear what she already knows. Plus, she hears the instructor is a real hardass about race, according to her other peers. Nonetheless, Rebecca keeps sight on the children she is going to affect.

JULY 22, 2017

A month later, Rebecca's schedule starts to pick up. With her preparing for her student teaching placement in a few months, Rebecca frequently relies on her experiences thus far. Using her years as an attorney as a crutch, she begins planning well in advance about piloting a project for her race, school, and society class that will knock the socks off this professor who can't seem to get enough about race.

Rebecca hits up Libby and says, "Are you ready for this?"

"Gosh, ready as I'll ever be! I can't believe how long this class has been and now it's time for a project? Let me guess what the professor wants . . . starts with an R and rhymes with base." Libby quipped.

"I get it, but let's stay positive! We have to empower these people. In the end, I just hope this class is worth it and I get a good placement in a up-and-coming neighborhood. I don't really have any expectations for someone telling me what I know already. I just want to be in the classroom already." After their conversation, Rebecca digs through her drawers trying to find a special shirt she wore a few months back. "Ah! Here it is!" Rebecca laughs gleefully.

The next morning, Rebecca jots down musings about making it as a millennial in trying times. She ruminates about her role as a teacher and to change lives. She certainly doesn't want to lose touch with what has motivated her to become a teacher. She also makes a note of the hot yoga class she scheduled in order to support her self-care ritual. Rebecca beams when she sees the shirt she will don in class: a bespoke tee with the statement, "black lives > white feelings." "This is what I'm here for." Wearing this t-shirt for Rebecca is a statement of solidarity and to show her dedication toward racial equity, among other issues related to social justice. What's more, she sports a 14k white gold safety pin necklace crafted exclusively for her from Etsy. The safety pin, which she was inspired to wear based on its popularity on Instagram, seemingly represents Rebecca's stalwart commitment to ending hate and being an ally for all marginalized folks affected by Trump.

The class is fairly large and includes students from outside the school of education. There is one Black woman in the class named Andrea in the predominantly white class. The instructor, Justin, introduces himself, a queer Filipino-American who has spent years teaching and researching race, gender, and class within education and cultural studies. He has the students position the desks into a circle. Justin begins the class with some working assumptions, "We're not building comfort zones in this class; but inviting space for the things we don't know and can't possibly know." Many of the students groan at this statement and are seemingly disinterested in what they are hearing.

Grumbles from students in the class include, "Is this person for real?" "I don't want to be here. I'd rather take a multiple-choice exam with Sandy. She makes me laugh!" "This is all stupid." Rebecca rolls her eyes while also catching Libby's roving gaze around the room. As Justin speaks about the course objectives, Rebecca mouths out slowly "BORING" to Libby, as the two eye Justin up and down as if to size him up. Justin quickly calls the class to order and requests that students get into pairs to begin an interview activity.

Rebecca swiftly chooses Libby and listens intently on instructions.

"Before you begin, I want you to think carefully about these questions: Why do you want to be a teacher? Who are you and how do you know?"

Begrudgingly, Rebecca obliges and quickly conjures up descriptions of teaching and education, hearkening to her reflections in Sandy's class. Always the overachiever, Rebecca begins to write a long missive to her instructor,

I want to be the voice for the voiceless. Urban youth need champion educators who demand excellence and are fiercely dedicated to empowering them. I am a fierce advocate for social change. I am a concerned citizen, former attorney, and human. I cannot describe how proud I am to have been the one to have had the honor of being the one to have stood up and gone to bat for those who had been charged with and even found guilty of certain crimes. I know who I am because I just do. I am a do-gooder. Social justice to me is about listening, but also about keeping people responsible and accountable of their stories and the consequences and products thereof.

Rebecca shares these goals with Libby. "You're so amazing." Libby swoons over Rebecca's statement, "You're meant to be an elementary teacher."

When Justin invites those to share parts of their responses, Rebecca is quick to raise her hand.

After the session ends, Justin assigns an extension of this activity to write a personal narrative that critically examines their background, formative educational experiences, and looks in retrospect of how investments in certain knowledge productions are shaped.

JULY 26, 2017

Rebecca is keen on detailing her formative years and life at Cedarwood Elementary. While the assignment only asks for seven pages, she is resolute on writing what will probably be a twenty-page legal memo recounting significant episodes. She wants to demonstrate that she, too, has experienced adversity. On a legal pad she even scrawled some vignettes of her difficult childhood. Rebecca furiously types, "It was hard having to move a lot during my childhood. My mother had to relocate to advance her career, and we as a family wanted to support her mobility. Eighth grade in New York City was bad, and I thought the students were dumb. They expected I lived in the projects or in the Bronx. I got into fights because some of the students suggested that I couldn't have lived in the city because I had lived in a house."

She is impelled to write about issues of diversity. Rebecca states emphatically,

> *I defensively believe that I am culturally competent and that I embrace and honor diversity in a way that is productive for persons of different backgrounds. I offensively concede that tomorrow, I will be more culturally competent than I am today.*

With tears streaming down her face, Rebecca deftly types,

> *I become defensive in asserting my ability as a culturally-competent teacher. I know that I can make a difference for my students. I get angry when I feel people are telling me that I will not be able to relate to my students, to understand them, to teach them, just because I am white and they will come from different worlds. Maybe this is a good thing. I am fired up because this is wrong. I know this is wrong.*

She concludes her story,

> *I want to save public schools and the deplorable conditions our students are subject to. Call me crazy, but I want to be able to save the children who grew up in not so great areas by being that teacher who cared, that made them feel like they could do anything. Kids are impressionable, and I want to impress to them that they matter. Because for me, they are special, and I believe I am special for them. They are my martyrdom. I love the idea of public schools . . . It is a romantic and naïve idea, but so what. You don't decide who or what you love, you just do.*

JULY 28, 2017

Rebecca was not looking forward to the class session on identity, race, and whiteness in education. After all, why discuss something so sensitive, so seemingly unproductive to the general purpose of becoming an effective teacher? She had already enumerated all her experiences about being different from the racists. The readings assigned for the week only fomented her indignation. The former attorney was ready to be a devil's advocate in class to show her legal prowess. She had a bone to pick with Charles W. Mills and this thing called "the racial contract." She was already familiar with the works of Audre Lorde and Gloria Anzaldúa. She read terms that in her mind aren't meaningful to her. She dismissed Mills' suggestion that there is a knowledge system that perpetuates ignorance.

Justin begins with a discussion of whiteness, a pervasive movement and sensibility that structures the values and realities of the world.

"Excuse me, don't you think you're being a bit harsh about talking about white people the way you are? This is why white people feel discouraged, guilty, and ashamed when they try to do good in some way. I mean, just a suggestion . . . we need to work on this aggressive tone and unnecessary rage . . . Not all white people are bad people. I, for one, am doing the work. This is the problem; we can't make any progress with race relations if we harp on about how bad things are." Many students in the class slyly grin at Rebecca's proposition. She boldly continues, "Maybe it could just be an issue of semantics. How about if we just reframe whiteness to a culture of domination?"

With a look of incredulity, Andrea, the sole Black woman teacher candidate in the room who is working toward her licenses in elementary and special education, delivers a compelling rebuttal. "We can't just push these issues under the rug, because race and whiteness are very much a part of our everyday lives. It becomes convenient for white people, who don't recognize their own marked and privileged beings to not think about their impact on people of color. Whiteness *is* the culture of domination. And, just because the word offends you, doesn't mean you can stop talking about it altogether. What gives you the right to place your defensive feelings of learning about whiteness above the academic and social reality of learning what it is all about?"

Justin offers, "Well, we often miss opportunities to confront the systemic violence of race and how these get reprises over time. It's great that one can say they're committed to diversity, one's actions often get disconnected from the rhetoric that supposedly espouses a more racially just future."

Andrea chimes in, "The message is about how can we all collectively restore humanity. That is not to say we're taking on a color-blind mentality and seeing things through rose-colored glasses, but what are we going to do to disrupt these structures and processes of oppression. We're not implicating all white people, but you need to understand how you white folks are complicit in perpetuating violence despite good intentions of not wanting to hurt someone."

Rebecca retorts, "But Andrea, why are you indicting those who are trying to do good? Why are you making people like me complicit in all of this? I'm not one of them. How can you say that I don't support black people? I've done a lot! I won't stand for this. If white people can't do anything, if I'm hearing you correctly, what do you expect us to do?"

"Well, you're not hearing correctly. You just need to listen to what people of color are saying. It isn't about your feelings and it's more about your impact. Right now, you're doing a lot of damage by being so defensive of your whiteness," Andrea says.

Rebecca, flummoxed by this entire exchange, storms out of the classroom, feeling that everything she has accomplished was in vain. Her close colleagues, white women, following in tow, their Tumi backpacks adorned with Hillary buttons, and equality stickers, also leave the classroom trying to console her. "They don't understand that we're trying to help. It's okay, Rebecca. You're doing great things. Some people just take things too personally."

"I guess, so." Rebecca still distraught. "It shouldn't have to be this hard. I don't like being shamed. Aren't we all here to help students? Race this and race that. I'm so over it. It's like I can never please *them*. I guess you pay a price for being nice and white."

That evening, Rebecca is still trying to come to terms with all that had happened in class. She wants to prove to her instructor and Andrea that she has their best interests in mind. As a gesture of good-will, she takes out some textured crème cardstock embossed with her initials and begins to write a note to Justin and Andrea. Each letter is the same. A glass fountain pen in hand, she writes,

Maya Angelou often said, "When you know better, you do better." Audre Lorde made clear "It is not our differences that divide us. It is our inability to recognize, accept, and celebrate those differences." I thank you for sharing how you feel and I know how it can be difficult being a minority to express yourself. My foremothers were a part of the women's suffrage moment, so I understand struggle and oppression. I am not unlike you. I think we can all learn a valuable lesson from what transpired yesterday. You should be proud of where you are today. I don't ever want to take that away from you. But, I think in order to work toward social justice, we need to come together as one. People are not out to get you. Instead of chastising one another, we need to assume people have the best intentions.

Rebecca signs it affectionately, *Love, Becky*.

AUGUST 4, 2017

At the end of the next class session, Rebecca delivers the note to Justin and Andrea. Andrea opens the card first, scanning the content with her mouth gaped in disbelief. Justin is in the background trying to diffuse the situation, but was also attending to last minute questions from students.

Andrea looks squarely at Rebecca and responds, "I don't know what you are trying to convey in your message. Honestly, Rebecca, this is not only offensive to me, but not a constructive way to confront what happened last week."

Exasperated, Rebecca points her finger at Andrea and yells, "Are you freaking serious right now? What do you people want? Everything is such a big deal. Professor, hello? Help me out!"

Rebecca turns to her instructor, to which they remain stoic. As a professor, Justin speaks in a calm, yet stern tone, "You need to realize, Rebecca, that your message is condescending. You are invalidating Andrea and putting all this labor on her to have to explain everything to you."

Rebecca chides both of them, reiterating how she felt Justin and Andrea were ignorant about the real issues affecting black children.

When home, Rebecca pens a lengthy email to the dean of the college and describes how rude the professor and Andrea have been and how this class does not fulfill the institutional promise of inclusive excellence. Furthermore, she states how the instructor is unqualified and theoretically ignorant. Rebecca can't seem to understand how Justin and Andrea are being "racist" to her after everything she has done professionally.

AUGUST 6, 2017

Sipping her green smoothie at the nearby juice bar, Rebecca receives a reply from the college dean. It writes "Thank you, Rebecca, for your message. We are evaluating ways to make this a better educational experience for you."

Meanwhile, Andrea speaks to Justin about what transpired in class the other day. She details how she constantly feels surveilled, dehumanized, and demoralized in the university. Andrea yearns to feel heard and to not be taken as a pawn who readily accommodates those who are "being lovingly, yet knowingly ignorant" and who preserve this ignorance through self-righteous arrogance. For Andrea and Justin, this is not just about an unfortunate encounter with a disgruntled student, but rather about the continual struggle to survive and flourish in the present apocalypse; that is, reckoning with a (white) lifeworld and conditions whose maintenance is dependent on the perpetual suffering of marginalized people.

Together, Andrea and Justin form an undercommons study group for teacher candidates of color to discuss, critique, and envision healing ways to be in, but not *of* the academy. Andrea and Justin hope this group is a breathing space where people of color do not have to be under the scrutiny of white feminism.

AUGUST 11, 2017

Class resumes, but Andrea is nowhere to be found. She seemingly dropped from the program. Rebecca lets out a sigh of relief knowing that she does not have to deal with Andrea anymore. She turns and acts surprised to see Sandy at the lectern, with Justin. Justin looked defeated and exhausted, but that did not bother Rebecca. Sandy greets the class, "Hi everyone. Starting today, Justin and I will be team teaching this course."

Rebecca is confident. She feels like she has an ally in Sandy who takes care in talking about issues of difference in ways that are palatable to her. Rebecca is glad that there is no one threatening her motives. Rebecca is wide-eyed and quickly smiles at Libby before taking out her legal pad. She's now ready to take notes and eager to learn the *right* way. After all, she really just wants to be a good white feminist.

Chapter Six

This Ain't No "Wizard of Oz," Becky!

G. L. Sarcedo

BECKY IN GENTRIFYA

The blue sky turned gray as Becky threw her "We should all be feminists" sign in her hybrid. She felt exhilarated leaving the women's march and taking a visible stand against patriarchy with a sisterhood of like-minded women. She had met many other self-proclaimed "woke" liberal feminist college students who positioned themselves as allies to people of Color committed to smashing the patriarchy. Yet Becky had failed to have any substantive interactions with any women of Color, only connecting with other white women, the same way she moved through the rest of her life without question. Parked next to Becky was a curly-haired Black woman wearing purple glasses, who offered her a warm smile. Becky avoided eye contact upon seeing her "white feminism is trash without intersectionality" sign.

In her rearview mirror, Becky glimpsed her dark University of Gentrifya sweatshirt contrasting her paleness as she removed her pink pussy hat and continued to ignore the Black woman in the next car, who was wearing the same college sweatshirt as Becky. Rain started falling while thunder began to rumble amid lightning flashes. The weather couldn't dampen Becky's unbridled empowerment after the women's march as she drove past the drab University of Gentrifya campus to her hip converted loft apartment.

The rain made the recently repaved streets of Gentrifya glisten. Gentrifya was once a booming community of Color known as Blacktonia, but had been declared blighted by the City Council until the recent "revitalization" efforts. All the white college students like Becky and young urban professionals like her boyfriend Chad pouring into the neighborhood increased property values while driving out long-time Black and Brown residents.

As the city changed, even the former Blacktonia State College transformed into the University of Gentrifya. Though adjacent to a historically Black neighborhood, the "urban" campus of Blacktonia State had been a historically white institution. With renewed visions of inclusive excellence, University of Gentrifya, or UGen, continued to brag about its "diverse" student body, yet graduated an alarmingly low number of students of Color compared to white students. UGen's purported diversity had cemented Becky's desire to attend.

The storm intensified as Becky drove past the yoga center she frequented after it replaced a Black-owned dance studio, which was "too ethnic" for her. A stocky Black woman with long braids matching the stormy sky was busy moving signs into the UGen-branded building next to the yoga studio, but Becky barely noticed her.

The rain-drenched storefronts reminded Becky that Gentrifya boasted the most "authentic" soul food in the city. Becky smiled at how thrilled she was when The Café on campus and the city location began serving kale and pumpkin spice beverages. Oh, how Becky loved consuming the supposed authenticity of Gentrifya, ignoring that her neighbors and fellow students were becoming increasingly white.

Lightning illuminated the deep gray sky, and Becky saw a tall, regal Black woman running into the Blacktonia Community Center of Gentrifya. A thunderbolt struck a newly transplanted tree along the street. As a large branch fell, Becky slammed on her brakes and her hybrid fishtailed on the wet road. She eased the brake and turned into the skid as she had learned during her private driving lessons, but to no avail. As Becky's panic grew, her car continued pitching back and forth in the raging storm. Her car hit something on the passenger side and began spinning. Her mind spinning along with each rotation of the car, Becky's fear reached its crescendo as she lost consciousness and the car came to a skidding halt.

THE WONDROUS LAND OF NY

As she came to, Becky blinked her blue eyes wildly. Beyond her windshield, Becky no longer saw the stormy streets of Gentrifya, but a bright and vibrant college campus like she had never seen before. It was so very different from the stodgy UGen campus. The shining sun highlighted the brightly colored buildings. She saw art hanging in a gallery, depicting only Black and Brown people. Some unknown savory smell wafted across campus. She imagined the scene as a new Harlem Renaissance, though she had only studied it briefly that one semester she took an African American history class to fulfill the single-course diversity requirement at UGen.

She emerged from her car to see she had hit a signpost, which declared "Welcome to the University of Ny." Confused and disoriented, Becky looked at the seemingly empty campus, noticing the white paving stones beneath her. Just then, a familiar-seeming stocky Black woman with long gray braids ran out from one of the bright buildings.

"Are you hurt?" The stranger asked as she hugged Becky in a motherly embrace. The woman felt Becky's body stiffen and stepped back to check Becky for injuries. She could acutely sense Becky's nervousness as Becky avoided her gaze.

"Where am I? I was driving through Gentrifya . . . " Becky glanced down and folded her arms, her body language declaring her discomfort.

"You're in Ny," the stranger said warmly.

Stepping back from the stranger with an alarmed look on her face, Becky burst into tears and reached for her phone. "I'm calling the police . . . " Becky sobbed into her dead phone.

"Stop your crying; white tears have no power here. This isn't a utopia, but Nyans understand the ways of whiteness, unlike Gentrifya," said the stranger, still with warmth in her voice.

Flabbergasted, Becky's thin lips twisted angrily, then instantly softened when she presumed she could still get what she wanted. She wiped her eyes and faked a smile. "You know Gentrifya? You *need* to get me back," she said with feigned earnestness.

"I don't *need* to do anything, but let's get something to eat and make a plan." The stranger motioned for Becky to follow her into the bright building from which she had emerged. Reluctantly, Becky followed the woman into what she discovered was a student center full of Black and Brown college students and source of the delicious smell wafting down the street. Becky and the stranger sat down at an empty table.

"I need to get back to Gentrifya," Becky reiterated, still nervous yet confident she could achieve her desired outcome.

"I briefly studied Gentrifya in comparative educational and political systems in my doctoral program, but frankly, I have no idea how to get you home." The stranger offered another warm smile.

Avoiding the stranger's gaze, Becky looked at the students at other tables, only slightly embarrassed she couldn't recall another time where she was the only white person in the room.

"If you can't help, I need to talk whoever's in charge." Becky pounded on the table, "I'd like to speak to *him* now."

"I'm Dr. Jeanetta Harper, President at University of Ny, and I'm in charge here." Dr. Harper said, her tone conveying the authority Becky had assumed she lacked.

"Thank you, Jeanetta . . . I'm Becky," she scoffed with forced politeness, extending a reluctant hand to Dr. Harper.

Dr. Harper shook hands firmly, looking Becky directly in the eye. "Becky, it's Dr. Harper . . . Excuse me, let me arrange our meal." Dr. Harper disappeared into the back of the student center, her exit a coping mechanism in the face of whiteness.

Interrupting a conversation at the table next to her without a second thought, Becky asked the two "non-threatening" young Black women to tell her about the University and land of Ny. They explained Ny to be a constitutional monarchy and bustling Black- and Brown-inhabited land, with a small white minority. Ny had a rich history of cultural, literary, artistic, and intellectual traditions and economic growth. They further explained the University as the premier urban research institution in Ny. Such a wondrous place, Becky thought to herself. She wanted to take Ny back to Gentrifya, reducing an entire civilization to a souvenir for her benefit.

Dr. Harper returned with two students holding platters of food. The now-familiar savory scent she had encountered earlier filled Becky's nose as she looked upon the generous spread. The offering reminded Becky of the supposedly authentic soul food she prized in Gentrifya, but was so much more flavorful. It was the best meal Becky had ever had, so thoroughly seasoned unlike anything she had eaten before. Nyan cafeteria food made Gentrifyan food seem utterly bland.

As Becky ate, Dr. Harper told her about the Queen of Ny, a statuesque dark-skinned Black woman who was democratically-elected based on her community activism in Ny. If anyone could help Becky return home, the Queen could. Becky, who had never interacted with a woman of Color in authority, looked at Dr. Harper with skepticism.

Dr. Harper described how White Road, the stretch of white pavers Becky had noticed earlier, ran through the urban campus and terminated at the Capitol Building where the Queen was housed. Becky finished her meal as Dr. Harper offered to arrange a ride for her.

"That's not necessary, thank you, just point me in the right direction," Becky said with more feigned politeness. Dr. Harper knew that Becky's polite tone masked disgust for an offer of help from a woman of Color.

"You seem so confident, despite being an outsider here," said Dr. Harper, certain of Becky's arrogance drawn from a lifetime of white privilege. Without bothering to contradict Becky's white self-assurance, Dr. Harper walked Becky outside and pointed toward the ornate Capitol Building at the end of White Road.

BECKY ON WHITE ROAD

Becky strode confidently away from the student center down White Road. She passed the art gallery she had seen earlier, still marveling at the Black and Brown depictions. It was unquestionably novel for her to see faces of Color centered. Coming upon the University of Ny quad adjacent to White Road, Becky saw a group of students listening to a Black woman speak. Maybe it was a poetry reading, Becky thought to herself as she eavesdropped. The speaker's brown curls framed her face, with purple glasses popping against her medium-toned brown skin. She spoke of smashing the patriarchy through political activism, shocking Becky but piquing her interest as she reminisced about the women's march. Becky noticed all the students wearing "Hello, my name is" tags.

"I just did a women's march and would be happy to share organizing strategies!" Becky interrupted the speaker, whose name tag said Zayla.

"Excuse you?" Zayla asked with a puzzled look on her face.

"Oh, I'm Becky! I'm on my way to the Capitol to meet the Queen, but I couldn't help overhear. I'm all about smashing the patriarchy!"

"Look, Becky, you might mean well, but you interrupted us to offer help we don't want or need, and you have no context for what we're discussing."

"Zayla? I might be a relative stranger in Ny, but patriarchy is patriarchy. I . . ."

Zayla raised a hand that shocked Becky into stunned silence, as her cheeks flushed with anger at the thought of a woman of Color cutting her off, while ignoring that she had just interrupted Zayla.

"I'm trying to be civil. Why are you being so rude?" Becky pouted like a sullen child.

"Becky, don't ask for politeness after interrupting us. You choose to interrupt. Please leave us alone." Zayla crossed her arms and broadened her stance, her posture an act of resistance to whiteness. Becky couldn't understand why they didn't want her help.

"I'll be on my way to meet the Queen then, since you clearly don't value coalition and ally-building," Becky thought the women's faces were growing angry.

"This isn't about our values," Zayla said flatly.

"Whatever, you wicked witch!" Becky retorted indignantly, turning so she didn't have to look Zayla in the eye.

"*You* are the problem Becky, not us!" Zayla said calmly, yet Becky took her words as a threat and began to run down White Road like a bewildered animal. Becky did not see Zayla simply turn back to her audience and continue speaking.

Becky ran until the quad was out of sight. Continuing toward the Capitol, Becky felt paranoid that "angry" Zayla was going to ambush her on White Road, remaining hyper-vigilant and peering over her shoulder. No harm came to her, but Becky steadfastly believed she had made a mortal enemy in Zayla.

BECKY & THE QUEEN OF NY

Becky approached a grand white paver staircase as she came upon the end of White Road at the Capitol. The ornate building had intricate architectural moldings, making Becky gasp at its details. Atop the stairs sat a muscular, uniform-clad Black man behind a desk, his uniform nameplate designating him, "Officer Howlett." His dark skin and blue uniform contrasted the carved honey-colored wood doors behind him.

He offered Becky a friendly smile. "Good afternoon, ma'am. What's your business at the Capitol?"

"I was sent by Jeanetta Harper at the University to see the Queen."

"Dr. Harper, you mean," Officer Howlett said matter-of-factly as he began typing into the computer at the desk.

"Sure," Becky replied tepidly with an unconscious eye roll. Officer Howlett did not look up as he typed, making Becky nervous she would be unable to see the Queen. She inched closer to the desk as she waited, until she was leaning on the edge. With a flirtatious twirl of her blond hair, she leaned in and unzipped her UGen sweatshirt to show her cleavage and began stroking Officer Howlett's arm as he typed. "Officer," she said with a giggle, "what are you typing?"

Officer Howlett knew this wasn't the first time Becky had attempted flirtation to get what she wanted from a man of Color, unbothered by her manipulative display.

"Ma'am, back up. You're not going to expedite this." Officer Howlett continued typing, not even looking up to see Becky zip her sweatshirt and cross her arms. He then pointed above his head and Becky saw the security camera. Her cheeks turned red, embarrassed she had been rebuffed.

"Whatever . . . " Becky said dismissively to herself. Unbeknownst to Becky, all Nyan officers learned about the dangers of white femininity during training.

"Ma'am, I'll escort you to the Queen. Fortunately, Dr. Harper called in a favor; otherwise, you would not be granted this opportunity." Becky smirked at his words, as if she did not need Dr. Harper's assistance. Officer Howlett disappeared behind the large wood doors and emerged with another officer.

The other officer assumed the seat at the desk and Officer Howlett motioned for Becky to follow him beyond the carved doors. Becky's eyes widened as saw the marble floors and wood columns inside the Capitol. It was statelier than she had imagined possible, because her white mind couldn't conceptualize something so grand in a land of Color.

At the end of the corridor Officer Howlett and Becky met an aide, who escorted Becky to the Queen. Just as Dr. Harper had said, the Queen was a statuesque dark-skinned Black woman. Sitting opposite the Queen across an ornate desk, Becky was unsure how to behave in the presence of a queen.

"Dr. Harper told me you are from Gentrifya and seem desperate to return home?" As Becky nodded, she thought the Queen had a regal air about her, which Becky found intimidating at first. "Please tell me about your time in Ny." The Queen's seemingly magical aura made Becky want to be totally honest in a way she had never experienced before, like she was talking to Oprah or Michelle Obama—the *only* commanding Black women Becky knew, because her advanced feminist theory course at UGen ignored Patricia Hill Collins, bell hooks, Audre Lorde, and other foundational authors of Color.

Becky recounted to the Queen the storm in Gentrifya and her mysterious arrival in Ny. She described her initial "fear" of "Jeanetta" and how she was "shamed" for crying, then praised Dr. Harper's hospitality. Becky detailed her "terrifying run in" with the "wicked witch" student and "being nice" to Officer Howlett while waiting and his astonishing lack of customer service. Becky even mentioned her surprise at the grandeur of the Capitol. The Queen sighed deeply and Becky smiled, assuming the Queen was impressed with her.

"Becky, your attitude and behaviors in Ny—and in Gentrifya—are unacceptable. You continually exude whiteness."

Becky sat in stunned silence for a moment as her smile faded, then retorted indignantly, "How dare you call *me* racist! I *am* a good ally! I don't even *see* color! Back in Gentrifya, I would never—"

"—your behavior didn't magically change in Ny," said the Queen pointedly as she cut off Becky. "You *do* see color. Your privilege in Gentrifya shields you from understanding how you benefit from racism and when you wield whiteness."

"But I didn't do anything wrong in Ny!" Becky protested.

"Becky, you tried to call the police on *Dr.* Harper, who you refuse to call by the proper honorific. You think emphasizing her care-giving nature is a compliment, but it's deeply rooted in racism. The student you had a so-called run-in with? You were extraordinarily rude to her, and then actually thought she was going to hunt you down like some mythical wicked witch. You created that narrative because it makes you the damsel in distress up against the big, scary angry woman of Color. Even in your attempted flirtation with Officer Howlett to try to manipulate the situation, you spew whiteness."

"I *cannot* believe that is what you think that of me!" Becky said with disdain for the Queen, but not her own actions.

"You continue to show your whiteness. Only when you truly grapple with what all this means and how you can work to dismantle it can you return home to Gentrifya." The Queen's expression was stern but tender. "I want you to close your eyes and contemplate what I've said. When you truly understand it, you will be granted passage home."

Becky sat quietly with her eyes closed, breathing deeply, like she was at yoga, as she started to consider the Queen's words.

"You have always possessed the ability to return home, Becky, to comprehend your whiteness and start to work toward disrupting it. You didn't need a mystical journey or magical leader to show you; you needed to be put in a position where you could no longer ignore it. I will slap back to Gentrifya with that knowledge." At the Queen's words, Becky felt the Queen's hand slap her hard across the face.

RETURN TO GENTRIFYA

Becky bolted upright as she came to, realizing she was on a gurney in an ambulance. Just beyond the open ambulance doors, she could see the storm had cleared but her mangled car was wrecked along Gentrifya's main drag.

"Ma'am, please lie down," said a familiar voice that Becky couldn't place. She smiled as she saw a muscular Black man in a blue uniform.

"Officer Howlett?" Becky said in astonishment.

"Sorry ma'am, my name is Andes. You sustained a minor head injury and were unconscious. Confusion is normal." Andes flashed a polite smile as he took her vitals.

A crowd was gathering around the ambulance. Three Black women in particular stood out in the crowd: the curly-haired woman who had parked next to Becky at the march, a stocky woman with long gray braids, and a statuesque, regal woman. Becky called out to them, "Zayla, Dr. Harper, your Majesty!" The women looked at each other in confusion.

"My name is Calla. We left the march at the same time and I was driving behind you when you crashed," said the woman Becky thought was Zayla.

"I'm Dr. Desna, the Executive Director of the UGen Community Outreach Center down the street, next to the yoga studio. I saw you pass as I was putting our signs away and heard the crash. I called the ambulance." Dr. Desna offered Becky a warm smile reminiscent of Dr. Harper's embrace.

"You can call me your Majesty," the tall Black woman laughed, "but my name is Amma Tabbot, the Director of the Blacktonia Community Center of Gentrifya across the street. You crashed in front of the center."

"Amma *is* a queen in this community," said Dr. Desna, as Calla and the others in the crowd nodded in consensus.

"We need to get to the hospital," Andes said as he jumped out of the ambulance.

"Wait," said Becky as she sat up to address the crowd. "My name is Becky and I will no longer embrace whiteness and hide behind its privileges. Calla, Desna—"

"—*Dr.* Desna!" Amma corrected her.

"Yes, Dr. Desna, and especially you Amma, your Majesty, I return from the land of Ny a changed woman. I'm developing an understanding of what I must do to break down whiteness in Gentrifya. I'm committed to changing myself and asking other white people, especially white women, to change also. Dorothy in the 'Wizard of Oz' said, 'there's no place like home.' I'm telling you there's no place for whiteness in Gentrifya. No, there's no place for whiteness in *Blacktonia*!"

The three women looked quizzically at each other and back at Becky. Although they didn't understand what Becky was talking about, they exchanged a knowing glance. The three women, and all the people of Color in the crowd, desired to have every white woman they had ever met experience whatever Becky had just been through—they didn't know Becky, but, they all *knew* Becky.

"I've heard that speech before, Becky. Your epiphany doesn't mean anything until you back it up with action," Calla challenged Becky, to agreeing nods in the crowd.

"No, really, you can trust me! I'm changed," beseeched Becky.

"Oh no, Becky, you're not. Expecting us to trust in whatever your supposed transformation is, *is* an act of whiteness," said Dr. Desna with a sigh.

"That's right, you're not changed Becky! You can miss me with that mess!" Amma said to cheers from the crowd. "You can't dream away whiteness like Dorothy dreamed away homesickness."

Becky felt those last words in her soul. Indeed, her experience in Ny was no fantasy. The sense of humanity she now felt would haunt her dreams, felling compelled to harness the brief lessons learned in Ny and change her behavior in Gentrifya. She knew she needed to seek out the tools to do so without burdening communities of Color.

This change in Becky felt similar to when she had returned from a mission trip to Africa, but this time she was committing to making real, lasting changes. She could not pat herself on the back like she had upon return from Africa. Becky believed she finally understood that she was not the "woke" white woman she thought she was. Never again could she treat "wokeness" as a destination rather than a constant, bitter journey toward racial justice. Ny was just the beginning of unhooking from whiteness.

"If Dorothy can change, rest assured, I _will_ work to show my change is heartfelt and sincere!" Becky smiled at the three Black women, pleased with her promise.

"This ain't no 'Wizard of Oz,' Becky!" exclaimed Calla, Dr. Desna, and Amma in unison. The thinning crowd responded with laughter as the women shared another knowing glance, all with the full realization that the binds of whiteness made Becky's purported transformation practically impossible.

Andes then closed one ambulance door, blocking Becky from the crowd's view, so no one saw her pale cheeks flush in embarrassment. Without Andes in the back of the rig with her, Becky turned to see the driver was another Black man. "Excuse me," she said in a breathy whisper to get his attention.

He turned to see Becky bite her lip playfully and smile seductively "Is there any way we can stop to get a pumpkin spice latte? I need _something_ to calm my nerves after dealing with those angry Black women!"

Outside the ambulance, the three women heard Becky as Andes stepped back in and closed the other door. As the ambulance drove away, Calla, Dr. Desna, and Amma shared a deep sigh at Becky's continued display of whiteness.

Chapter Seven

Surviving Becky in Space

Melva R. Grant

The Earth's third World War was initiated by the 45th US President to avoid incarceration for himself and his children in late 2019; the nuclear devastation killed more than 200 million people, and left the Middle East, parts of Africa, and most of Asia uninhabitable. The mass devastation and migration was the final impetus for the Great Warming of 2020, accelerated climate change, famine, and disease; these events decreased the Earth's population by half in record time. In 2021 the Earth's climate followed patterns once predicted for 2050; the severe weather and population distress forced a global governmental collaboration committed to planetary evacuation within a century. These war survivors ushered in an era of planetary innovations that rivaled the nineteenth century Industrial Revolution, and gave rise to a technological renaissance for human survival. The goal was met, and the final mass migration from Earth to life-sustaining space stations was completed and the Democratic Council emerged as a structured governing body to maintain order and communications among the myriad human space stations. The last people to leave Earth were the least privileged and poor. The Earth imploded in the early twenty-seventh century, just before the worst prisoners and criminally insane were evacuated due to planetary instability according to governmental records, but little history remains about that time period or those left behind. They are affectionately referred to as *The Remembered*, and their "loss" is commemorated annually with parades and gatherings. Some historians liken it to the historic US, Earth holiday called Thanksgiving.

Over the next five centuries, intergalactic space travel technology grew and intergalactic space exploration led to meeting non-human cognizant beings and uncharted planets, some able to support human life. These discoveries led to a portion of the Democratic Council being absorbed into an inclusive multi-being governing body, the Intergalactic Collective Council

(ICC). Over time, the ICC determined research priorities for meeting the needs of the collective cognizant beings, and then followed by the proliferation across the intergalactic space stations and planets. For example, improving communications and multi-being life sustaining systems were priorities of the ICC. Now, in the year 3017, the ICC governs beings inhabiting almost 10,000 space stations and planets and supported by a fleet of 500 Star Cruisers, each the size of a densly populated city. Currently, the ICC is upgrading space station infrastructure (ICC-SSI), an effort requiring rapid training and deployment of Rocket Scientists (R-Sci), of which I, Dr. Mammy Jones, am one of the most renowned R-Sci team leaders in the ICC Research Labs. My ICC species categorization record describes me as Planet 0, Sector 1 ancestry, child producing, enslaved descendents. Translated, I am a Black woman from the Earth, North America's United States. The previous year, the ICC Research Lab recognized me for leading the teams that implemented my power system research that led to several fusion reaction power systems fueled with dilithium crystals—a breakthrough technology that generates massive amounts of power for minimal costs. This discovery has the potential for powering major ICC infrastructure well into the next century, powering systems including warp drives for space-time travel and multi-redundant fail-safe life support systems.

Every 10 years, the most productive lab researchers are placed in rotation—for 10 years, ICC Lab researchers train scientists to implement the most consequential technologies since the last rotation. Given the potential of my research, I was selected for field rotation and because of my special recognition for team mentoring and leadership, I was assigned ICC Commander. My rotation assignment is to lead the ICC-SSI to train and upgrade the power systems across the Collective. I was stationed on the USS-121 Star Cruiser. The Star Cruisers in the ICC Fleet were first and foremost schools of higher learning, built to spread new technologies, travel between space stations and planets transporting newly trained scientists, support personnel, supplies, and technologies. The ICC Commander appointment also included becoming a member of the USS-121 leadership command. This made me responsible for the ICC-SSI Mission and all of the R-Sci Researchers in rotation aboard the 500 ICC Star Cruisers assigned to the mission for power system upgrades. For this mission, the Mammy Jones Power System, officially named to memorialize my achievement, was affectionately called Ma's Power across the Collective. At this level of command, my work is generally self-directed and monitored only at the highest levels within the ICC command structure; for research I report to the Research High Fleet Commander (i.e., Fleet Cmdr.), and also on the USS-121, I report directly to the Cruise Cmdr.

The USS-121 Star Cruiser is docked at Space Station 007 in the Silver Supremacy Star System to pick up five new R-Sci recruits. Recruits are typically selected using Station selection protocols coupled with ICC Lab criteria that included performance measurement benchmarks established by me, the ICC Cmdr. However, for recruits assigned to train directly with me, ICC Cmdr., additional permission from the Fleet Cmdr. is required. Of course, most recognize that the additional requirement opens the door for political maneuvering versus objective measures. For example, the first group of recruits I trained had elite lineage; they included children and relatives of Star Cruiser or Space Station Command, and the niece of an ICC council member. This group of new recruits would be no different, I was sure. The question for me to figure out, however, is what are the politics and how do I maneuver unscathed?

The Space Station 007, home of the new recruits, is one of the first space stations following Earth's evacuation from the Great Warming. The first 12 stations are referred to collectively as The Dozen, and were created for the most privileged Earth populations during the twenty-first century migration. Unlike the other stations, Outer Stations, the population of The Dozen had not changed much over the centuries. According to the latest ICC counts and categorization data, The Dozen population was 75 percent Planet 0, Sector 0 ancestry. Translated, that means the population is predominantly White people mostly from the US and the rest is not reported. The Dozen population was once described by US, Earth twenty-first century historians as the 1 percent, meaning the most wealthy citizens from Earth. This moniker is no longer used, but is still applicable by today's intergalactic wealth measures. After all, The Dozen's wealth continues as it always has and continues to grow, even in space. The resources afforded The Dozen continue to be over-allocated when compared to other populations across the ICC. For example, technology and infrastructure enhancements are always implemented in The Dozen as soon as the kinks have been identified and fixed, and their scientists are always trained by the ICC Cmdr. Prior to becoming ICC Cmdr., the privilege of The Dozen had been less transparent. For example, I saw first hand how the Mission Plan changed and our Star Cruiser preemptively rerouted following the stellar Power System upgrade and test at Station 227. This was our third consecutive success, and any R-Sci would label the milestone as Gold Star; our power system is now free of errors. Without consultation with me, our schedule was changed by the Fleet Cmdr.; I am assigned to train the 007 R-Sci recruits, and now we await their arrival.

As I make my way to greet the new recruits, I wonder why I still had not received the recruits' performance benchmark data indicating their preparedness for R-Sci training. I thought about how strange this seemed and how it was so unlike any of the other recruit groups I had been assigned to train as the ICC Cmdr. I had been told that I would receive the benchmark data upon recruit arrival. Benchmarks were a diagnostic assessment required of all who applied for R-Sci training. These minimum requirements were designed to ensure recruit safety and competence, while policy prevents accepting recruits who do not meet performance standards. However, it appears that the Station 007 recruits bypassed these safeguards.

As I approach the docking bay to greet the new recruits, I realize that I have never met anyone from The Dozen, but like most US-Earth descendants with slave ancestry, my generational family stories were full of negative encounters with White people, their wealth, supremacy, and privilege. As a scientist, however, I am a healthy skeptic of stories that lack empirical evidence. Even so, the long-held Dozen tradition is clear: the peope of The Dozen limited co-mingling with Outer Stations and they have maintained a "pure" culture and hold privilege unlike people from the Outer Stations. As a Black woman raised in an Outer Station, I encountered many new and different types of beings, human and others, who in time became friends. I am looking forward to working with scientists from The Dozen; perhaps the face they show will contradict my held sterotypes. In spite of the unprecedented circumstances—new recruits without benchmark data and my familial-inspired mistrust—I have made new friends since being in rotation, one or two in each recruit group, and I expect nothing different from this group.

The vibration from my communicator shakes me out of my thoughts as an incoming holo-message captures my attention as the buzzing pattern indicates high priority. To my surprise, the call originates from the Fleet Cmdr., my boss. I stop after finding a small alcove that affords a modicum of privacy to accept the holo-message—a holographic life-like interaction among two or more beings. The holographic technology replaced the historical text or video-based virtual technologies for communication, and offers enhancements like near-reality, and 5-D technology; touch and smell are part of it. Before my eyes, as I shift my postion to stand at attention, the Fleet Cmdr. takes shape. She smiles and offers her usual warm greeting as she waves an arm indicating that I be at ease. I relax and respond to her greeting warmly. Then Cmdr. Helen asks, "Have you met the new 007 R-Sci recruits?"

My curiosity was peaked, as I responded, "I'm about two minutes away from the docking bay. Stopped to take your holo-message." The commander let out a relaxing breath before explaining, "Mammy, take care with these recruits. The cultural norms of The Dozen are *different* [intended emphasis] from those of the Outer Stations. It is most important that every Star Fleet officer and commander value these *very special beings*." After a pause, Cmdr. Helen continues, "Mammy, these recruits have only met two of the three benchmarks. Actually, they each scored low on one component of the Scientist Personality Profile, the empathetic collaboration scale. What I'm getting at is that they struggle to cope when they perceive a threat, even a very slight threat. In fact, this perception of threat is especially heightened when the 'threat' comes from one who is not white. They experience a type of *fragility* that manifests in psycho-analytic cranial overload which is known to impair one's emotional response and the logic center of the brain shuts down." In response to what Cmdr. Helen shared, I naturally asked, "So, how does one compensate for this, *fragility*? I cannot recall having heard of such a condition."

After a brief silence, Cmdr. Helen advised, "As I said, this is a condition that emerges from The Dozen's homogeneity and isolation from the Outer Station people. There may not be a way to compensate. The recruits are all women—Rebecca, Becca, Beckie, Reba, and Beckzilla—but she prefers being called Beck-z. Their *fragility* response can be quite emotional, but is not typically violent. The Star Fleet personnel and command must take *care* when interacting with these recruits. We must all value their ideas explicitly, ensure they see you considering them or providing rationale when they are not used, and address their concerns with empathy. In fact, Mammy, your transformative and gentle leadership style factored into selecting you as ICC Commander. We believe you are uniquely qualified and prepared to judiciously support these recruits. Getting this right is very important for us all, especially considering that one of the recruits is the granddaughter of the ICC Past President."

As a Black woman, I understood all to well what I was being asked to do as I considered what had been said. The commander smiled brightly with a sense that her message had been received, and I reassured her by saying, "No worries, Cmdr. Helen. I'm adept at ensuring that all voices are heard and valued in ways that everyone is explicitly informed about when and how their ideas were used, as well as addressing concerns among team members with transparency, grace, and appropriate humility."

The commander smiled and responded, "Precisely. I knew we chose wisely by sending this *special* group of recruits to you. Mammy, these recruits need special care because of their innate fragility, but take care to never refer to their condition as they are unaware of it and they would not be receptive to learning about it from someone not of The Dozen. Feel free, however, to discuss this communication with the Cruise Command to ensure success for this R-Sci training."

"OK. Thank you for informing me, is there anything more I should know? I need to get to the docking bay so our *special* recruits are not kept waiting." The commander had nothing more to share, she offered me good luck, and told me we should talk soon. Cmdr. Helen's holo-image disintegrated and I felt a flutter of nerves in my belly as I contemplated the implications of the commander's briefing. As a Black woman leading predominantly male scientists in Labs for more than 10 years, I hoped that this *fragility* would be similar to the egg shells I'd walked to assuage the men so they felt comforted. Like a bad habit, I pushed the flutter of dread aside and entered the docking bay to greet the new recruits from The Dozen.

I put on a smile worthy of the brightest star in the galaxy, gathered my salt and pepper locks to the nape of my neck, and smoothed my fitted silver and gray uniform with its iconic symbols communicating my professional preparation as well as Star Fleet rank and appointment. My uniform included three bars topped with three stars on my left chest marking me as Cruise command; four bars on my upper right arm indicating my status as ICC lab leader and distinguished researcher; and on my left chest a colorful rocket ship set upon an open book for R-Sci educator atop a bold red bar super-imposed with my title and name, ICC Cmdr. Mammy Jones. The uniform icons make each officer's biography transparent to all Star Fleet personnel. During new recruit orientation, new recruits learn Star Fleet cultural norms and traditions, including reading uniform icons and how to address ship commanders and other personnel properly.

I finally arrived at the bey, walked the short distance to the shuttle, and stood in front of the recruits and two Star Fleet Escorts. The five Station 007 female recruits were of average height, pale skin color, and varying hair colors and lengths. Interestingly, the top half of each woman was was covered with glitter. Stopping in front of the recruits, the escorts try to get the recruits attention, but to no avail; the escorts and I exchange glances. The escorts carry out an appropriate formal greetings in unison and I respond, but the recruits fail to notice. The escorts and I refocus our gaze on the recruits who continue to take no notice of my presence. The recruits gather around one woman attempting to comfort her; she sobs, loudly. I think to myself, *"Fragility???"*

The escorts and I watch the spectacle and wait. After about 15 minutes, I say using a soothing sympathetic voice, but loud enough to penetrate the commotion, "Excuse me, but has someone experienced a trauma that requires a medic?"

The recruits, in unison, turn their attention to me for the first time since my arrival in the bay. The center recruit's nametag reads, Beckzilla. "An odd name," I think to myself. When I look at Beck-z, it seems she is looking at me with an expressions of distaste, as if she were looking at something, or someone in this case, that smelled bad. Miraculously, her tears stop as if in response to a silent command. Beck-z looks up and exclaims loudly, "OMG! I was unable to reach Daddy to tell him to deposit more credits into my Star Account. I cannot go to the Recruit Gala next week without proper preparation! It would be the end of the galaxy to go without fresh plasto!" I attempt to decipher Beck-z's trauma-laden expression of what ails her. I understand plasto was slang for plasto-tweaks—the USS-121 is equipped with a state-of-the-art plasto-tweak lab, but the service is for personnel injured in the line of duty. The service is not a commodity sold to ship personnel, and especially not for newly arriving recruits. Even so, it is not clear why Beck-z is so distraught.

Before I can construct a reasoned response, tears begin streaming down the recruit's face again, leaving trails of colorful make-up dripping onto her uniform. Immediately, the recruits resume comforting Beck-z. After a short while, Beck-z's wails calm to a whimper. Becca, another recruit, says, "We are all just devastated about Beck-z's account balance. How will she ever purchase the right look for the Gala with only a mill-cred? She's almost destitute! Sorry, Beck-z. But really, how does one survive on only a mill-cred for six months?" Becca's comments are heartfelt with an air of innocence that emanates from her facial expressions. I am truly flummoxed, Beck-z's six months budget surpasses that for the USS-121 Star Cruiser that includes thousands of crew members.

My thoughts are interrupted when Beckie, the third recruit, notices I am looking at her glitter-sparkling uniform. She explains, "It all started when I shared a waist-up glitter puff on the transport. The dreary color palette was killin' my vibe. Drab grey uniforms on more grey seats, yuck. After the puff, there was vibrant sparkle that totally improved everything inside the transport! This led to a star-blasted dance party, which brought our conversation to the Gala and this crisis. I feel awful for Beck-z."

Not missing a beat, Rebecca, the fourth recruit, shouts out, "But, even you fleet officers must admit that the sparkle looks AMAZING!?! Recruits! Strike a pose for holo-pics to send home. Let's show off our amazing sparkle!!!" Before I can say anything Rebecca launches a photo drone, it begins taking photos of the group as they strike pose after pose, each one featuring a new facial expression, pouty to smiling faces. If I didn't know better I might have been fooled into thinking I was watching Top Model. The escorts and I shared a look and a smile; we did not believe our lying eyes. At that moment, I believed these recruits felt that the galaxies had been created for them alone. What could be said? So, I said nothing.

My silence went unnoticed by the recruits, and Beckie soon filled it saying, "We were under the impression that a Class A Star Cruiser like the USS-121 would offer state-of-the-art plasto. During the R-Sci orientation that droned on and on, we asked the trainer, and we discussed it at length. So, don't tell us what you think, because we know." Turning now to Beck-z, Beckie says,

"Beck-z, I cannot imagine what your dad was thinking. Did he expect you to go cold turkey with no plasto during the whole six months of R-Sci training?" Beckie spoke as though she and the others were entitled to anything in the galaxy. Again, before I could speak, the last of the five recruits who had been on the fringe of the group spoke up. Reba says, "Now that we are on the Star Ship, maybe Beck-z can get a holo-message to her dad to straighten this situation out. Personally, I have not started plasto yet. My family's gene pool does not require them until later in life. I'm kind of like you," Reba points to me and continues, "even though I don't have slave-ancestry like you, we're a lot alike. You know, Black don't crack, but my family doesn't either. But I do not begrudge those who get plasto sooner. I hope Beck-z gets what she needs. It has been hard for us all. Can we get on with this whatever we are doing here so we can be escorted to our quarters? It's been a long morning. When will the training begin and with whom?" From my vantage point, these recruits were in full fragility, and I planned to keep my distance and do my best to heed Cmdr. Helen's advice.

I took a deep cleansing breath to settle myself and contemplate how to address the recruits and what, if anything, I might do to assert Fleet hierarchy given their state of *fragility*. I straightened my posture, shoulders back and head high to reach my full 1.65-meter stature. Using my most professionally modulated voice laced with syrup, I say, "Recruits, welcome to the USS-121 Star Cruiser where the finest R-Sci are trained. We will learn to build, install, and maintain the most efficient power system in the galaxy using custom designed simulation pods, sims for short. These sims were developed using research from the top R-Sci's, including mine, and I will be your trainer, Commander Mammy Jones, lead inventor of the power system." The recruits, for the first time, looked at my face. Their expressions of grief now changed to varying looks of disbelief. They looked me up and down staring at my dark skin and kinky hair, and frowning at my robustly full and curvy body.

As I look at each of the recruits directly and in turn, they avoid my eye contact. So I continued, "In an effort to mitigate this unfortunate situation, it is my understanding that there has never been a Gala on board the USS-121. However, because you believe a Gala is eminent, I will get more information right away, and share what I learn. Policy, per regulation 7-10196-2, stipulates that personnel wear Star Fleet-issued gear at all times, which unfortunately, does not include sparkle for skin, hair, or uniforms. Finally, there are state of the art get-and-go plasto-tweaks available on this vessel for fleet personnel injured in the line of duty. These services are not a commodity that can be sold at this time, but perhaps there has been a change." Turning to face Beck-z, I continue, "Please, contact your dad. The Star Cruiser has full communication coverage that can accommodate a holo-message to your dad. Also, worth mentioining, I believe the mill-cred balance you have should suffice for the six months aboard the USS-121; there really is not that much to buy aboard the Star Cruiser. If there are no further questions, then, Escorts, please show the recruits to their pods."

Beck-z, spoke up no longer teary-eyed but with indignation, "Did you say there is no Recruit Gala? You put the kibosh on new plasto, too?! Luckily for me, I thought ahead and had a full-body plasto-tweak last week, which will have to do." She ran her hands over her slender but shapely figure as she spoke. "But how will we be introduced to the ship's crew?" Her tone with me appeared to have gone from indifference to outright hatred. Beckie quickly adds, "I suggest you call someone who is more informed than a, comm . . . , uhm. . ., a you, Mammy, did you say. We have it on good authority that there is a Recruit Gala next week, a coming out event for us in welcome."

"Not to mention," Becca offers in her sweet innocence, "it would be really poor form to not introduce us to the crew. Without a proper introduction how will the crew know we were even here? It is the polite thing to do. I don't want to have to call my grandpa, the past ICC President. I wonder what he has to say?"

In an effort to not let the recruits devolve into more *fragility,* I add, "In the past, recruits were not introduced to the ship's crew. However, it is clear that you are unlike other recruits." Then continuing in more measured tones, still draped in honey sweetness, in spite of my waning patience with the insolent recruits who lack respect, "Your points are well taken. I certainly did not say there is no gala and if one is planned I did not cancel it. However, I will inquire to see the gala status immediately. I can postpone the R-Sci training start for a day while you all get acclimated to ship life. Please, take your leave to freshen up and align your attire to Star Fleet regulation. The escorts will show you to your personal pods." Without a millisecond delay, I turned on my heels with practiced precision and left the silent recruits in the docking bay.

Taking my leave and feeling anxious after the recruits' overt hostility, I need peace and tranquility. I walk quickly to my personal pod, prepare a cup of spicy chai tea, and retreat to my favorite chair that sits beside a table top waterfall. As I sit, I realize that I have not been breathing efficiently. I close my eyes, feel the warmth of the teacup, smell my spicy sweet tea, and breathe. I imagine my family members one by one and feel their love. When I open my eyes, I see their pictures on a collage board floating on a flat wall screen on my right. I feel the inner strength and peace that come with meditation. Before I move, I thank the generations of Black women for passing the mind centering meditation technique that calms me this day, and so many days before. I also think about the women I have shared the meditation technique with and hope that their need is less than mine today. I quietly encourage myself by saying, "Strength, girl. Have strength. This is going to be a trying rotation. That which doesn't kill you will make you stronger, remember that."

By the end of the first training week, from the daily sim reports I knew the recruits had not been making progress on the sims for two days. I wanted to know why because this had not been reported in other trainings across the galaxy. To center myself, I stand in the front of the lab and savor the smell of my fragrant blueberry coffee. The lab entry system alert sounds; the recruits file into the room. Facing them, coffee in hand, unbeknownst to me, they are ready for battle. I, on the other hand, maintain my professional calm as I smile and report, "Recruits, I notice there has been no progress on R-Sci sims for two days. Please, help me to understand what is going on so I can ensure you are supported." The recruits look at me with incredulity. Becca takes the lead in what feels like a coordinated response, "Miss Mammy, you put on your fake smile and ask about sims, but did you offer anyone a cup of coffee? Maybe if we had morning coffee, we could make more progress on sims."

"You all continue to not address me by title, which is against policy" I say more directly than I intended. But before I can continue. Rebecca scoffs, "I don't see what the big deal is about your title. Aren't we all just people of equal importance? Why should one person be better than another?!" I take a cleansing breath before saying, "The R-Sci training was designed for maximum learning in a very short time. What's keeping you from the sims? And, please help yourself to the coffee, just keep it away from the equipment."

Reba's feminist critique of the training made my jaw drop, "As women, completing sims on schedule is oppressive. Why do you proliferate such oppression? As a woman, you should know better. We thought, given racism and your ancestry, that you would care about other women, you know, like us." Shock, my jaw drops. I close my mouth. Before I can say anything else, Beckie adds, "Also, being free to get coffee is really not the point, what about kindness? I once had a Black friend. Her momma and family have served our family for generations and she would never drink in front of me without offering me a drink first. It's common courtesy. But, you never serve us coffee and always help yourself to your own before us." I choose to redirect the conversation, "I hear your concerns about coffee, but what about the sims? Are you stuck? Is equipment operational?"

Beck-z, spoke up antagonistically, "I do not see what the big deal is about the schedule. We should be able to work at our own pace. We have been working every day since we got here and we needed a break. So, we took one. We are from The Dozen. Never were our people slaves, and I'll be damned if I start now." Beck-z shot me a devilish look, full of hatred. Shocked at the obvious display of insubordination and entitlement, I left the scene.

My authority over The Dozen recruits continued to devolve after that incident. Over the next few months, the recruits took liberties in reporting small infractions they perceived I perpetrated against them. They regularly lodged complaints to both commands lines, Fleet Cmdr. Helen and the Cruise Cmdr. In turn, my workload increased in addition to leading the ICC-SSI Fleet Mission and supporting R-Sci training for the very disgruntled 007 recruits, I defended charges. Charge after charge the recruits were painting me as a horrible trainer so much so that I struggled to reclaim my narrative. According to the recruits, I was sabotaging their success. Miraculously, in the last month, my chain of command changed tactics. They started resisting the recruit complaints, refuting them with the many strengths and achievements I have earned, and they start requesting evidence to support their claims against me.

Honestly, I believe my commanders grew weary of repeatedly reviewing my 20-page responses defending what we all knew were unfounded charges. Each response detailed my actions per ICC-SSI Fleet Mission policy and procedures, and ended with questions that required command responses in writing within 2 days per Fleet Code 04-23196-0. Fleet command was working harder, and they were probably not as used to the grind as I was. Not to mention, my preparation, the quality of my work, and the integrity of my character were reflected in my actions and responses, and I would like to believe they were reminded of why they selected me as ICC-SSI Commnader.

Training the recruits from The Dozen Space Station 007 will be memorable for me and I am pleased that today begins the final week for these recruits. Yes, they successfully completed the R-Sci Training by building an operational power system, which they made sure to never refer to in a way that acknowldeged me as it's inventor, and they are as prepared as they can be to install the power system on Space Station 012. Try as they might, they were not able to have me decommissioned and dishonorably discharged from the Fleet, but they were able to encourage the Cruise Commander to host the very first closing ceremonies ending with a Graduates Introduction Gala. Interestingly, I was selected to make the introductions. The recruits also got clearance from the Cruise Commander for get-and-go plasto-tweaks in time for the event. I plan to purchase and share a Full-body Glitter Puff with the recruits to sparkle as I introduce them as the newest Rocket Science graduates. I wonder if I will receive an official reprimand?

Section Three

Guiding Questions

1. All three stories dealt with the theme of entitlement and privilege. What are some ways that the Becky(s) in each story expressed entitlement and privilege? How did it impact the other characters? Are there times you see this in your own environment? How so?
2. Why is it so important to recognize when a Becky is using her privilege? What happens if it is left unchecked?
3. In "The World According to Becky" the main character believes herself to be a social justice advocate because of her prior experiences as an attorney. How can this belief be problematic? How does it influence her learning about race from a person of color?
4. In "Surviving Becky in Space" Dr. Mammy Jones is a highly decorated scientist. Speculate as to why the author goes to great lengths to explicate this. How does whiteness work in ways that discredit Dr. Jones' status, expertise, and position? How does this relate to your own environment?
5. If you are a white woman and begin to notice that folks of color steer clear of you, consider the ways you might be using your privilege or feel entitled to something. Why do you feel you have a right to something? For example, why might one feel entitled to be right, have emotions coddled, or be considered the expert in any given topic?

Section Four

Becky(s) as Terrors

That white women can be anything other than innocent bystanders of atrocious racial bigotry is difficult for society to accept. Hollywood films, for example, often employ racial stereotypes to depict whites as saviors or messiahs redeeming people of color from themselves, their communities, or their cultural depravities. After all, as Vera & Gordon (2003) assert, "we continue to live in a media-manipulated society, saturated in the imagery of white supremacy" (p. 192). Particular to white women, Vera and Gordon (2003) observed how films like *Gone With the Wind* often characterize white women as "complete, 'normal,' [given] a full character" whilst Black female characters are only given one dimension (p. 101). The same can be said in more recent films depicting white women as saviors in urban classrooms. From blockbuster hits like *Dangerous Minds* to *Freedom Writers*, the oft trope of white women is that they are well meaning, pure and innocent, and victims of brutalities of people of color—even if those people are but mere K–12 students (see Matias, 2013). In these movies, the children of color are given grossly unidimensional characterizations whereas the white teacher is given a more complete characterization, complete with a full range of emotions, actions, complexities, and circumstances. In doing so, "society falls to their knees when white women cry because their pain is felt by society . . . their pain becomes real" (Matias, 2016, p. 9). But what of the students' tears? Because their characters are so watered down, so one dimensional, viewers see the students as nothing more than antagonists only used to the comfort and sensibilities of a kind-hearted white women.

As a professor, I often belabor this point of who gets full characterization by referring to the television show *Walking Dead*. The character Michonne, a Black woman, is introduced into the series without any background story to complexify her character for almost an entire season. In fact, in that introductory season, she is given no words, only grunting like an animal. To further animalize her character, she carries around two dead family members like dogs on a chain. Later in the series, she becomes both a mammy to a white man's child (see Vera & Gordon, 2003) and his sexual fulfillment, only after his love companion, a white woman, dies. In contrast, the other white characters and the one Asian American male are given more complete characterizations, complete with flashbacks of their lives prior to the zombie apocalypse. In doing so, viewers come to identify them as whole beings whereas the one Latina and one Black woman characters, who are given no such backgrounds, are not. In fact, the Latina enters the story as a sexual "side piece" for another white man, and the show completely erases the presence of Latino men and Asian American females; a curious phenomenon when acknowledging that the largest growing ethnic minority populations in the U.S. are Asian Pacific Americans and Latinos. However, the character, Maggie, a white woman, is given great complexity. She is given a love story, background context, and complete ranges of emotions from anger and grief over the loss of her husband to strength and determination when saving (yes again) her group of survivors. Later in the series, she even gets pregnant and thus sets the basis for why she needs the most protecting. But I digress.

The point of my belabored analysis is characterization matters because it disseminates who counts as fully human and who doesn't. And that discernment establishes the basis of how people are treated in this white supremacist society. With respect to white women, society, media, and people alike go to great lengths to characterize them as nothing but innocent full human beings always worthy of consideration. They are never outrightly deemed malicious or terrorizing. Yet, the behaviors of Becky(s) are straight malicious and terrorizing. Though intentions matters, the focus is not on her intentions. In fact, that becomes a weapon. She need only say I did not intend or mean to offend and be swiftly relinquished from the culpability of her actions. Simply put, she may be well meaning but at the end of the day, the impact of her actions and behaviors coupled with knowing she need only say she never intended to cause harm as a way to absolve her actions, are terrorizing. It is almost as if we, people of color, moreover women of color, must tiptoe around a Becky(s)' sentimentalities merely because we know to upset her would be to set off a ticking time bomb. And the worst part is, once that bomb is set off, she assumes no responsibility for her action by simply saying, "It was not my intention."

In my experiences, Becky(s) have no remorse for their acts of terror. Take, for example, white women administrators at predominantly white universities who create the context for which women of color experience hostile work environments (see Gutierrez y Muhs, Niemann, Gonzalez, & Harris, 2012;

hooks, 1995; James, 1999; Matias, 2016). This type of Becky will go to great lengths to mischaracterize women of color. She might even focus on one particular woman of color as a strategic maneuver to isolate her. She picks this particular woman of color precisely because this woman sees past Becky's false niceties and employments of victimizations and sees her as she truly is: a fucking terror. Once she isolates this particular woman of color, she will abuse her administrative power to discredit this woman of color's research, teaching, and service. In fact, she will construct a narrative based on "creative liberties" of the truth just to further discredit and isolate the woman of color. In the end, her goal is to get everyone to believe, including the woman of color herself through the process of her gaslighting, that the woman of color is not collaborative, is "the problem," or refuses to take responsibility for actions not of her own. And the worst part is this Becky knows she never has to take responsibility for discriminating, harassing, and bullying this particular woman of color, all because she can send an email and CC the provost saying, "It is not my intention."

Becky(s) as terrors are the worst of its kind because in their boldness to engage in terrorizing, malicious, and manipulative behaviors, they reveal how much they do know about whiteness and how it protects them. Meaning, they know in the end they will always be deemed—to borrow from Godfrey's (2004) title —sweet little white girls and thus their gaslighting, coercion, aggression, and manipulation will never be checked. However, the stories in this section highlight the behaviors of Becky(s) as Terrors so that these behaviors are not left unchecked. In fact, one author describes why she submitted her story to the book. She writes, "To share what it feels like to suffer from prolonged exposure to Beckys(ness). I needed to vent." Another writes, "I wanted to be a part of the larger conversation on white fragility & toxic whiteness." Clearly, there is something detrimentally terrorizing about Becky(s) who behave in this manner. To leave it be by remaining silent about these terrors would be to accept this act of abuse as normal. Indeed, if society is truly committed to a more humane world, then it is not above reproach to investigate these behaviors more deeply.

When pushed and asked what these authors wanted the readers to come away with, their answers reveal the depth of this terror. One writes, "I want readers to know that dealing with white fragility is scary and very toxic to people of color's safety and general existence." The other provides a long explanation that details some of the negative impacts of these behaviors. She writes the following:

> I want them to realize they (Beckys & co) are toxic . . . There is nothing they can do to erase the harm they've cause individually or as a group. There will

never be a time that their presence (and engagement with us) will not be trig-gering. Only through acknowledging, accepting and actively working to be honest in your relationships can you move toward a place of being an anti-racist accomplice. Beckys (and co) need to understand that their relationships with BIPOC, womyn & queer people in particular, will always come to an end. They will always fuck up. There is no avoiding that. They can only be sincere and apologetic and hope that they can eventually be considered a friend and build enough trust that BIPOC are willing to be vulnerable. Beckys must strive to be accomplices and recognize that they will have to sacrifice to be committed to the cause of anti-racism.

Both authors clearly described how writing the story was in and of itself a challenge because it triggered trauma while still being cathartic. One writes, "I didn't realize how re-traumatizing it would be. Receiving feed-back was eye-opening and at the same time, it was provocative. I mean it brought to the surface feelings that I had not expressed about the *current* Beckys in my life. I had compartmentalized this experience to a particular place/space/time in my life and thought I was largely 'over it.'" The other author describes how writing the piece gave her the strength to fight back. She writes, "During this process I felt empowered being able to give voice to people of color's lived experiences." In the end, though the stories are fictionalized, they draw from personal traumatic experiences of women of color who must survive these behaviors.

Based on my own experiences, I doubt that Becky(s) as Terrors will ever take responsibility of their toxic behaviors, but I do hold out for hope. How-ever, the hope is twofold. One, I hope Becky(s) as Terrors will own up to their aggressive enactments of whiteness that ultimately reify white supremacy. And, in doing so, make a turn for a more humane co-existence; one that is willing to learn and listen about how the impact of her actions is not always so innocent regardless of her intentions. However, if that fails to happen, I hope that after reading these stories people can more clearly identify Becky(s) as Terrors, especially when people fruitlessly attempt to reason with them. Clearly, one cannot reason with unreasonable people.

As I documented in my first book, whiteness is nothing but narcissistic. In this case, the emotionality of narcissism in whiteness, one in which Becky(s) as Terrors embody, is egregious because to "overlook how whiteness hege-monically positions itself as the apex of humanity will continue to oppress people of color while distorting who is *actually* getting oppressed" (p. 72). Meaning, in the case of the white administrator above, she will come away looking as if she is the benevolent white administrator doing what is best to "strengthen" the research, teaching, or service a woman of color, when, in fact, all she is doing is distorting her wrongful actions against her and placing the blame of her actions onto the woman of color herself. My caution to readers is to not be fooled by the behaviors of Becky(s) as Terror. Society has already characterized her with full humanity and innocence such that she is always given credence and the benefit of the doubt. Becky knows this. That is why she loudly professes falsities of her commitment to justice, antiracism, and cultural responsivity. And, in knowing this, she can do no wrong when she engages in acts of terror onto people, moreover, women of color. Becky knows the woman of color will never be given the benefit of the doubt. Becky knows the woman of color's truths will never stand in par excellence to the narrative Becky has already constructed for her. One should not be fooled because in the end, Rebecca is, like the stories dictate, nothing but a terror wreaking havoc in the lives of people of color, moreover, women of color.

REFERENCES

Godfrey, P. (2004). "Sweet little (white) girls"? Sex and fantasy across the color line and the contestation of patriarchal white supremacy. *Equity & Excellence in Education, 37*(3), 204–18.

Gutierrez y Muhs, G., Niemann, Y., Gonzalez, C. & Harris, A. (2012). *Presumed Incompetent: The Intersections of Race and Class for Women in Academia.* CO: University Press of Colorado.

hooks, b. (1995). *Killing Rage: Ending Racism.* New York: Owl Books.

James, J. (1999). *Shadowboxing: Representations of Black Feminist Politics.* New York: St. Martin's Press.

Matias, C. E. (2013). On the "flip" side: A teacher educator of color unveiling the dangerous minds of white teacher candidates. *Teacher Education Quarterly, 40*(2), 53–73.

Matias, C. E. (2016). *Feeling White: Whiteness, Emotionality, and Education.* The Netherlands, Sense Publishers.

Vera, H. & Gordon, A. (2003). *Screen Saviors: Hollywood Fictions of Whiteness.* Lanham, MA: Rowman & Littlefield Publishers, Inc.

Chapter Eight

Nightmare on Black Magic Street

The Reality Of Staying Woke

Rebecca George and Alexanderia Smith

This tale of horror unfolds in the most unlikely place, on Black Magic Street. You see Black Magic Street is no ordinary Street. It is a street where some of the most brilliant and powerful people of color reside. Black Magic Street houses a community of Black owned businesses, a world renowned school system, museums, banks, and culturally inclusive spiritual centers. Black Magic Street is indeed every person of color's utopia.

Nicole is a sixteen year old African American female who lives on Black Magic Street with her mother, Angela, and her father, Malcolm, the founder and primary developer of the Black Magic Community. Nicole is an honors student at her school and ranks among the top five students in her class. She is athletic and exudes confidence in her abilities. Nicole's goal was to graduate from Greenwood High school, attend college, and then eventually go to Law School to become a Civil Rights Attorney. She spends her free time with her boyfriend Shawn, her best friend Cindy, and Cindy's boyfriend Tom. They usually frequent the town mall, Noir Mall located on Tulsa Avenue.

One night, just like any other night, once Nicole's family finished eating dinner, she retired to her room to prepare for bed. After showering, Nicole curled up in her bed with a book and eventually succumbed to sleep. During the course of the night, Nicole experienced a horrific and disturbing nightmare.

The track meet was finally over and Nicole was showering in the girls' locker room. Nicole did not realize how long she had been in the shower until she got out and noticed that everyone else had left. So, she got dressed in a hurry and as she was giving herself a final once over in the mirror, she noticed an image behind her. She turned around to face the person and saw that it was a white woman. However, this was no ordinary white woman. Unbeknownst to Nicole this was Surveillance BeckyKrueger.

Surveillance BeckyKrueger was just staring at Nicole with her pale blue eyes. She didn't blink. She didn't move. Instead, Surveillance BeckyKrueger locked eyes on Nicole. This made Nicole feel extremely uncomfortable, but Nicole tried not to let her nervousness show. Hoping for a better interaction Nicole calls out, "Hi, I'm Nicole," she said. The white woman responded, "Oh I know who you are, but do you know who I am?" Nicole said, "No, I am afraid I do not." Surveillance BeckyKrueger smiled a sinister smile and slyly whispered, "Good." At this point, Nicole was in a state of total confusion and fear. She asked Surveillance BeckyKrueger, "What do you mean, good?" Surveillance BeckyKrueger replied, "It's good that you do not know who I am and it's good that you are afraid."

At this, Surveillance BeckyKrueger immediately raised her hand, exposing a glove that had been bedazzled with gems. As Surveillance BeckyKrueger removed the glove, however, Nicole saw that connected to her hand were razor blades for fingernails. With one swift motion of Surveillance Becky-Krueger's hand she began to slice into Nicole's face, causing blood to splatter on the mirrors and walls of the locker room. Nicole did not retaliate because she was in shock, but instead screamed holding the side of her face, which was now scarred by Surveillance BeckyKrueger's razor fingernails.

Nicole struggled to gather herself, as she had fallen against one of the lockers, stricken with fear. Through tears she asked Surveillance BeckyKrueger why she had done that.

Surveillance BeckyKrueger retorted with, "Why did you think it was okay for you to stay in the shower so long? Do you think you're more important than everyone else and deserve to take such long showers? What about if I wanted to take a shower? You stayed in the shower ten minutes longer than everyone else."

Nicole said, "But I don't understand, there were other showers available that you could have used."

At this point, Surveillance BeckyKrueger told Nicole to shut up. Becky-Krueger said "It's not about if other showers were available for me to use. It's about the fact that you should not be able to stay in the shower longer than everyone else."

By this time, Nicole was too weak to even speak. Still backed into the locker, she began to feel herself slowly slide down to the floor. All Nicole could think about was the amount of blood she must be losing. She was horrified as she noticed that what used to be her beautiful mahogany colored skin was now red.

Surveillance BeckyKrueger then stood over Nicole and in a demonic voice that felt as though she were spitting venom, bellowed, "My only objective is to put your soul back in the place where it belongs."

In that instance, just as BeckyKrueger was about to penetrate Nicole in her gut with her razor nails, in walked the coach who yelled, "What is going on here? Move away from her now. Who are you?"

At this point, Surveillance BeckyKrueger spun her head around as if she were spineless. Then, a different face morphed from the first face. The hardness from her eyes disappeared and was replaced with sorrow and sadness. Surveillance BeckyKrueger turned into Reverse Victimization BeckyKrueger right before their eyes. She quickly put her glove back on to cover her hand and began to cry uncontrollably, stating that she was a part of the visiting track team. Between her sobs Reverse Victimization BeckyKrueger told the coach that Nicole took longer in the shower than everyone else and because of this she did not have enough time to take a shower.

Reverse Victimization BeckyKrueger's eyes became puffy from her excessive crying. As Reverse Victimization BeckyKrueger stood over Nicole, crying, Nicole suddenly felt as though she was on fire. Nicole was horrified when she saw one of BeckyKrueger's tears fall on her arm. Once the tear hit her skin, a small puff of smoke rose from Nicole's skin. Nicole winced in pain and let out a blood-curdling scream. It was at this moment when shock spread all over Nicole's body as she realized she was being subjected to more punishment as a result of staying in the shower longer than Surveillance BeckyKrueger felt she should have. The punishment this time, however, was that she was being showered with Reverse Victimization BeckyKrueger's tears, which were actually toxically acidic.

Coach Ebony walked over to Nicole who by this time was lying on the floor going in and out of consciousness. Nicole felt the coach gently shake her and whisper in her ear over and over, "Just stay woke."

Nicole was jolted from her dream and sat straight up in her bed gasping for air with sweat dripping down her forehead and back. "What the hell kind of dream was that?!" cried Nicole.

To calm herself down, Nicole got up and went over to her bathroom to get a cloth to dry her face before returning to bed. But, when she returned to bed her mind and heart were still racing. As she lay in her bed slowly breathing trying to figure out what was going on in her dream, she focused on the ceiling fan spinning around and around as she slowly drifted off into another slumber.

The next morning, Nicole was waiting at a local coffee shop for her boyfriend Shawn, her best friend Cindy, and Cindy's boyfriend Tom to arrive. They were supposed to be working on a school project together, but last night's nightmare was still fresh in Nicole's head. Pushing ahead Nicole found a spot near the door so that her friends would see her when they entered. She sat quietly looking over her social media accounts and "liking" photos of her friends. In order to be productive while she waited, Nicole began to make an outline that detailed some facts about historical racism and white supremacy and the many forms it takes on since slavery, through Jim Crow, the civil rights era on until today.

Just as she finished typing her notes, there was a shadow that came across her phone that caused her to look up, half out of curiosity and some fear. Standing over her was a white woman talking loudly on her phone, sharing with the person on the other end that "some woman was in her seat!" She continued to rant and rave until everyone was looking in her direction. The woman got louder and louder and yelled for a manager.

Once the manager came over, she said pointing her finger at the manager, "You need to remove her. She is not a paying customer! Why is she allowed to be in here with paying customers? She does not belong!" The Entitled Becky-Krueger's shouts were so loud that the entire coffee shop was staring now.

While shouting Entitled BeckyKrueger flips her bangs to the right side of her face, purses her lips and says, "I come here every Friday at 3pm and sit at that chair to drink my pumpkin spice soy latte. And I come here today and I find a nonpaying customer just chillaxing here. This girl simply must go!"

The manager, siding with Entitlement BeckyKrueger first tried to appease Entitled BeckyKrueger by offering free gift cards, apologies, even a new seat brought to the window. But Entitled BeckyKrueger refused them all.

Nicole decided to speak up. "The chair didn't have your name and I was just waiting for my friends before I ordered."

At this, Entitled BeckyKrueger looked appalled. "How dare you scream at me?" She turns to the manager and says, "Did you see that? Did you see how she talked to me? You better call the police. I feel threatened."

The manager resigns and calls the police. The police arrived moments later. Nicole, still in shock and disbelief, was still sitting down knowing she was not doing anything wrong. She attempts to share with the police that she is a high school student waiting for friends to work on a project. The police did not want to hear her explanation. As a police officer places the handcuffs on Nicole's hands all she hears is the click click of the cuffs. Click click. Click click. Click CLICK. Then louder CLICK CLICK.

Feelings of terror rush over her body, Nicole hears someone yelling, "WAKE UP, Nicole!" Nicole realized she was having another nightmare. Upon waking up Nicole realizes it is her mother calling from the kitchen for her to get ready for school. Oddly, Nicole notices her mom is stirring her tea with a silver spoon and she hears an unnerving click click. The sound of the spoon scraping the tea cup lingers in her mind.

"Whoa," Nicole whispers to herself. "I have to talk to my friends about these dreams." She returns to her room, dresses quickly and races off to school.

Nicole arrived at school early so that she could catch her friends before their Advanced Calculus Class. She shared with them each of the dreams that she had experienced and was a bit surprised when the horrific description of her subconscious was met with complete silence. She looked at her friends with a puzzled expression and asked, "Why are you all so quiet?"

They looked at her and then looked at each other with terror consuming their faces, and almost as if they had rehearsed their responses. They told Nicole, "Because we have been experiencing similar nightmares."

They each began to share their frightening experience with BeckyKrueger. Each of Nicole's friends were being haunted by the terror of this Becky-Krueger, but they had no idea why.

After conversing with her friends, Nicole decided she needed to confide in her father. So, after school, she walked into her father's study only to find him reading, as he usually does.

Nicole, said "Hi Dad."

Her father responded by saying, "Hi there, Chocolate Puddin! Uh oh, what's with the long face?"

Nicole responded, "Dad, can we talk?"

He said, "Sure, you know I am always here for you."

Nicole told her father about her dreams and the similarities between her dreams and her friends' dreams. Nicole was a little confused by her father's nonverbal response. He did not appear surprised, shocked, nor horrified. It was almost as if he had been anticipating her very words.

Nicole's father, Malcolm, leaned back in his chair, closed his book, and removed his glasses. He said, "Well Puddin, I had always hoped we would never need to have this conversation, but I'm afraid the time has come."

Nicole became frantic and her voice began to tremble as she saw a level of concern in her father's eyes that she had never seen before. Nicole questioned her father, "What is it Dad? You're scaring me."

Nicole's father motioned for her to sit on the couch and he joined her. He put his arm around her shoulder and said, "It's happening again."

Nicole anxiously responded, "What Dad? What is happening again?"

Her father explained, "There is something you don't know about, exactly how Black Magic Street came to be Black Magic Street."

Nicole said, "What do you mean? You and a group of other Black people decided that you wanted to establish a community built where Black people can live, grow, and thrive together."

Nicole's father responded and said, "Yes, that is the case, but there is more. You see, Black Magic Street was actually founded not just because we wanted the community, but because we also needed it."

Nicole's father explained that back when he grew up on Snowflake Lane, he and his friends knew people who were physically attacked by Becky-Krueger. As a matter of fact, BeckyKrueger was permitted to terrorize whomever she pleased. So, once he and his friends left for college, they never looked back. Even more, they decided after college to stay far, far away from Snowflake Lane, in an attempt to escape BeckyKrueger's wrath. They also hoped that Black Magic Street would serve as a safe place for them to raise their children away from BeckyKrueger's grip.

Nicole's father stated that he and his friends thought they had left the nightmares of BeckyKrueger behind, but fears they are still haunting them, out of revenge, because they were the ones who got away.

Nicole's father turned to her with regret in his eyes and said, "Puddin, my friends and I found our way to deal with BeckyKrueger and you and your friends will have to find your way, but one thing is for sure; we will never be displaced from Black Magic Street, so leaving is not an option." Nicole's father went on to explain that she and her friends are the new generation, so they must come up with their own strategies for surviving the Becky-Kruegers of the world.

Nicole's father stated that he and his friends knew that living on Black Magic Street would protect them from BeckyKrueger's physical attacks, but they never imagined that the monster would become more sophisticated and even more relentless by attacking their children when they are the least guarded, in their sleep.

Nicole found her father's final warning to her the most chilling of all. He said, "Puddin, unfortunately BeckyKrueger targets young adults of color with the most promising futures. So, this is why you and your circle of friends are being attacked. BeckyKrueger views your intellect, confidence, and potential for greatness as threats and honestly, the only true weapons of mass destruction against her evil ways."

Nicole usually felt more at ease after speaking with her father, but this time was different; she felt confused and afraid. One thing was for certain, though: Nicole decided her father was right, and that she and her friends must fight against these injustices. Nicole told herself, "We are the next generation and should take a stand against the BeckyKruegers of the world!"

To this, Nicole immediately texted her boyfriend Shawn, her best-friend Cindy, and Cindy's boyfriend Tom, asking them to meet at the library after school. She instructed, "I have something very important to discuss with you all." In the meantime, however, Nicole wondered how she could possibly get a good night's rest with the possibility of BeckyKrueger waiting to wreak havoc on her subconscious.

Everyone met up at the school library during lunch time. Nicole quickly gathers everyone together to review her agenda of what she thinks will stop the terrible nightmares. Nicole assigns each of her friends tasks to research in the library. Cindy is assigned racial microaggressions. Shawn is assigned white supremacy. Tom is assigned racism and power, while Nicole decides to stay in the small meeting room to work on strategy. Shawn, Cindy, and Tom all find their way to different aisles of books to research the assigned topics. As each of the locate books and articles, they sit down to peruse the literature only to find themselves lulled to sleep by the hum of air blowing from the overhead vents.

Cindy, Tom, Nicole, and Shawn are awakened by noises of metal screeching across the window. They all find themselves in the print shop reviewing the school newspaper for a feature on being unapologetically Black in the twenty-first century. Each student adds vibrant photos of glowing Black girls from their high school who radiate confidence and pride.

No sooner than they each selected another photo for print did they hear screeching again. This time it was closer. Screech. SCREECH! Then suddenly the door flew open and there stood Reverse Victimization Becky-Krueger! She had a target on her forehead just below her layered locks that she placed there. She wore a red and green cardigan with pearls. She threw her backpack on the copy edit table and proclaimed, "Why does the issue have to be about Black girls? They are only 12 percent of the student body. Isn't it reverse discrimination to only focus on Black girls? Those girls do not represent everyone here." Her voice rolled like a high-pitched poodle afraid to go outside for relief.

Amazingly Nicole and Cindy attempted to share the facts about previous issues over the years that only featured white guys or girls. Reverse Victimization BeckyKrueger did not see the value in equality or equity in representing students at the school. She goes on to say how much her family has donated to school functions and the football team, and that she should not have to be subjected to images that do not reflect her Great American way of life! Reverse Victimization BeckyKrueger walks just outside the door and calls to the school counselor.

While on the phone with the school counselo, Reverse Victimization BeckyKrueger is overheard saying that she felt uneasy about all of the inappropriate images that were planned for the upcoming newspaper. She eluded that they were somehow prejudicial in nature.

The school counselor assured Reverse Victimization BeckyKrueger that she should not concern herself with this, because all school newspaper issues are thoroughly reviewed before they are ever distributed.

Reverse Victimization BeckKrueger replied by stating that such conduct would have never been tolerated at the school she came from.

Reverse Victimization BeckyKrueger viewed the school counselor's response as dismissive in nature. In anger, she ended the call and decided that she would deal with this situation "her way."

Reverse Victimization BeckyKrueger returned to the print room and began crying and screaming at Nicole and her friends about the injustice they were promoting by featuring a Black topic. Reverse Victimization BeckyKrueger's flood of toxic, flammable, and acidic tears proved to be a dangerous mix with the copy paper stacked up on the floor near her. Before Nicole and her friends knew it, they were engulfed in flames and Reverse Victimization Becky-Krueger was backing out of the room completely unscathed.

Nicole and her friends are abruptly awoken from this nightmare by an announcement that came over the loudspeaker stating that the library would be closing in fifteen minutes. As they exited the library, they said, almost in concert to each other, "You won't believe the dream I just had."

It was in this moment when the group of friends realized that this could not go on. BeckyKrueger had to be stopped and she had to be stopped now. The group of friends were not sure just how many more dreams they could survive.

That night, as Nicole lay in her bed, tired, but too afraid to fall asleep, it hit her. Nicole knew that never falling asleep was not an option; however, "staying woke" just might be. Tomorrow was Friday and Nicole decided that it was time for her and her friends to have an afternoon slumber party.

She asked her parents if her friends could come over after school the next day to hang out in the basement. Once her parents agreed, Nicole sent out a text message to everyone who agreed to attend.

Once everyone arrived Nicole shared her epiphany. She told her friends that she realized their solution was not to avoid going to sleep, but to simply to "stay woke" at all times. Needless to say, Nicole's friends were confused. She explained that BeckyKrueger kept winning, because we continue to forget that we can be in control, even in our dreams. "We cannot allow Becky-Krueger to dictate what happens to us."

Nicole went on to share with her friends that she remembered reading an excerpt from a Black History Book that discussed the power that Black people are equipped with to repel the force of internal racism. The key, however, Nicole went on to explain, "is that we must first tap into it. We do this by transcending the messages of self-degradation that permeate our conscious and subconscious minds. Instead, we 'stay woke' with the truths of our gifted ancestors. This self-knowledge, you see, will be our ultimate weapon."

Nicole and her friends went on to further strategize how they would take BeckyKrueger down once and for all, but first they would all have to simultaneously fall asleep.

Nicole decided that the best way to help them fall asleep would be to watch an episode of *Family Matters*, so she found an old episode and within minutes they were all asleep.

Just like clockwork, BeckyKrueger showed up with a smug look on her face. She giggled and stated "I see you all just can't get enough of me. You really must be stupid."

Nicole said, "See that's the thing, you know we are far from stupid, which is why you continue these senseless attacks against us."

The smile slowly fell from BeckyKrueger's face and she said in a menacing voice, "I see you've been talking to that no good father of yours. He thought he outsmarted me by leaving town, which is why I found a way to inflict harm even as you sleep, because you can never leave your dreams."

Nicole said, "I actually don't want to leave my dreams, but you will."

BeckyKrueger said, "Ha, this I've got to see."

In unison, Nicole and her friends began to chant the following words while holding up the Black power fist. "I am Black! I am proud! I am glorious! I am Black! I am proud! I am glorious! I am Black! I am proud! I am glorious!"

Each time Nicole and her friends recited the chant one of BeckyKrueger's razor fingernails fell off. When BeckyKrueger saw this, she began to cry.

Nicole stated you will never be able to penetrate Black flesh again with your vicious assaults.

As the teenagers chanted, they noticed that the more BeckyKrueger cried, the more her tears turned to stone until her entire face and body became concrete right before their eyes.

Nicole screamed, "Your forced and fictitious tears will no longer pull at the heartstrings of the world!"

Encouraged by this progress, Nicole and her friends chanted louder and as they did, BeckyKrueger literally cracked and crumbled until she was no more than a pile of dust on the floor, never to be resurrected again.

Nicole woke up to her mother shaking her. She was mumbling, "I am Black! I am proud! I am glorious!"

Her mother stated, "Nicole, wake up, you may be Black and proud, but you are about to be LATE, late for the big track meet that is."

The last track meet had finally arrived. This was the most important one of the season. Nicole's parents were there, along with everyone else on Black Magic Street. Nicole was excited, confident, and ready for the challenge. The weather was perfect. The sun was shining, and the crowd was buzzing with anticipation. Nicole glanced under the bleachers and caught a glimpse of a squirrel who had even come out to enjoy the event. Yes, everything was perfect in the air.

As Nicole stood up after completing her stretches and ensuring that her shoelaces were tied, she smiled to herself as she noticed the most beautiful black butterfly had landed on the cooler. As Nicole stared at the butterfly she found herself trying to make sense of the dream she had last night. She couldn't seem to get that chant out of her head. "I am Black! I am proud! I am glorious!!"

Suddenly, Nicole's state of Zen was abruptly interrupted when she felt a tap on her shoulder. When she turned around, she saw a white woman wearing the opposing team's uniform standing in front of her. The young lady had a long blonde ponytail and blue eyes. She extended her hand for a handshake to Nicole. Nicole reached out to shake the young lady's hand and as she did, chills ran through her body and the hair on the back of her neck stood up.

As Nicole pulled her hand back, the young lady said, "I was just wondering, do your shoes meet regulation standards?"

Suddenly a grey cloud appeared out of nowhere in what was a clear blue sky, just moments ago. Nicole felt an uneasiness, as if she were about to be sick again. There was a flash of lightning and a piercing boom of thunder rang out as the young lady continued with a grimace on her face and said, "Oh and by the way, hi, I'm Becky."

Chapter Nine

When You Cross a Becky

A Monologue

Scott D. Farver

Shitshitshitshitshitshitshit

Why does this always happen to me in the shower?!

Every.

Damn.

Time.

A wave of regret mixed with fear mixed with nausea mingled in my stomach as the shampoo ran into my eyes.

My mind always decides to do the most racing while I'm getting ready in the morning. Most of the time, it likes to take me back to conversations where I said things I regret or something stupid that I said. Most of the time, my mind makes me think about something I said twelve years ago, and I get embarrassed all over again. Often I finish, get out, dry off, and get over it, shaking my head at how ridiculous I was being.

This morning it was different though. This morning, it was more than embarrassment. I was scared. My hands were shaking as I tried to lather up. It was the email I had just read. I shouldn't have opened it. But that's what I do. I wake up. I look at my emails. I get in the shower. Usually, there's just junk in there so early in the morning. Amazon telling me about something I should buy. Someone sending a LinkedIn invitation that I ignore. Stuff like that. I usually wake up just to delete all the junk so I can start the day with a clean, empty, email inbox.

Wouldn't you know, though, the first email of the morning was from a real person. Emailing at 6:08am.

Who the hell sends email at 6:08am?!

The Dean, that's who, dummy.

As a graduate student, I have learned to fly under the radar as much as possible. I have a pretty sweet deal right now. I'm fully funded and don't want to lose that. I can't lose that. What would I do—halfway through my program and then nothing? I don't know what I would do. It's not like I got into other programs. I would have to spend another year applying and waiting and then moving and starting all over again? That's if anyone would want me. I feel like no one would want me if I got kicked out.

While it would seem nice if the Dean of a respected department at a big time university would know my name, experience has shown me this is not a good thing. It seems the Dean *not* knowing your name is better. A number of friends and faculty aren't here anymore because the Dean knew their name. I can think of a few right off the top of my head. Juanita was doing fine in the program. Three years in. Then her Op-Ed got published last year. Decrying the way the academy treats Women of Color. It didn't name names or anything, but, according to the Dean, it was too much. She is no longer in the program. No more funding. They said something like, "This isn't the environment we want to create at this institution" or something like that. Dr. Oh didn't get tenure. Apparently his views don't represent what the Department stands for—that microaggressions happen every day on college campuses like ours. Apparently our campus is more progressive than that. Apparently his research must be flawed. Roberto had to move, too. He did CRT. We don't do CRT at Midwestern University. At least not the way Roberto did it. He was told something about how this might not be the program for him. That his scholarship was too much. Those are just the people I know about. Who knows who else left because of stuff like this? Not kicked out, but forced out. Like, you can stay, but . . . don't.

I had gotten a lot of emails from the Dean over the last four years. Almost all of them were about grants or fellowships or departmental news—forwarded messages that didn't have my name at the top. Rather, it was sent to a listserv of doctoral students and faculty.

Just passing this along to those who might be interested in this.

Or.

Thought you should see this.

This email was different. This one had my name on it. It wasn't forwarded. It was definitely just for me. My name right at the top. 6:08am.

The nausea hit again as I rinsed off and remembered what she wrote. Thinking of the possible implications.

Shitshitshitshitshitshitshit

My stomach continued its somersaults as I tried to remember exactly what I had read as the water beat down on me.

This wasn't good.

Was I in trouble?

Of course you're in trouble you idiot! Why else would she email you like this?

This wasn't good.

But I didn't do anything.

Did I?

I must have done something. Shit!

This was definitely not good.

My breathing became shallow as my mind raced through what seemed like my entire life history in a moment. What had she written again? Snippets of the email flashed in front of me.

. . . Becky . . .
. . . A formal complaint . . .

What did that even mean?

. . . Becky?
. . . EDU 101?

Was this about Becky's video? It must be. We talked the other day. That had to be it. Becky's damn video. It was totally about the video.

Shitshitshitshitshitshitshit

I got out of the shower and ran to my phone to read the Dean's email again, dripping on the carpet. What was happening?

From: Dr. Rebecca White
6:08am (37 minutes ago)
To: me

I need to speak to you face to face as soon as possible. I received a disturbing email from one of your students who claims you called her a racist after class the other day. Becky Jones, from your EDU 101, contacted me and shared how she feels discriminated against in your class and that you singled her out because she is white. You know that at Midwestern University that we strive to create safe spaces for our students, and that we respect all opinions.

Because this is a formal complaint being lodged against you, we need to take action as soon as possible. Come to my office this morning at 9am, so I can discuss next steps.

Rebecca White, PhD

Dean, Department of Education
Midwestern University
Chair, Research Association Division of Equality for All (DoEfA)
Treasurer, National Association of Deans
Former President of Research Academy of America (RAA)

Shitshitshitshitshitshitshit!

What did Becky say to the Dean?

I had never been asked to meet with the Dean before. What was she going to say? Becky must have said something. What did that email say again?

. . . She feels discriminated against in your class . . .

My head was swirling with possible ramifications of the meeting. This was going to be Juanita all over again.

Shit!

I got dressed, my mind still racing.

I took some deep breaths. I stood up and paced around the room. My mind racing through what was happening and how it had happened.

Shitshitshitshitshitshitshit

It was totally about the video and our conversation afterward. Why did I have to call Becky on this? I should have just let it go. Just give Becky the damn A and forget about her and her flock of friends. I could picture them sitting together—barely listening each week as I tried to talk to the class about systems of oppression. Becky was clearly the ringleader. Her eyes seemed to roll more each week. As soon as class started, Becky's phone would come out—below the desk as if I couldn't see. As if I hadn't been teaching for 10 years. Her friends finagled their phones out too. Becky would snicker and look at her friends, then roll her eyes as she saw me looking at her. The phone put away for a few more minutes before popping out again to repeat the whole scene. It was tiring.

Every damn week it seemed. Future fucking teacher right there, that Becky.

I had taught the course before. I had students like Becky before. Most of the time I could get students like her to engage. They would say things like all lives matter or that we were a country that was past race. Or at least if those students disagreed with what we were learning, they wouldn't derail every conversation. I'd had a few students who just sat there, silently begrudging everything we did in class.

Becky was different though. She and her friends seemed to be able to disrupt everything just by their presence. Becky was like the cool kid in class who dictated what others should think. So not only was she disengaged, but because she was, none of the other students wanted to share anything. Like, I would ask a question and everyone's feet suddenly became the most interesting thing on the planet. I thought the idea of popular kids faded with high school, but it was clear with Becky that this concept was still going strong. Becky seemed to dictate the direction of the course, and silenced everyone else. Every day, as soon as Becky walked into class—the

Greek lettering on her shirt, bag, and water bottle was incomprehensible to me—conversations would stop and the whole feeling in the room would shift. I just wanted to get Becky and her friends to engage in the ideas and allow space for the other students to share. I should have been more careful about what I wished for. Because when Becky engaged, she really fucking engaged. Just in really assholey ways.

I could picture the day Becky had been most animated. The day her phone went away the longest. I was talking about reasons why we should reconsider celebrating Columbus Day. How teachers contribute to dangerous interpretations of history through word searches and poems and teaching students about his "heroics." I put the question back onto the class. They were going to be teachers in a few years. What would they do in their classes as teachers? Would they celebrate the holiday? What would they do with *their* students?

I thought it was a softball topic. I thought it was going to be cut and dry.

Most students every other year joined me in my outrage. Why the hell were we celebrating this guy?

Most students every other year were embarrassed. Why hadn't we learned about this before?

Most students every other year talked about how they had never considered Columbus before.

Most students every other year would share what they would do. No, they wouldn't celebrate the day. They'd teach differently.

This year was different though. As soon as the topic was broached, Becky chimed in.

She always celebrated Columbus Day. She always had that day off when she was in school. To her Columbus Day was just a holiday. To her, this was ridiculous. To her, we can't judge the past like this. She'd say, "What was the big deal about him? He discovered America." Then she'd look at me and with her darting eyes shout, "Why did you always have to make such a big deal out of everything?"

The whole idea seemed like a slap in the face to her. Becky was insistent that I was blowing things out of proportion. Like I always did. Becky's family was Italian. They always celebrated Columbus Day. I was insulting them. I was making a big deal out of nothing.

While Becky had been annoyingly indifferent up to that point, after that particular class, she was indignant. Every reading was a bunch of BS to her. The eye rolling became sharper. I hadn't been able to get through to her since that day. She didn't share in whole group discussions. Or if she did, it was a snarky comment. I tried to let it go. I didn't want to make things worse than what they were. Just let her coast through, I thought. It irked me though. Every comment. Every derisive look.

Becky did the work though. Papers turned in when they were due. And. Becky was very excited about the final project. It was open. Students could do it individually. Or in groups. Becky wanted to work in a group. Becky wanted to make a video. I saw a win in that she was starting to engage.

The nausea came back and I thought about the video. It was horrible. Maybe the worst thing that I have seen as a teacher. No, definitely the worst. ten years as a teacher, and this was the worst thing I had seen. I was still pacing around my apartment. I cringed again thinking about that damn video. It was like being in the shower all over again. This whole Dean thing is all about that video.

But wait!

Maybe the video Becky made really wasn't that bad.

Maybe it wasn't as bad as I thought.

Maybe I had crossed a line.

Maybe I could just let it go.

Maybe I would tell the Dean that I made a mistake.

Maybe tell her that everything was fine.

Maybe give Becky the A that she wanted and forget all about her.

That's what this was all about right? For sure it was. It *had* to be about that damn video and my conversation with Becky afterward. Maybe I was blowing everything out of proportion and just needed to apologize to Becky and the Dean and everything could go back to normal and I could keep my funding and finish my PhD and get the hell out of here.

I sat back down at the table and opened my laptop. It hummed and whirred as I clicked around my desktop. Yeah. That's what I'll do. I'll watch the video and see that it was fine and everything will be fine. It's fine.

*EDU101. *click**
*Final Assignment. *click**
*Becky_Jones. *click**
*Final Video.mp4. *click**

My computer sounded like a diesel motor as the video loaded. I had only watched it once, but that had been enough. I hadn't ever wanted to watch it again. Most students had created posters.

They really took up the ideas in creative ways. One had written a spoken word poem about oppression. Those were amazing. Not this, though. This had made my stomach turn. A familiar feeling this semester with Becky.

As I clicked, Becky's face filled the screen. A black hoodie covered her head. Gold chains dangled on her deck. The camera zoomed out and a large boombox sat next to her. As she pushed play, a heavy beat started thumping from my laptop speakers and Becky began nodding her head. She put on oversized sunglasses and held up a piece of paper and began reciting the lyrics to her song. It was like she was trying to incorporate every possible stereotype about rappers into one scene.

Becky looked into the camera.

We're all equal, me and you
Don't matter the color
Black, white or blue
All lives matter
That's what I'm trying to say
Why do we need to talk about race today . . .

She disappeared as I clicked the red X in the corner of the video player.

Nope.

Nopenope

Nopenopenopenopenope.

I couldn't watch anymore. It was too much.

I wasn't going to let this go.

It was just as bad as I remembered.

I remember the first time I had opened it. I remember that I was excited that Becky and her friends had wanted to create a video for the final project. I remember thinking that maybe I had read too much into Becky's actions in class. I remember thinking that maybe I had been too cynical about her. I remember how excited Becky had been at the idea of making a video. I remember the feeling I had when it played for the first time last week. Almost like getting the email from the Dean. Stomach dropping. Hands shaking.

What.

The.

Hell!

I couldn't make it through the first 20 seconds without feeling sick. The "rap" was cultural appropriation in its worst form. And the content—we talked all semester about race, power, oppression, and the importance of movements like BLM. How did she think this was ok? All lives matter? It was a slap in the face. I was glad I had called her on this. I felt redeemed. Reinvigorated. I was in the right. This was horrible.

Right?

After seeing it, I had thought long and hard about how I should confront Becky about this. Should I send an email? Do it all at distance? Or should I ask her to meet me somewhere? Public? Private?

I decided I needed to do it face-to-face. I stopped her after class last week before she left with her friends. *I just want to talk to you real quick about your video.* I remember how big she had smiled as we walked back to my office.

She seemed proud. Like I was going to compliment her on doing such a great job. Like there was a fucking Oscar in my desk drawer waiting for her.

We sat down. I talked. The video was problematic. It was full of cultural appropriation. The ideas she presented were problematic. But I wanted to give her another chance. If she could re-do the video, I would grade it again. No penalty. *Here's two articles on cultural appropriation that might help.*

She had sat silently there in my office as I talked. I could tell she was trying not to cry. But I remember a single tear working its way down her face. She huffed as she walked out the door. I naïvely thought she would go home and read the article and realize that what she had done was not ok. That she would be embarrassed at what she had done. Full of contrition. I was actually expecting an apology email from her this week. Instead, a different email. From the Dean. At 6:08 in the morning! That made my stomach churn at what might happen to me.

My mind flashed back to the email again.

. . . we strive to create safe spaces for our students, and that we respect all opinions.

Was I in trouble for making Becky feel uncomfortable? For making a white women feel uncomfortable? It sure seemed like it. Would I be asked to leave the program? What was the Dean going to say to me? It didn't seem like she was going to back me up. What would this mean for my funding? For my research? Or for the job search next year—the Dean sure knows a lot of people. Would she not recommend me? Or worse, would another program even let me in if I got kicked out? Would she actively tell people not to hire me?

Shitshitshitshitshitshitshit

I kept thinking about Juanita and Dr. Oh and Roberto. Their lives had been destroyed because of the Dean. Because they didn't "toe the line" in her favor.

No.

I was going to be fine. All I had to do was show the Dean this video and explain the conversation I had with Becky the other day. It was going to be fine. Maybe I could tell her that I would meet with Becky again and talk through why the video was so problematic. I mean, how can she be equipped to teach in our K–12 schools if she has problematic thoughts about race and most of our K–12 students are students of color?! Surely the Dean would see that.

No problem. That video was so bad. The Dean would see my point and it would work out.

I felt better. I knew that I was doing the right thing. If Becky was going to be a teacher, I needed to intervene here . . . while she was a student. Before she had a classroom of 10-year-olds. I was going to take a stand. I sat down and start typing my reply. To let the Dean know what really happened and why I had called Becky on her video. I was going to be fine.

To: Dr. Rebecca White
7:43 am
From: me

Dr. White

I would be glad to stop by today, though I have to rearrange my schedule to meet at 9am. I am a bit confused—is this about Becky's video that she made? I can bring it with me and show you and maybe we can talk about next steps? I hope that

My phone dinged mid sentence. I stopped typing and glanced down. A text. It was from a colleague at work. It was a link to ProfessorRater.com. They told me I needed to take a look at this.

I clicked and saw my name. I had a 1 star rating. There were at least 20 comments. They were all bad. What the hell? It had been fine last week. 5 stars.

Worst professor ever. Totally racist toward white people.

This teacher sucks. Unless you agree with everything they say (like white people suck), they will fail you.

MU needs to fire this professor. Can't believe they are actually allowed to teach a course.

My head was spinning. I stopped reading because my phone was dinging again. And again. And again. Twitter. It looked like my handle @MUteacher was being tagged. I'm horrible at Twitter. I had like 20 followers. Why would I be getting so many alerts? I opened the app.

@MUteacher is totally a #racistprofessor

Can't believe @MUedProgram has people like @MUteacher. #racistprofessor who shouldn't have a job. Fire now!

Hey @MUedProgram. Program is a disgrace because of people like @MUteacher. #racistprofessor

I began to legitimately freak out now. *What the hell was going on?*!

First the email from the Dean. Then the website. Now Twitter? This was crazy—I could *see* who was Tweeting. It was Becky and her friends. They were launching an all out campaign against me. I needed to be fired? What the actual fuck!?

Shitshitshitshitshitshitshit

I was trembling now. This had never happened before. All because of what I said about Becky's video? My mind replayed the scene in my office. The single tear running down Becky's cheek. That wasn't a tear of sadness. Instead, that was the tear that undergirded this nightmare. It was as if by shedding it she felt justified in her shaming tactics . . . but I had nothing to be ashamed of. I am not a racist. I teach race and racism. This was all too gaslighting!

How was I going to stop this? I needed to meet with the Dean and tell her my side of the story. This was not email material. I needed to talk to her face to face. Like now. I needed to make sure she knew what had really happened. To make this better. To work things out.

My head was spinning as I left the Dean's office. What had just happened? I remembered bits and pieces—images and words swirling together, a Dali painting of whatthefuckedness. Some things were vivid. Like, her safety pin on her desk. Some things were messy in my mind. Her words. What did she really say? I had tried to take notes, but couldn't concentrate. It was a blur. I had been blown away by the turn our talk had taken. It had not been a two-way conversation. She had listened—or at least appeared to listen—at first. She watched the video. Or at least the 20 seconds I shared with her. I said my piece. I thought it was going to be fine.

But.

There was no ambiguity. She heard nothing of my side because Becky's tears were more powerful than the mission of social justice.

I had been wrong. Snippets of what had been said rang in my ears as I tried to process the last half hour in the Dean's office as I walked aimlessly through campus trying to make sense of what she had said.

. . . *this is a sensitive time in our country* . . .

What is going on right now?

. . . *Becky's claims of racism are taken seriously* . . .

It couldn't be. This wasn't happening.

. . . *this is not the environment we are creating here at the university* . . .

No, everything is going to be fine. Right?

. . . *it is clear this is not the program for you* . . .

What just happened?!

. . . *you'll land on your feet somewhere* . . .

What am I going to do?!

. . . *it's for the best. For everyone.*

I shouldn't have crossed a Becky.

Section Four

Guiding Questions

1. In "Nightmare on Black Magic Street" the authors playfully use the story of BeckyKreuger. How are these Becky(s) terrors in the story? What impact does it have on the main character, Nicole and her father? How have Becky(s) been real terrors in your life?
2. "When You Cross a Becky" describes the terrorizing behaviors of a Becky in academia. Have you had experience with these terrorizing behaviors in your organization or academic setting? Why are the behaviors of Becky(s) so routinely produced in academy? Who or what supports these kinds of behavior and what are some ways to shut it down?
3. How does terror in the behaviors of Becky(s) impact people? How do we listen and support those who are most terrorized by Becky(s)?
4. If you are a white woman and a person of color shares with you that your behaviors might be construed as terrorizing or imbued with whiteness, why is the first response defensiveness? How can you lower your defensiveness and aggression in ways that invite better interactions between you and a person of color, particularly toward women of color? How does simply admitting that your actions were terrorizing—whether intention or not—begin a process toward healing? What will you do to atone for past transgressions?

Section Five

Becky(s) As Presumed Experts or Usurped Authority

Sworn in as the 2017 U.S. Secretary of Education, Betsy DeVos' appointment was greeted with protests from the educational community. From her failed attempt at spearheading the Detroit charter school system that left that entire educational system in shambles to her lack of formal training in education—she earned a bachelors in business from Calvin College— DeVos, who is not supported by teacher unions across the United States, is still presumed to be the expert who has every right to usurp authority. That is, she embodies someone who enacts their privilege in whiteness to appear as if she is qualified for a position that she is unqualified for. Or, as I have written before in an analysis of the re-emboldening en-whitening epistemological moment (see Matias & Newlove, 2017), this phenomenon is simply "equating plain vanilla to that of the crème de la crème" deeming themselves "experts without expertise" (p. 925).

Suffice it to say that those individuals who pompously self-presume themselves to be experts is one thing. However, for society to readily accept someone as an expert without any corresponding credentials, qualifications, or educational or professional training is another. Because to do so speaks directly to how a society operates in racial power and privilege; for a person of color, more precisely a Black person, is not so readily presumed to be an expert without the credentials to do so. In fact, in my own experiences as brown-skinned Pinay, I have had individuals question as to whether I have a doctorate degree as a tenured professor. While teaching my class at the university, an unknown white male popped his head one day and in front of my class asked me if I was the professor. As if standing in the front of the class while lecturing with a PowerPoint were not enough, this white male then asked if I had a PhD. Despite the obvious racial and gender microaggression, what interests me most as a scholar of whiteness is his racial presumption to feel entitled to ask such a question, moreover, his confidence to use my racial and gender phenotypes as justification enough to warrant the inquiry. The interpellation between his presumed authority over me based on my racial and gendered differences was not only appalling; it was telling of how whiteness and patriarchy operates with authority.

This entitlement where one presumes to be an expert and authority is no different than when applied to how Black and Brown college students are treated. Oftentimes Black and Brown students are presumed to be affirmative action admits regardless of their scholarly abilities or acknowledgment that white women make up the largest beneficiaries of modern affirmative action policies (see Beeman, Chowdhry, & Todd, 2000). Even more, white males are also never considered affirmative action hires or college admits despite being the recipients of one of the United States' largest affirmative action policies qua GI bills, FHA loans and housing preferences, and federal employment programs. Again, the interpellation between the presumption of Black and Brown college students as affirmative action admits is interesting, yet more telling is the presumption of those who so regularly assume they have the right to make that erroneous judgment, especially while they turn a blind eye to their own historical preferential treatment.

Or, how Black and Brown women in the academy or any work related position are presumed to have only gotten the job due to some diversity quota for the organization or are automatically presumed incompetent for the position for which they were hired (see Gutierrez y Muh, Niermann, Gonzalez, & Harris, 2012). Truth be told, these racial biases are what makes doing the work so difficult for Black and Brown women. Simply put, women of color are "surviving and even thriving in what are often foreign and hostile environments" (Gutierrez y Muh et al, 2012, p. 503). And, to be precise, that hostile environment exists because the preexisting conditions of whiteness and patriarchy operate in the space, which does not welcome those who do not subscribe to whiteness or patriarchy. If this space operates within this paradigm, then those who hold similar ideologies feel entitled to their presumptions of authority or expertise, which then, in turn, undergirds their racial and gender microaggressions of women of color. Meaning, if a space operates under the presumptions of whiteness then those individuals who engage in whiteness ideology will embrace such entitlement because that is what whiteness does: it elevates whites and whiteness ideology to the racial apex. And, in doing so, they will feel righteous, entitled, and justified in their engagements of racial microaggressions, which then racially oppresses people of color. In this case, the dynamics of having negative presumptions of women of color in the workplace is predicated on one's presumption of their own authority in that same workplace.

Frankly speaking, even our former president, Barack Obama, an African American male, could not escape critiques of being unqualified, despite his degrees from Columbia University and Harvard Law School. Conversely, all my white students feel they need to justify their qualification for teaching in urban schools despite never having interactions with people of color is to say, "Well, I did a semester abroad in Costa Rica." Clearly, unlike whites who can self-presume themselves as experts without expertise and have society readily accept them as such, the same is not true for people of color, especially for Black and Brown individuals.

Interesting to note here is that whereas the racial presumptions for people of color are laden with negative associations, whites are given preferential presumptions. In other sections, readers see how white emotionalities are given credence over that of the humanity of people of color or how white entitlement and privilege are used to assert control over people of color. Regardless of the strategy, the essence remains the same: whiteness facilitates the conditions ripe for Becky(s) to falsely presume expertise and usurp authority. Therefore, Becky(s) are white women who under the existing white supremacist society, use their whiteness in ways that entitle them to presume themselves as experts, and usurp the authority behind that presumption.

The stories in this section highlight how Becky(s) have not only presumed themselves to be experts in matters where they do not truly possess knowledge, but in making that presumption, they negatively exercise authority over others. In fact, Becky(s) exert their authority in ways that silence the expertise of people of color, reify their usurped power and authority, and obscure the real dynamics of power. And interestingly enough, Becky(s) as Presumed Experts and Usurped Authority operate under a mal-informed understanding of equity, justice, and diversity but since they are the authority or experts, they have created the condition for which they can never be challenged on that mal-informed understanding. In fact, one of the authors in this section writes about how Becky(s) as Presumed Expert and Usurped Authority attempted to sabotage her scholarship precisely because Becky(s) did not like to be challenged. She writes, "I've had so many experiences with Becky(s), especially since starting graduate school, that have really gotten to me. They've ranged from white women weaponizing their tears to stories of white women attempting to sabotage my progress because they didn't like how I challenged them." The author, a woman of color herself, describes how fearful she was to even speak out when she writes, "The call for the book felt like an outlet for me to express everything I've been holding in without the danger of ramifications. Clearly, speaking truth to power is dangerous when the truth simply means to challenge these kinds of Becky(s).

However, the focus on Becky(s) shifts when asked what she wants her readers to come away. Instead of focusing on identifying Becky(s)' behaviors which is important, what the author wants more than anything else is communal healing from other folks who are surviving the abusive behaviors of Becky(s). She writes the following:

> I think more than anything I want readers to know that they're not alone. That they're not the only ones experiencing these thing[s] and that when Beckys try to make them feel crazy for articulating their struggles, they shouldn't. They should know that what's happening is real. I want them to feel validated. I also want them to know that in spite of it all, there is almost always one person who is in their corner and fighting for equity and justice in the same ways they desire it.

Notice how the author urges readers to understand the psychological abuse incurred upon people who are surviving Becky(s) as Presumed Experts and Usurped Authority. Instead of allowing Becky(s) to use her power qua gaslighting tactics that wrongfully makes Becky's victims "feel crazy for articulating their struggles," the author demands validation for the real and lived experiences of victims. Essentially, though these Becky(s) attempt to gaslight the realities of their victims, the authors offer these stories to speak truth to power. Whether it is erroneously being labeled an affirmative action college admit or a diversity quota hire, the truth is whiteness works in ways that associate negative presumptions on people of color. This much is known. What is not commonly known is how these Becky(s) work whiteness as a way to gain power as experts and authority when the truth is their existence is nothing but an exemplar of mediocrity over true meritocracy.

REFERENCES

Beeman, M., Chowdhry, G., & Todd, K. (2000). Educating students about affirmative action: An analysis of university sociology texts. *Teaching Sociology*, 98–115.

Gutierrez y Muhs, G., Niemann, Y., Gonzalez, C. & Harris, A. (2012). *Presumed Incompetent: The Intersections of Race and Class for Women in Academia*. CO: University Press of Colorado.

Matias, C. E., & Newlove, P. M. (2017). Better the devil you see, than the one you don't: bearing witness to emboldened en-whitening epistemology in the Trump era. *International Journal of Qualitative Studies in Education*, *30*(10), 920–28.

Chapter Ten

Waiting to Excel

Justine Lee and Autumn A. Griffin

At 6 AM, the blaring alarm clock wrested twenty-three-year old Neveah from yet another night of not enough sleep. As she readied herself for work at Clinton Charter School where she taught tenth grade English, and class at Reagan University later that evening, Neveah mentally prepared for what was to come that day. First, she knew she would have a staff meeting to discuss changes in admissions. After, she would head to a meeting with Dr. Beck Zilla, the chair of her department at the prestigious and predominantly white Reagan University about the latest and third failed attempt to fill a faculty position with a person of color.

As she walked to work, wrestling with the wind that refused to let her fresh twist out be great, she pondered these things; she took note of how much her neighborhood had changed over the past few years. A Whole Foods had replaced the grocery store owned by Mr. and Mrs. Banks, whose daughter she attended Zion AME Church with. An Apple store stood where the town's community center had once been, where her and all of her girls would practice their rendition of Destiny's Child's *Say My Name*—where she attended her first dance and her younger sister had her first kiss. Then she passed what used to be Gloria's, a West Indian restaurant where her uncles played cards every Sunday and her aunts got together to gossip with Miss Gloria, whose grandchildren Neveah used to babysit. When the White folks bought out Gloria's, they rebranded it "Jamaican Me Crazy" and changed the menu.

It wasn't just the buildings that had changed. Faces that were once recognizable sources of comfort were replaced with foreign, whiter ones. These transplants kept to themselves, except in times when they felt threatened and called the police on a neighbor for playing music too loudly. Neveah saw the changes in her classroom as well. Since her old high school was converted into Clinton Charter Academy, she thought as she walked through its doors, so much about the school had changed.

On her way to the 8AM staff meeting, Neveah was approached by Becca, the school principal, who said, "Before we have the meeting, I wanted to ask for a local opinion about the school board's request to implement an admissions test for Clinton Charter. What are your thoughts?"

Neveah replied, "I think it would be an exclusionary measure. Standardized tests tend to be culturally biased against Black and Latinx students."

Becca, taken aback by this thought that had clearly never occurred to her, responded, "Well, the board just wants to accommodate the changing demographics of the neighborhood, and so they think adding an admissions test is the best way to do it."

Neveah, realizing Becca had already made up her mind, replied, "Great. Let me know what they come up with."

Sensing she had misstepped and confused over how, Becca asked Neveah about her weekend. Neveah replied, "It was fine, thank you. How was yours?"

Becca excitedly chattered, "It was so great! I had my second date with John, this Black guy. We went to Jamaican Me Crazy because, let me tell you, it is my absolute *favorite* place to eat! Anyway, the date went really well! He hasn't called me back yet. I hope he does because I really *love* Black men. I mean, I have loved them ever since I did Teach For America. Did you know I had dreadlocks in high school? In Kansas, if you can believe it! I guess you could say I've always had jungle fever!" Becca laughed prolongedly at her own joke while interlocking her arms with Neveah's as if they were best friends. Neveah inhaled quietly, pulled away, and appeased her with a simple, "That's . . . good for you."

Becca said, "*Thank* you. I mean I *do* think it's good for me. I'm *so* glad you're not offended by it, because sometimes online I read articles that say . . . "

They were interrupted by Rebecca White, Neveah's classroom neighbor and teacher of history, who declared, "Becca, I heard we might be implementing an admissions test, and I fully support it. After all, kids should *earn* their place here and prove they have what it takes to succeed."

The first period of the day occurred without much incident; Neveah and her students engaged in a rich discussion of the third and fourth chapters of Carter G. Woodson's *The Miseducation of the Negro*, analyzing his rhetorical strategies and delving deep into discussions about the relationship between race and education. At 10:30 AM, about fifteen minutes into second period, a class that was going just as well, Rebecca barged into Neveah's classroom while Neveah's students were reading, despite the fact that Rebecca was supposed to be teaching next door.

Rebecca said, "What are you reading? Oh, *this* book. I read it in my diversity education class. It's too controversial. Plus, he really shouldn't be using the word *N-word* in his title." She turns to the class and says, "Don't you think Mr. Woodman is combative?"

Jay, a Latino student, said, "I don't think so. He's just protesting against unfair conditions. Also, it's *Doctor Woodson*."

Rebecca quipped, "Young man, raise your hand before addressing an adult. It's rude to correct people in public." Jay and Neveah exchange looks and both stifle a smile.

Rebecca continued loudly to Neveah, "This is what I meant during the meeting, like we need more respectful kids. I can't wait 'til we get kids who *actually* want to learn."

Instead of responding with, "My experience with our students has been that they all love to learn"; "Please don't talk about my students as if they are not sitting in front of you"; or "If you cared about the well-being of the school, wouldn't you be in your classroom teaching right now?" all of which would have been appropriate responses, Neveah chose to end the foolish interruption to her class as quickly as possible and said, "Did you need something, Rebecca?"

Rebecca said, "Oh! Yes. You need to talk to Jeffrey. Every day with him is a battle. He's always so aggressive. It scares me. You know! You have him fifth period!"

Neveah, trying to get Rebecca to leave, said, "Ok, send him to my room once the period is over."

Rebecca said, "I need you to do it now. I'll teach your book while you talk to him."

Neveah glanced at the mixture of disgusted and pleading looks from her students, who seemed to silently scream, "Please do not leave us alone with her," and responded to Rebecca, "You can go back to your class. Have Jeffrey meet me in the hallway." Neveah felt how her students looked. Rebecca *always* had a problem with critically-minded Black students like Jeffrey, and while she did not seem willing to address her own racist biases, Rebecca was more than willing to spew them to Neveah, on more than one occasion.

"You're such a sweetheart," Rebecca said patronizingly, leaving without at least a "thank you."

Neveah exited her classroom to meet Jeffrey, and they stood at a vantage point so that Neveah could still keep an eye on her class.

"Hi Miss," Jeffrey said warmly. "Sorry you had to leave your class. Hope you had a good weekend."

Neveah said, "Thank you, Jeffrey. Good to see you. What happened in Ms. White's class today?"

Jeffrey sighed exasperatedly and whispered furiously, "Miss! She doesn't know how to teach, and she's *so* disrespectful. Today, she called the Black Panthers 'terrorists.' You *know* that's not what they were, and it's offensive 'cause I have family members who were in the Black Panthers, and I know other students in the class do, too. I'm proud of coming from that activism and belief in the community, and that's all I said to her. Then she wanted to be all like, 'Well if you have family like that, it makes sense why you think you can be so disrespectful to me, maybe they need lessons in respect, too.' I was like, 'YOU'RE the only one *being disrespectful*, and you're not even right. I don't care if you're my teacher—don't talk about my family that way.' Then she just *ran out of the classroom crying*! Like what? Aren't you a grown adult with a job that you just decided not to do?"

Neveah drew in breath and fought the instinct to let out an exasperated sigh. Rebecca, like many terribly misguided White women at Clinton, thought they were saving poor Black and Brown children through one painfully boring lesson at a time. She turned to Jeffrey and said, "I'm sorry she did that, Jeffrey. It's not right for her to say that, and you *should* be proud of your legacy."

Jeffrey responded, "But why are you the one apologizing? I swear I'm not going back in there until I get an apology from her. She owes me one and the class one. I hate going there. We don't learn anything. It's all propaganda and lies."

As Neveah and Jeffrey spoke, Rebecca's shouting at her students and the sound of Neveah's students rearranging their desks to start a Socratic seminar served as background noise. Neveah smiled at Jeffrey and said, "I'm really proud of you and how much you've taught yourself. You have a sharp mind that makes you wise beyond your years, and that's not always easy. I'll talk to Ms. White and try to get her to apologize, but as a piece of advice, if you're waiting for proud and ill-informed people to apologize, you'll be waiting the rest of your life. You and I both know that people get away with doing wrong all the time. You shouldn't stop standing up for what you think is right, but what you're experiencing right now happens when you point out injustices. You're absolutely right—that doesn't make it OK, but you stick with the mentors and the peers you know bring positivity, learning, and love in your life, and you hold onto that."

Jeffrey smiled sheepishly at the ground and said, "Thanks, Miss." With a quick change in mood that so characterizes adolescence, he excitedly began talking to her about their reading homework last night, chapter 3 of *The Miseducation of the Negro*, before Neveah said, "I'm so happy you're this excited to talk about it, but let's save it for class discussion later." Jeffrey nodded and walked away, feeling bittersweet about returning to class, and Neveah returned to her class, where her students were already engaged in a lively discussion about the text.

Running from the bus stop to Reagan University Neveah could barely catch her breath as she arrived at the door of her department's office at exactly 3:58 PM. She couldn't stand the thought of being late for her meeting with the department chair. She already knew what the White folks at Reagan thought of her and the other critical students of color in the department and she didn't want to add fuel to that fire. When she arrived, Wanda, the sweet elderly woman at the front desk, looked up at her and smiled warmly. "Hi, Neveah! I haven't seen you in a while! How are you?"

"I know! I'm still trying to adjust to this work-school-life balance thing. How are you? How's your family?"

"I understand. Make sure you're taking care of yourself. We're all good! Thanks for asking. Are you here for a meeting with Dr. Zilla?" Wanda asked with a slight smirk on her face. Neveah returned the smirk and nodded her head yes. "You can go on in. I think she's waiting for you."

"Thank you," she said. Just before she reached the threshold for Dr. Zilla's door she turned, crossed her fingers, and mouthed to Wanda "wish me luck." Wanda chuckled and returned to her work. Neveah let out a deep breath, and knocked softly on Dr. Zilla's already opened door. Dr. Zilla, who was at her desk working, did not lift her head or pause from her work to greet Neveah in the same pleasant manner that Wanda had. Instead, she briefly lifted her eyes to look over her glasses and lifted a single finger, which instructed Nevaeh to wait patiently at the door until she saw fit to allow her to enter. Nevaeh waited awkwardly, staring at her shoes and reviewing her grievances in her head: "professor of color, students of color, outdated hiring policy."

After what seemed like an eternity, Dr. Zilla lifted her head and asked, "How can I help you?"

"Hi, Dr. Zilla, I'm here for our meeting."

"There must be some mistake, I have a meeting with Dr. Jones at 4."

A mistake indeed. Dr. Jones was a professor in the department upstairs and a long time mentor of Nevaeh's. Nevaeh, whose last name was also Jones, took a deep breath, praying that the patience she would need to sustain this meeting was somewhere in the air around her. "My last name is Jones. Do you think maybe the two meetings have been confused?"

Dr. Zilla fiddled with her computer and after a moment asked, "Is your name Nevaeh?"

"Yes," she replied.

"Yes, you're right. I'm meeting with you at 4. Please, come sit down."

Nevaeh walked toward the table at the center of Dr. Zilla's office, sat down, and took out her notebook. "So, what are we meeting about today?" Dr. Zilla asked.

"Well, first I want to thank you for taking the time to meet with me. I appreciate it. I know the department has been looking for a professor of color to add to the faculty and I greatly support this decision. Last week, Dr. Bell interviewed here. I love her work. It's informed a lot of my thoughts about race and hers is a major framework I'm using to support my Master's thesis. Her presentation was wonderful, and she really seemed to gel with the students and some of the faculty." Dr. Zilla nodded, but sat silently, staring blankly. Nevaeh continued, "I know the department decided not to hire her, and as a student who is interested in her work, potentially going into academia someday, and the well-being of this department, I was hoping you could give me some insight as to how that decision was made."

"Well, unfortunately, that's a personnel decision, and we really can't discuss those issues with anyone not on the hiring committee."

Personnel, huh? Nevaeh had heard that excuse in issues of hiring before. It was White women's way of saying "I don't care to discuss this with you and I'm going to invoke my White privilege and organizational power so that I don't have to." She would have to find another way to engage Dr. Zilla in this conversation.

"That is fine. Generally speaking, is the department's hiring practice a personnel matter?"

"No, it is not."

"Ok. Can you explain the hiring process to me please?"

Dr. Zilla's lips tightened. She sat up straight, clearly trying not to seem annoyed with this meeting that she perceived to be a waste of her time. "Well, after a professor is invited for an interview, they come to campus and give a departmental presentation and meet with students and faculty. Then, a committee of their peers votes on whether or not we should make an offer for them to join us here."

"When you say *their peers*, who are you referring to?"

"Other faculty members at the same level as them. So if it's an associate professor, then other associate professors vote. If it's a full professor, other full professors vote."

It was all starting to make sense. Dr. Amber Bell was a full professor at Iowa. If she were to come to Reagan, she would be the only Black woman in the department with full professorship. This was Nevaeh's in.

"So, for Dr. Bell, that means all of the full professors in the department voted?"

"Well, yes. But I can't tell you who that is or how they voted."

"Right. I'm actually less concerned with the details. But, I do have a question. I know that the only full professors in this department are White. They're also all people who are a bit older and don't necessarily value studies that center on race. I've taken classes with some of them, and I know they haven't read her work. So if they're the ones voting on whether or not Dr. Bell should come, doesn't that perpetuate the problem the department is currently facing—the one of us not having enough faculty of color?"

"I resent this implication. Are you calling me racist? I am *nothing* of the sort. You should also know that all faculty who vote are required to read one to two pieces written by the potential faculty member before voting."

"Oh! Is there a discussion of those pieces prior to the interview?"

"No. But because we're a department that values diversity, it's also suggested that they attend some of the diversity forums on campus."

Nevaeh was a bit confused. She didn't understand what one point had to do with the other, but she figured she'd play along. "If it's suggested that means they don't have to attend, correct?"

"Correct."

"Dr. Zilla, I think that's the point I'm trying to make. It seems like there really are no initiatives to encourage the faculty members on these voting committees to consider the value in diversity of personhood or thought. I think unless the departmental voting structure changes, we're going to continue to let highly qualified faculty slip through our fingers."

"Unfortunately, Neveah, the decision has been made. Dr. Bell was just not what the department needed at this time. Besides," she said, almost smirking, "it would be unfair to hire someone based solely on the color of their skin. That would be reverse racism."

Neveah felt her heart sink. It was clear the conversation was over. There was no point in continuing a discussion with someone who was irrational and clearly hellbent on remaining ignorant. The department, led by Dr. Zilla, had no intention of hiring a faculty member of color. That would require revisiting some of its racist institutional policies and it seemed that *that* was out of the question. Neveah put on her best passive closed-lipped smile and said, "Thank you for your time, Dr. Zilla. I don't want to hold you up."

"Yes, thank you for coming in! Feel free to stop by anytime."

Neveah slipped her notebook back into her bag, stood, shook Dr. Zilla's hand and turned to exit.

As she walked down the hallway toward the bathroom, she felt her face getting hot. She fought the tears welling up in her eyes. *"Please just let me make it to the stall first,"* she thought. As soon as she entered the first empty stall, Neveah let it all out. It was a loud, sad, snot-filled cry, and she didn't care who heard. They couldn't see her. They would never see her. Not through the stall; not in this building. But if they came into the bathroom they would have to hear her. She wanted them to hear.

She thought back to the meeting she sat in that morning with Becca. She was reminded of the way Becca felt legitimized in limiting Black student enrollment in their very *public* school. She thought about Rebecca and the way she disrespected kids and adults; always knowing the least and assuming the worst. This meeting with Dr. Zilla had been the last straw. Here she was at the pinnacle of higher education, still unable to make a difference at any level. It was becoming increasingly clear to her that the words in Dr. Woodson's book were not to be taken lightly: "the highly educated Negro often grows sour. He becomes too pessimistic to be a constructive force and usually develops into a chronic fault-finder or a complainant at the bar of public opinion." It seemed like the more education she received, the more critical she became. And the more critical she became, the less people wanted to hear from her.

As her breathing returned to normal and the tears began to slow, Neveah thought about her options. She could go on with her day pretending as if nothing had happened. That's how she usually handled things. That's how the world expected her to handle them. This time didn't necessarily have to be any different. She could talk to her professors and the school board to try to make a difference both in her department and at Clinton. But if she was being honest with herself, she didn't have the time or the energy for any of that. She was barely keeping her head above water trying to manage school and work.

Then, Nevaeh had a thought: she could walk away from it all. It was clear that some things were just too deeply ingrained for her to change. Maybe she could pursue her dream of writing. She always loved to write. And there were some stories inside of her that were burning to get out. Plus, she'd always wanted to start her own nonprofit hosting writing workshops for kids. She had the experience and the skills. And leaving it all behind would provide her the time to be able to work on her projects.

Her phone buzzed in her pocket, interrupting her thoughts. 4:55. Five minutes until the start of class. She wiped her face and took a final deep breath. She splashed some water on her face and wiped it away to try to camouflage the fact that she had been crying. Trying to forget about the day for the time being, she took a quick look in the mirror and mustered up a small smile before leaving the bathroom.

Neveah took a seat in Dr. Davis's class, and was reassured by the presence of her peers—three black women, one Latina, one Asian American woman, and one White woman, all critically minded—and her professor.

Dr. Davis, an assistant professor and the only tenure track Black woman in the department, began class: "Now, normally, we launch into a discussion of the readings, but I think we should take some time to unpack the failed hiring of Dr. Bell."

At this, Alyssa, a student, got up out of her seat and closed the door. The whole class, including Neveah exchanged knowing looks and giggled, sharing in the knowledge that they were about to be honest, critical, and vulnerable in a way that they were never free to be when overwhelmed by the presence of whiteness.

Dr. Davis continued, "I know many of you are disappointed with what happened, since just last class we were speaking about her work. Believe me, I am also disappointed, since Dr. Bell is a dear friend and mentor, and I can't help but feel frustrated that I continue to recommend my friends for them to be rejected and humiliated in this manner. As a Black woman in the academy who studies issues of race, it's disheartening to me that a scholar who is nationally renowned as a leading voice in this work was turned down for a job by this department. It makes me wonder how my work and my voice are valued and whether or not this space is making a concerted effort to show they value people of color. But enough about my feelings, I want to know how you are all feeling."

Toni, a Black student, said, "It's just ludicrous. I'm sick of waiting for and working toward the day academia stops moving the bar or giving racially coded responses to marginalize our work and tell us why we're not good enough. What happened to all of the president's promises about 'commitment to diversity'?"

Sandra, a Latina student, added, "Seriously. I think we need to organize and protest. We can't be the only students of color who feel this way, and our collective voices need to be heard."

Peggy, the sole white woman, continued, "I don't mean to spotlight Neveah, but she's been doing an incredible job with the student union. And Neveah, I would defer to you to organize this, but I know you're also teaching full time, so please let me know what I can do. I don't think I should be the face of this, though, for obvious reasons."

Neveah chuckled and said, "Thank you, Peggy. I appreciate that. I agree that we should do something about it, but if I'm being honest I'm just so frustrated and disheartened at this point. Between the blatant and covert racism at my school and here, it feels like we're just barely chipping away at such a massive problem." Her voice quivered, "It's just hard to maintain the hope we need to keep going." She paused and attempted a lighthearted tone: "Dr. Davis, you've been working in education so long, got any pearls of wisdom?"

Dr. Davis smiled and responded, "I can't lie, Neveah. I *still* get frustrated and disheartened, and I'm not sure those feelings will ever go away. It's not easy to pour your heart and soul into work for the uplift of people you care about and people who look like you. But what I've found is that solidarity and community can make all the difference. Find your people. Check in with and support each other. Work together. Knowing that you're not in this alone is more powerful than you might think."

Neveah nodded in acknowledgment, and looked around the room realizing that Dr. Davis's class was the only space she had felt safe all day. She let out the long, slow breath of relief she had been waiting for. As she and the other students exchanged pointed smiles, quietly swimming in the solidarity they all knew they felt in that room, Dr. Davis allowed for a moment of silence while she watched her students process. "Alright. Is everyone ready to jump into our readings for today?"

Chapter Eleven

Racism

Becky's Dance Around the Other 'R-Word' in Student Affairs

Nolan L. Cabrera

PART I: "WE HAVE A PROBLEM WITH OUR 'DIVERSE' STUDENT POPULATIONS"

It was a familiar scene. I was among a group of middle-class, White women, each sporting a larger, flashier diamond engagement ring than the next. Then there was me: the ponytail-wearing, goatee sporting, Chicano in Dickies, a tanktop (refuse the misogynistic "wife-beater"), an over-sized White t-shirt, and a silver chain with the *Virgin de Guadalupe* hanging in the center of my chest. My inner monologue runs wild in these meetings, and I have that song from *Sesame Street* running through my head, "One of these things is not like the other. One of these things just doesn't belong." The crazy thing about it is that despite my appearance, I am more than qualified to be at the table having completed nine graduate-level statistics courses, and one of my analyses cited in a federal desegregation case. Self-aggrandizing aside, I tend to be quiet in these meetings because the celebrated in the room are regurgitating satisfaction survey results. They tend to go something like this, "95 percent of our students are happy with the offerings in the rec center."

My role in these meetings was to provide statistical quality control in hopes of creating bridges between Student Affairs research and theory (me) and practice (everyone else in the room). This was a noble goal, and three years earlier I started bright-eyed and bushy-tailed as the university continually moved toward "data-driven decision-making." However, I soon lost patience for this mantra for a number of reasons. Students of Color are the least likely to respond to these surveys, which means university policy is normed around the experiences and views of middle-class, non-first generation, White women. But Student Affairs is frequently self-congratulatory; recognize the effort people put into their assessments and honor their commitment to our students. I put up with it because it allowed me to conduct my survey of all students, which in turn, allowed me to explore issues of campus racism, sexism, and homophobia: issues that were muted in these meetings despite my gregarious protestations.

I really shut down when I discovered the ethos of self-congratulation did not hold for programming that targeted Students of Color. A few years earlier all of the retention programming was taken out of the cultural centers (e.g., *El Centro*) because the students taking the programming had lower GPAs than the rest of the campus population. What the adminstrators forgot was that these students came into the university with lower GPAs than their White peers, did not attend as academically rigorous high schools, oh yeah, and they had the added benefit of having to overcome a hostile racial campus climate. I digress . . .

Ultimately, we were waiting for Becky, the head of Student Affairs, to grace us with her presence. She stumbled in about fifteen minutes late waving to everyone saying, "Oh, sorry I'm late." She didn't mean it. It was her passive-aggressive way to signal that she was the most important person in the room.

She took a breath, exhaled deliberately, and connected her iPad to its portable keyboard. She started abruptly, "We have a problem with our 'diverse' student populations." Multiple underlings chimed in with some version of, "What do you mean?"

Becky continued, "Their persistence and graduation rates are significantly lower than the rest of the student body, and we need to do something about it. This is directive coming straight from the regents."

Feeling like a smartass, I piped up, "Point of clarification. What do you mean by our 'diverse' student populations?"

I could tell Becky was annoyed by the question because we both knew what she meant. It was an obvious reference to Students of Color, but race and racism had become what I refer to as the other 'r-word' ('retard' being the original). In Student Affairs, we tend to use euphemisms and avoid the real problems. Becky avoided my question, facilitated by another person in the meeting asking a question "So, what is causing this problem?"

"Well," Becky replied, "our diverse student populations are coming into our university with lower high school grades and standardized test scores. We need to figure out quickly how to identify these students and get them into remediation courses quickly."

"Is this the entire problem?" I prodded further, "What about issues of the campus racial climate? What about sense of belonging on campus? What about microaggressions? Wouldn't those also affect student graduation rates as well? These variables are well known and documented in the literature."

"Maybe," Becky replied, "But you and I both know that our campus climate survey showed that all students found the campus to be generally supportive and we significantly improved since the climate survey five years ago."

A bit of context is warranted here. Yes, Becky was correct that the numbers were on the rise. What she failed to mention were the following inconvenient truths:

- Approximately 80 percent of the students responding to the survey were White (compared to 60 in the undergraduate student population)
- There was no disaggregation by racial/ethnic group
- The terms 'race' and 'racism' did not appear on the climate survey
- None of my aforementioned constructs (e.g., sense of belonging) was measured
- She rejected my offer to actually do an assessment of the climate

She knew she had the upper hand on this one. She had a predetermined outcome for the climate survey she approved. She set the rules of the game. And, surprise, the climate research showed a university improving during her tenure. Unfortunately, the folks in the room did not have background on the issue or statistics to understand how the game was fixed. I thought about breakin' it down, but it would have been like trying to explain the pitfalls of three-card monte to the dude who is convinced he has a fool-proof system and can't lose. Most of the folks were at the table simply because they were 'yes' people.

On cue, another one of the Student Affairs folk in the room piped up, "We've had incredible success with our Academic Ambassadors program. A few weeks ago, I presented on how their graduation rates are actually higher than the rest of the students on campus."

Becky was nodding, "I love it. Let's keep going."

What Becky failed to realize was that the Academic Ambassadors program targeted higher performing (largely White, middle-class) students on campus, and their impact was largely a function of selection bias. Damn my stat nerdiness—but I have not found a way to effectively communicate these critiques to this group. I tried for a year, and now kept getting annoyed at the phrase "diverse students." Regardless, dear reader, I will not bore you with the rest of the details of this meeting. You get the general idea, and honestly, I cannot remember how the rest of it went. After a dozen bad ideas floated, I just started drawing snarky comments and cartoons on my yellow pad, while making sure to draw from the top of the page down and left-to-right so it would look like I was taking notes. I guess I cannot get too mad at my students for doing the same thing in class.

The meeting came to an end, and I exited the building quickly not wanting to get trapped in small talk. I opened a door and the Tucson sun hit my face like the light above the dentist chair. A wave of heat engulfed my body and I immediately started sweating. Ah, the feeling of being free from another assessment meeting!

PART II: BACK WITH MY PEOPLE

Given the pressures to assess, I joined a meeting of the six campus cultural center directors. This meeting stood in stark contrast to my usual Student Affairs work. Amy, the head of LGBTQ Affairs, wore a rainbow flag on her lapel, and all the colors of the rainbow were present at this meeting. Actually, two of the other center directors were also sportin' the pins even though they were straight. Instead of eight different shades of beige in my Student Affairs assessment meetings, one of us was sporting handmade turquoise jewelry from a local Native tribe; another dawned a simple blouse with intricate, hand-woven animals along the neckline (each had a significance which I cannot currently recall); and one sported a t-shirt that simply read, "The Gender Binary Sucks." It should go without saying, I fit in so much better with this crew. Unfortunately, this was the extent of diversity within Student Affairs. Despite all of our differences, there was a fundamental understanding that our students were not full-fledged members of the campus. For example, when they (Students of Color and LGBTQ students) hosted campus scavenger hunts at night, we had to remind them to warn the police ahead of time because they would otherwise be seen as threats. I mean, let's be real. My campus had a long history of police stopping Professors of Color, let alone Students of Color. I found it interesting that my race-conscious inner monologue was generally silent during these meetings. Maybe that was because we could talk freely and openly about these pressing issues that faced our minoritized students.

Cindy opened the meeting, "We have a problem."

"What's going on?" asked Maria.

"Becky has a new edict. Going into the new academic year, the cultural centers need to be more inclusive," Cindy replied.

Charles piped up, "What does that mean?"

"I think you know," said Cindy with more than a hint of sarcasm in her voice.

"All right, is this more of that bullshit—pardon my language—that Millennials are post-racial?" Charles continued.

"Yes, but it's more complicated than that," Cindy said in a tone that foreshadowed the knowledge she was going to drop in the next sentence. As the matriarch of the cultural centers, she enjoyed being the wise sage of the group. "You're right that Becky doesn't believe in what we do. That's part of why she always refers to us as serving our 'diverse student populations' and will never, I mean *never,* say racism. That is her 'r-word' and woe to he who dares to use it in her presence. I digress. The other issue is that she is feeling pressure from the regents."

"Why is that?" I decided to chime in.

"Because," Cindy continued, "You remember her bright idea to combine all of the cultural centers into one 'unity center'?"

This story was all-too-familiar to me. A couple years back, Becky unilaterally decided to consolidate all of the cultural centers into one "unity center." We all knew it was a bad idea, but Becky thought she always knew best for us—nothing like a little patronizing Whiteness to wake you up in the morning! She tried to enact her plan during the summer time, which is pretty standard practice if an administrator wants the least pushback possible. She claimed she knew the community well, and she seemed stunned when her plan failed miserably. She should have known that she overestimated her cultural competency. After several angry Op-Eds by alumni, social protests, and a town hall that turned into a public shaming, Becky withdrew her plan. At the townhall, Becky requested that campus police be present including a number of plain clothes officers spread throughout the crowd. She thought the community would not realize what was going on, and she wonders why we have difficulty trusting her . . . I digress.

Cindy continued, "While the protests and angry letters saved the cultural centers, they also put a giant spotlight on what we do. Some of the regents are not happy and they say stupid shit like, 'Where is the White cultural center?' Or, 'Why are my tax dollars going to an organization that promotes racial segregation?'"

"So, what does this mean for us?" asked Jenny who had been quiet up to this point.

Cindy replied, "It's just like I said. Becky's new edict is that we are more 'inclusive' of the entire campus. It is a giant PR stunt that she hopes will get the regents off her back, and it gives her the ability to reassert her power over us. It's not like she's asking the housed frats to be more racially inclusive even though that's the most segregated spot on campus."

"I'm sorry, but even that tone pisses me off," I offered. "This means that we are currently being exclusive right now!"

"Exactly," said Cindy. "In an ironic twist of fate, Becky told me the other day that she actually blames us for the political pressure we're under right now. She said something like, 'If you people had just let unity center go through, we wouldn't be in this mess right now.'"

"Shut up," interjected Jenny. "C'mon, she did not really say 'you people' did she?"

"Bet your ass she did. The sad part is, she does not even understand what is wrong with that. I personally think she truly believes in this post-racial B.S. Easy to take that position as a nice White lady." Cindy's sarcasm was seething. "That was just a heads up. Now we need to get to our other matter—assessment."

This was my time to chime in, "All right folks, as you know, I'm in charge of the longitudinal surveys that go out to all students on campus. Well, I don't know if you have had a chance to look over the survey, but hidden among the usual constructs of student engagement are constructs of racism, sexism, and homophobia."

I continued to describe what the survey offered and how we could use it as climate assessment for our students, and Jenny offered some words of validation, "Finally, we can get to the heart of the matter. Here is our opportunity to really start assessing something larger than GPA."

Cindy was cautiously optimistic, "This is great, but I have a bit of a problem. I don't have the statistical background to run the analyses you're proposing."

I responded, "Don't worry about it. That is my job. All we need to do is keep a dialogue going about your respective centers' assessment needs. This should allow you to do your job as practitioners."

Charles also chimed in, "I always get concerned about assessments. They seem to be used against us."

"You are correct," I said. "We all remember what happened with the retention programming." The group let out a collective groan. A couple years back, retention programs were housed in the campus-based cultural centers, and the student participants showed marked improvement in grades and retention. However, they did not reach parity with their White and affluent peers, so these efforts were deemed "a failure" and moved out of the cultural centers. It was just another in a long line of examples where Becky misused data to justify a power grab, continually expanding her empire.

I continued, "These edicts of demonstrated effectiveness are going to be here for the foreseeable future. They are not fair. They are not equally mandated. The housed Greeks do not have to continually prove their worth to the campus, and we know how they impact college life: increased levels of binge drinking, eating disorders, sexual assault, hazing, and code of conduct violations. However, their alumni base is so strong that for now, they are untouchable. It's a racist double standard and we can choose to do one of two things. We can avoid assessment altogether and get shut down. Or, we can conduct assessment on our terms—kind of like a stats version of FUBU ("For Us, By

Us")—exposing some of the dirty secrets of the campus like our students of color, female students, and LGBTQ students, are the regular targets of harassment on campus. The choice is yours."

Charles responded, "I get it. Let's do it."

We all stood up, hugged each other goodbye, and returned to our respective sides of campus.

PART III: DIVERSITY BECOMES TOO EXTREME/NARROW AND BECKY DROPS THE AXE

Fast forward six months, and I was feelin' pretty good about my meeting with the cultural center directors. We formulated a plan, developed our own surveys, convinced other Student Affairs units that the constructs were relevant to their practice, and from that, gained momentum to the point that the larger Student Affairs administrative unit endorsed the survey and helped get students to participate. These endless strings of '1s' and '0s' were available to support the development of programming—programming for the worst served in the university. I also felt I had gotten over on Becky a little. The survey itself had a ton of "traditional" measures about student engagement and development, but there were also a number of constructs related to race hidden throughout. Rather, I naïvely thought they were hidden until Becky called me into her office. There was no explanation offered for the meeting being called, and I regressed twenty years—feeling like a grade school student getting sent to the principal's office. I actually caught myself drooping my head as I walked to the meeting, and my inner monologue took on the voice of the drill sergeant from *Full Metal Jacket*, "Straighten up! If you don't carry yourself with respect, no one's gonna respect you. Now go in there and if you ain't got confidence, fake it."

I approached Becky's administrative assistant to let her know that I was here for the 10:00AM meeting to which she responded, "Becky is still in her other meeting. If you want to take a seat, you can over there."

I knew this was going to happen. In three years of meeting with Becky, I have yet to see her on time. That said, I cannot show up late because I know that will be the one time she actually makes it on time and of course would police my tardiness. This coupled with the lack of an agenda are all the ways she demonstrates her power. I have to keep reminding myself that this is part of her game—being vague, keeping those under her guessing and never sure, changing the protocol for her convenience. The good news for me is that my hand is steady, and my face is stoic without being hardened.

Becky finally pokes her head out of her office, "Hi! C'mon in!"

I stand, keep a cool appearance, and keep telling myself to think before speaking. Situations such as these are kind of like being read your Miranda Rights, "Anything you say can, and will, be used against you."

Becky cuts right to the chase, "Let me blunt. I am not happy with your survey."

"Ok, what about it do you not like?" I asked.

"I think it is too narrowly focused on our diverse populations," Becky replied. "This is supposed to be a survey for the whole university, and some of the items seem a little biased. A little extreme."

"All right, maybe you could show me what you are talking about," I tried to probe.

"I really don't have time to get into that right now. I know you study diversity, and of course that is really important, but I am not sure that this survey is the best use of our energies right now."

"I run this ship by myself," I said. "The only person's energy it takes is mine."

"Well," said Becky, "Kind of. As you know, the students are surveyed to death through Student Affairs."

"I am aware."

"Well, it's time to start cutting out some of the noise so that our students can focus on those that will provide the most bang for the buck," Becky continued.

I began to have a knot in my stomach. I initially thought I was being called into Becky's office to be chastised. Now it seemed like there was more to this meeting, and I was getting increasingly nervous. While messing with my survey could hurt me as a junior scholar, the truly insidious impact is that it would cut off data for the cultural centers—some of the only places I actually care about in Student Affairs. I tried to pick my next words carefully, "Ok, how about this: Let me take a closer look at the survey, and I see what I can cut and reword."

"I'm afraid that won't work," Becky replied. "The amount you focus on diversity on the survey is simply too much for it to have appeal to the general student population. I mean look at this item here," she gestured to a print out of my survey. "'How often do you think about race?' These students are Millennials. They are post-racial. We need to move beyond this stuff."

"While I disagree with your assessment, diversity-related questions are less than five percent of the survey, what do you propose?" I asked.

"This survey needs to be shut down," Becky replied. "It's insufficiently broad and takes too much attention from the real assessments we need to conduct."

I didn't say anything, and there was an uncomfortable silence Uma Thurman's character talked about in *Pulp Fiction*. "Insufficiently broad" was that same euphemistic language like "being more inclusive." It meant that the survey did not primarily focus on the experiences of middle-class White students. The irony is that it actually did with ninety-five percent of the constructs addressing issues of general student engagement. This, however, was not enough for Becky. I waited for what seemed to be hours, but it was more like 45 seconds. Finally, Becky broke in, "Well, don't you have any response?"

"I have to say I'm disappointed. I never even had a chance to modify the approach."

"I know this must be hard for you," Becky continued. "But we simply don't have time to make changes, and even then, I'm not sure that you would be able to modify the survey enough for it to be broadly applicable. I had to make a choice under a time crunch, and this is what I had to do in the best interests of the university. You'll understand this better in the future when you have greater administrative responsibilities."

My inner-monologue snapped, "Mother fucker patronizing asshole! I've forgotten more about assessment than you will ever know, and you have the nerve to lecture me and pull the age/experience card in the process?!?!?!" While this went on in my head, I stayed externally calm—formulating a simple question that I was finally able to get out when my brain shut up, "So, is there anything else you needed to talk about?"

"Nope, that was it," Becky said. "I know this is difficult, but I really appreciate your understanding."

All right, that about set me over the edge. I can tolerate people talkin' shit because at least you know where they're coming from. What I can't stand is this Student Affairs-talk that is perpetually affirming, positive, and always using 'I statements' while still undermining marginalized people. What Becky never understood was that she never valued cultural differences. Perpetually using the hackneyed expression, "Diversity is a core value of our institution and we value our diverse student populations," does not actually demonstrate a commitment to them. Coming from a Student Affairs background, or hell as a person who passed kindergarten, she should understand the concept that actions speak louder than words. Focusing on her actions, Becky tried to shut down the only programming for Students of Color on campus. When that failed, she put forth the edict that they needed to be more inclusive of the campus (White) community. She then used assessment punitively against the community centers (i.e., demonstrate an impact or get eliminated), and then cut off their best source of data to demonstrate an impact. But she still, "values the diverse populations."

I stood up to leave, and Becky put her hand on my shoulder, and my inner monologue started screaming in my head, "Becky, I can't tell if you're trying to comfort me or remind me you won this round, but *Goddammit don't touch me!!*"

On my way out, Becky smirked, "Have a nice day."

I mumbled some response, and I headed for the elevator. I kept my composure, and the 300-yard walk to my office seemed to take an hour. My mind was racing, trying to figure out how I could have handled the situation differently to achieve a different outcome. By the time I arrived at my office I came to no conclusions, but I felt like I let down my community. Filling with rage, I slammed the door behind me and didn't realize I was shouting until "MOTHER FUCKERRRRRRRR!!!!!!!!!!!!!!!" echoed off my office walls. I then hoped in vain that the walls were sound proof.

For some reason, I had that stupid song running through my head, "I fought the law and the law won." In this instance it was more like, "I fought Whiteness and Whiteness won." Not only was actual engagement with racism too much for Becky to handle, evidently, even 'diversity' was too extreme as well. Down but not out, I picked up the antiquated technology that is my office landline and called Cindy. It cut to voicemail, and I said, "Hey Cindy. So, our data supply is cut off . . . The survey is dead . . . Becky dropped the axe five minutes ago . . . Forget this noise! We don't need her approval to do this work. Let's create a *real* assessment about how our students experience race and racism—not having to dance around Becky's 'r-word.' Give me a call. Peace."

Section Five

Guiding Questions

1. In "Waiting to Exhale" Neveah experiences different Becky(s) throughout her day who proclaim themselves as experts or abuse their power as authority. In what ways does this occur? How might this impact how Neveah interacts with them? How does it impact the trust between people?
2. In the same story, if these Becky(s) were not consumed with exerting their power how might they have responded more humanely? How would engaging with Neveah (and possibly her students) be more racially just?
3. In "Racism: Becky's Dance Around the Other 'R-Word' in Student Affairs" how does the Becky(s) in this story still express whiteness? How does she mask it behind rhetoric of diversity? How does this play out in your environment?
4. Have there been times when a white woman attempts to do what is right for equity and diversity but falls short? Why does she fall short and what happens if she is told about her shortcomings? Does she assert power or concede to learning? How is her response telling with respects to a Becky?
5. If you are a white woman in roles that support diversity, how can you learn from others, particularly women of color, and still be self critical about yourself to ensure whiteness never overpowers the work?

Becky(s) as Allies? Victims?

From safety pins that self-identify white women as "allies" to more complex, even questionable, practices of "allyship" from white women like Rachel Dolezal, who proclaims herself to be antiracist by posing as a Black woman, the curiosities of what constitutes an ally, who has the right to deem a person an ally, and what is considered a healthy relationship for allies to have with people of color must be considered. No doubt there are white women who are truly committed to the cause of dismantling white supremacy for a more racially humane society. However, more often than not this understanding of dismantling is still framed through the ocular of whiteness qua white saviority or missionary work. Consequently, the acts meant to serve people of color reify whiteness while coddling the fragile identities of white women. Therefore Becky(s) as Allies? are not truly allies.

Take for example the field of teaching where most U.S. teachers are white women teaching the majority of the nation's students of color. Applying racial psychoanalytics helps us better understand why white women, many of whom have never had any substantial relationships or interactions with urban people of color, would feel compelled to "give back" or "save" urban schools. For why would one feel so compelled to give back when they have never interacted with that group of people before? In fact, as mentioned in a previous section, most white teachers are aware that they grew up in stark contrast to their students of color, having lived in white, middle-class communities complete with privilege, access, and opportunities. Safe to say, they are aware of the racial disparities that students of color within urban schools face. But more interestingly, in their compulsion to give back, they own up to how the plight of people of color is connected to their sense of guilt and morality. Meaning, they are in some ways, whether consciously or subconsciously, aware of how wealth is racially distributed and thus, feel guilty for this unequal distribution. This guilt then propels them to give back as a way to assuage their sense of morality. It is as if they feel guilty for having opportunities, access, and privilege that are not afforded to students in urban schools and thus to feel better—for themselves—they opt to heal their own conscience by teaching in urban schools. Therefore, their efforts to give back are less about giving to urban schools and more so a mechanism to appease their culpability for reaping the benefits of racial discrimination. Essentially, they are trying to heal their own state of melancholy.

Cheng (2001) discusses white racial melancholia, claiming, "melancholia offers a powerful critical tool precisely because it theoretically *accounts* for the guilt and the denial of guilt, the blending of shame and omnipotence in the racist imaginary" (emphasis included, p. 12). Knowing that white privilege and whiteness are ridden with complexities surrounding guilt, there is no better tool to help us understand why white women—often depicted as the beholder of society's moral conscience—feel compelled to teach in urban schools. White women have been depicted as the moral leaders of the world. Statues of Lady Justice, for instance, depict her as blindfolded, holding the scales of justice as if her voice objectively weighs in the moral judgment of society.

But melancholia, morality, and guilt are deep-rooted sentiments that have deep roots and are complicitous. Cheng (2001) warns us of this by stating "in focusing on a structure of crisis on part of the victim, misses the violators' own dynamics process at state in such denigration" (p. 12). As such, though absolutely important, to focus too narrowly on how race, racism, or racial microaggressions oppress people of color, society then overlooks the violator's own complicity in the process of that denigration. Or, more poignantly, to focus too narrowly on the racial achievement gap, overrepresentation of Black and Brown students in special education and suspension, the underrepresentation of Black and Brown students in gifted and talented education, the harsh punitive measures applied to Black and Brown students—the list goes on—detracts from an analysis of the role white teachers and administrators play in this manifestation. To be clear, by no means do I advocate that these issues are unworthy of study. No. They are not only worthy of study; they must be studied to understand the impacts of white supremacy in education. What I am saying is that to focus too narrowly on the symptoms of white supremacy is to often overlook the complicity, operations, and culpability of those who maintain white supremacy. Meaning, what is the role of the perpetrator?

In this case, what is the role of white women who claim to be giving back to urban schools of color when in the end her own issues of privilege—one she bequeathed at the expense of urban communities of color—is precisely the reason as to why she feels morally obligated in the first place? Is then her teaching truly for the betterment of the community or is it for her to feel less melancholia over the guilt she feels about race? And it is within this complex state of relations and emotions where white women feel compelled to call themselves allies. Hence, the title "Allies?"

The notion of allyship is made even more complex with white women's historical depiction as victims always in need of protection. Anti-miscegenation laws were created part and parcel to protect the "purity" of white women especially with respects to how men of color have been racially stereotyped as sexual predators. Racial covenants and redlining were racially discriminatory practices used to preserve white families and to further protect white women and children from the racially stereotyped "perversities" of people of color. Within white supremacist ideologies, white women were portrayed "as chaste, pure, asexual, good mothers, exemplars of femininity" (Daniels, 1997, p. 56). And in portraying them as innocent bystanders, victims even, of the issues of race, society overlooks the fact that "white women are more than complicit in the white supremacist movement" (p. 57). Therefore, claiming victimhood has always been and still is a strategic maneuver used in gendered whiteness to relinquish a white women's culpability of her own wrongdoing.

Furthermore, using victim status becomes a manipulative ploy to enact more harm onto people of color. Take for example the many cases brought up earlier in this book about how pretending to be a victim led to the untimely death of Emmett Till and wrongful incarceration of the Central Park Five. The employment of victimhood from a white woman is a powerful one because as they engage in racial transgressions, even racial violence, they need only to say they are fearful of a person of color, which is justification enough for a swift and, at times, deadly retaliation. Though not all cries of false victimhood end up in deadly retaliation, they nonetheless end up harming a person of color.

Take for example, a white woman who feels wronged despite the fact that she was the one who initially engaged in an aggressive attack on a woman of color. Such an attack then warranted the disapproval made by the woman of color, who later decided to sever the relationship in order to self-protect herself from this white woman. Though this white woman may claim she is an ally and maybe even apologize to the woman of color, she may still publicly lament over the severed relationships as a strategic attempt to gain the sympathy from others. And in doing so, this white woman is able to impart negativity onto the woman of color, even though this Becky was the attacker. As such, is this woman truly a victim? Alas, no. Clearly, Becky(s) as Victims? are white women who engage in racially microaggressive behaviors onto people of color but then turn around and strategically employ victimhood to switch the balance of power from her wrongdoing to focusing on maiming, defaming, or discrediting the real victim: the person of color.

The stories in this section question whether Becky(s) are truly allies or the victims they claim to be. In fact, white women interrogating their own complicity to whiteness as self-presumed allies wrote two of the three stories. One story's authors write, "As self-identified 'liberally progressive' White women, it was [a] challenge to acknowledge and confront our contributions to and continued participation with white supremacy." Another author writes,

"I wanted to spend time thinking more deeply about my own 'Becky'ness as a white woman." Both responses clearly convey that to be a true ally, white women must deeply reflect on their complicity to whiteness at all times. Conversely, Becky(s) as Allies? Victims? are white women who refuse to deeply reflect on that complicity and instead focus on publicly labeling herself as an ally without doing the work of an ally.

As a brown-skinned Pinay and editor of this book, I had to offer feedback to ensure that the authenticity of how people of color survive the behaviors of Becky(s) remained true to that honor. For example, in writing the story, the authors of one story discussed how my feedback pushed them to understand some of the nuances of whiteness they may have overlooked. They write, "Her comments served as [a] mirror that helped us to gain a deeper (yet incomplete) understanding of Whiteness." For another story, the author reflects on her process of writing the chapter. She writes, "It was actually an incredibly important experience for me to further my understandings of how I affect others and others affect me. Parts of this were written to think through and understand some personally challenging experiences." In fact, this author wants to make sure that her story allows other Becky(s) to more deeply reflect on their own behaviors when she writes, "I would like all white women to own that we are all inescapably 'Becky's.' And by owning that, we can do a better job of recognizing it and fixing the issue we cause. All we can strive for is doing better and better. We will never be perfect." The other authors echo this sentiment. When asked about their goal or purpose of writing the story, these two authors state, "The opportunity to continue to unpack that way that we are, as White women, privileged by the current racial hierarchy."

Written as a metaphor, the final story was written by a woman of color who draws from Filipino *kuwentos* (or stories) and folklore to demonstrate how communities of color warn children of color of the lies behind the seemingly innocent smiles of the white lady. That is, to not be lured in by false niceties when history and reality have proven differently. In the end, the nice white lady is not the white lady preoccupied with self-aggrandizing herself as an ally. Instead, it is the woman who is willing to deeply reflect, apologize, and atone for her incessant complicity to whiteness. Until that happens, these Becky(s) are no allies to us.

REFERENCES

Cheng, A. (2001). *The Melancholy of Race: Psychoanalysis, Assimilation, and Hidden Grief*. New York: Oxford University Press.

Daniels, J. (1997). *White Lies: Race, Class, Gender and Sexuality in White Supremacist Discourse*. New York: Routledge.

Chapter Twelve

The Guilt of a Becky

Kara Mitchell Viesca

OBLIVIOUS BECKY, THAT'S ME

Dear Diary,

Today I presented research at a faculty meeting regarding the perceptions of our students toward race. Our students are teacher candidates in an urban focused teacher education program. I stood at the front of the room present-ing with my doctoral student and the results of our study proved that there are issues of race within the program itself. This finding caused great concern to some colleagues. Many were uncomfortable. One colleague was so angered that he questioned our findings, but then did something so ridiculous. He turned the conversation directly to Carol, the only tenure line faculty of color in the core teacher education program, and eventually stood up, shook his fist and yelled at her saying, "I do not feel collaborated with!" I couldn't believe my eyes. Then a White woman directly in front of me turns around to the back of the room to also face Carol. Then she starts screaming at Carol that it is not about race and that people are dying for being gay. This was all so intense. I am the White woman in the front of the room presenting findings from a study on race but my Colleague of Color got attacked. I guess this shouldn't surprise me. I have studied critical race theory for years now. I used it in my dissertation. My entire job talk when I came to be considered for this position was grounded in critical race theory. I know a lot about how race operates in our society and how it is central. I felt I got hired at this institution for that expertise.

But here I am. Almost a year and a half into my job and two huge things are clear to me today. First, I do not have colleagues or leaders who have done the work to understand race and race issues in our own spaces and engagements with one another. Second, FUCK, I'm one of them. How is it that I was hired into the same position at the same time with another woman, a Colleague of Color, and only noticed how she is being treated today? Her text is haunting me, "This has been happening since we got here." Damn! How can I be so oblivious?! And worse, have I been part of the problem? In what ways have I been participating in her marginalization and silencing?

It's devastating to realize, but *I am a Becky too.*

Intellectually, I know this. I know that White people are racialized and culturized to engage in the world in ways that uphold white supremacy. So, as a White person and woman, me-doing-me can often be me-doing-oppression. I know that. But why didn't I *know* it? Why did it take me a year and a half to see it within my new role as a professor? Honestly, there have been so many signs. Only two months into our jobs, I had a fellow White colleague come into my office and say that she didn't think Carol would make it. I was so puzzled how anyone could know or say that since it was the very beginning of our first semester at this university. I mean, we came in together after all. Is this how all the faculty thought of her? Let's be real. Carol is the only fulltime tenure-lined Faculty of Color in the program. We have subsidiary programs like literacy, special education, and science education who have some Faculty of Color but for the general teacher education program, Carol is it. DAMN! I've watched as courses are given to a male doctoral Student of Color over Carol, a tenure-track female professor with a PhD! I've noticed people responding to Carol's social interactions with eye rolls and sighs. Why didn't I realize the racialized nature of these assessments of the girl from L.A. in a professor gig in the Mountain West?

UNEXPECTED BECKY

●●●●○ Sprint LTE   **9:23 AM**   23% 🔋

❮ Messages   **Carol**   Details

> I feel like my efforts to combat whiteness in our program have just made things worse, especially for you.

> But it matters to me that you tried.

Dear Diary,

It's been weeks since I last wrote and a lot has happened at work. I notified our administration (all women) that I felt there were issues of race at play in that meeting with how Carol was treated. Instead of focusing on the harassment and hostile workplace that Carol was subjected to, it became a damnation of how dare I call my White male colleague "a racist." And, he's the one who stood and yelled at Carol in front of everyone. Trying to be an ally and support Carol, I was present in multiple phone calls and emails so that administration would understand what was happening. But they never listened. Instead they painted Carol as the problem.

Then, our dean forced us in a sequestered meeting. She denied Carol's mentor or members of the diversity committee attendance. I cried. A lot. It was awful. Several faculty and staff members gathered outside the door in support of Carol and I. There was no attempt to reconcile for how Carol was treated, let alone how we preach social justice but engage in racially oppressive ways in our own program. That was completely absent. What was present was empathy and solace for the White man who felt accused of being called racist. He pointed at Carol and accused her of calling him racist, something she NEVER did. I couldn't wallow in my own pain and horror anymore. I knew I had to say something. So I screamed, "She never called you that. I DID!" But he paid no attention to me. The dean quickly stepped in and made Carol and I say what we appreciate about this White male lecturer.

I left the meeting crying. I sobbed on the shoulders of my colleagues who stood vigilant outside the meeting in support of Carol and I. I tried. I was the whistleblower trying to stand up for a Colleague of Color but in the end, she felt the brunt of it. Turns out surviving Becky, even as a Becky myself, with all my flaws, white privilege and whiteness, is pretty tough. And here I am writing all about my pain and struggle when I wonder what it must be like for her?

STILL BECKY-ING

Dear Diary,

"No one was ever hated into loving." Wow. Years into my friendship with Carol, she still wows me with her grace, knowledge, forgiveness, and fortitude. She always finds ways to push me, to help me see things I need to see and does it in the most humane and loving ways possible. I feel so seen and accepted by her—even though I have forsaken her multiple times with my own Beckiness. This reminder from her is helping me move forward in some challenging contexts, but what about how I've treated her? Admittedly, there was a time during a faculty meeting where the director of the teacher education program urged all faculty members to sit at a table and talk to partnering principals, student teaching supervisors, and master teachers about their research in the upcoming all-teacher-education-stakeholders meeting with university faculty. All the faculty in this program are White and we were excited about the opportunity to share our research. It even appeared to be a welcomed opportunity for the Black male doctoral student that had been hired as an adjunct. Carol raised her hand and expressed her concern, almost fear, of doing that task. At this the same White male lecturer who screamed at her earlier, rolled his eyes and threw his hands in the air, "There you go again," he muttered. Sadly, I stupidly added to this microaggression by saying, "I don't know what you're afraid about. I research race too." When I said this the rest of the White faculty took this as a legitimizing statement to dismiss Carol's fears. Damn. What was I thinking? This event went horribly for Carol. Her expressed fears were legitimate and should have been attended to. Carol sat at a table for over an hour and watched how the White principals, master teachers, and student teaching supervisors refused to go to her table. She sat patiently and professionally, didn't say a word. But I can't imagine how she felt. I allowed them to dismiss her. *I* dismissed her. Damnit! How can I do all that to her? And look she's still here teaching me a thing or two about love. Her forgiveness is unparalleled.

OOPS! I BECKY AGAIN . . .

Dear Diary,

It happened again. FUCK. FUCK. FUCK. Why do I keep acting like a Becky? I sincerely don't want to. But I just keep on Becky-ing on. UGH.

I ran into Carol the other day. I've noticed she keeps to herself much more now. Recently a new "rule" was instituted in our meetings—that we couldn't have our laptops open in the meeting. This rule appears to have come from a White faculty member calling out Carol during a meeting when she had it open and was typing, asking with obvious annoyance, "What are you writing about?" Now we have a no open laptop policy that many White faculty (including me) break. But Carol never does. They police her so much—I can understand why she rarely smiles anymore.

Anyhow, I saw her in the hallway and we got into small talk. It was awkward especially since my last hiccup about the table talks. I wanted to encourage her. I want to do better. I want to be an ally to her. I offered her sincere and honest compliments about the national attention and accolades she was receiving (let's face it, she's a total kick-ass scholar) and suggested that she should go up for tenure early like me. I thought I was supporting her. I thought I was encouraging her. What I didn't realize was how she had already been treated around that topic. In fact, she seemed surprised that I was going up for tenure early. "Did the dean approve this?" she asked. I nonchalantly told her yes and relayed the fact that the dean even encouraged another White female professor to go up early with me. I thought by telling her this I was encouraging her. I could see Carol struggle to smile and say something polite like, "Good for you." I was so surprised by her response. Why wasn't she agreeing with me that she should go up early with me? Her publication record is stellar, she just won a prestigious national award, she is invited all over the country to give guest lectures . . . she's seriously a rock-star. Doesn't she see it? So, I kept telling her that she should go up early for tenure because the pay is better for her and her kids and it would be the best thing for her family. She again struggled to smile but managed anyway and walked away. I didn't get it. I wasn't sure why she wasn't excited about the idea of going up early with me. I left wondering to myself what had gone wrong with that conversation—clearly something had. But what?

I found out later that the dean had already proactively discouraged her in going up early for tenure, suggesting it would not look good if two junior professors both went up early. But two junior professors were already going up early, something she was supporting. So that's obviously just an excuse. Really the dean was saying she would not support *Carol* going up early. UGH. How do I keep putting my foot in my mouth? I'm always trying to compare our positions and roles in this university but she definitely experiences something far worse than I. Something I struggle to even see or recognize or know when I'm contributing to it. When will I just realize that because she isn't White, she is not protected in this white supremacist academy. Ugh. I Beckied again.

WHEN A BECKY GETS BECKIED

Dear Diary,

It happened. As much as I have been working on noticing my own Becky-ing, now I've noticed/experienced something new: being Beckied myself! And it fucking sucks. Like OUCH. Like, my life has literally been turned upside down by this, especially realizing how incredibly painful it is to be treated with such little care by someone you thought cared about you. And to see the ways that whiteness and Becky-dom perform so perfectly to marginalize, police, and silence . . . ME. This is new and hard and painful. Obviously it is not the same as when white privilege and whiteness is used to silence, marginalize and police People of Color. I know that even in this context where white cultural practices that sustain whiteness are being used against me, I still maintain a great deal of privilege and opportunity. And still. OUCH! It's awful!! Thank God for Carol. She really stepped up to help me process this. And see a way forward. She let me cry. She showed me so much love and empathy. I truly don't even feel like I've done enough to deserve this kind of care from her. But there she is, as she says, loving me into a better anti-racist accomplice (hopefully).

The situation is complex and I'm not in the mood to write all of the details about it. But basically, I engaged in a space where I needed to be heard. Something shitty had happened and represented a larger issue that I needed addressed. I shared some important information with a person I thought cared about me and valued me. However, what I got back from sharing that important information was judgement, policing, and silencing. While I won't say that this is the first time a Becky has Beckied me, it is the first time its happened since I've been working so hard to Becky less often and sincerely live and work in the world as an anti-racist accomplice. So, I see and feel it all very differently now: The maneuvers that were used to silence my hurt in order to amplify hers; The ways the issues I needed addressing were dismissed as the attention became focused on the hurt I had caused for just bringing them up; The predictability of it all, for Carol; But the surprise of it all, for me.

This is how it works. This is how we Becky. We perform typical white cultural practices that work to absolve us from recognizing or taking responsibility for something shitty we've done. Then, if someone dares to point out the shitty after, we respond with judgement, policing, and silencing. With this response pattern, we get to neither address nor fix the shitty issues we have caused. We also get to keep the attention and focus on us because it all becomes about our hurt and our needs, which in combination silences the person to whom the shitty was done (usually a Person of Color) and leaves the shitty that was done to them neither addressed nor resolved. And this happens ALL THE TIME. I'm starting to see it even more now that I've been through it. Carol and I talked about how this happens so much to People of Color that they all have to develop strong coping mechanisms to manage. One mechanism that she helped me recognize is the ability to see, much more quickly, when you are in a space where you can be heard and when you are in a space where you will not be. For some People of Color, this recognition means not even speaking up to begin with. Carol helped me see, that such a proactively silencing space can even be filled with people who voted for Hillary Clinton and think Trump is a complete racist. This is whiteness. This is how we Becky. We live in the world in ways that operate to silence, even when we think we are working from pure intentions and thus can't be contributing to racism. Ugh. This is a hard lesson to learn. But since I've learned it, I need to be sure to really do differently now that I know better.

NEVER TRUST A BECKY

●●●○○ Sprint LTE   7:57 PM   43% ▭

< Messages   **Carol**   Details

> I think I'm starting to understand something, but it makes me so sad and so…I don't know. Sincerely, I'm wondering, can you trust anyone?

I absolutely can. But the people I trust have earned it. And can lose it if they don't keep showing me that I can trust them. My circle of trust is not large, but it exists and is precious. But let's be honest. None of us are perfect. We're all human. Everyone makes mistakes. Part of my trust rests in those who seek to fix their mistakes.

🖸 Text Message   Send

Dear Diary,

I've been thinking a lot about trust lately as I've really started to see that there are people, especially in my professional life that I just can't trust. And as I think about it, I've been reflecting on all of the ways I've potentially been that person to other people, especially to Carol. It's funny to me to look back and think about our relationship from the perspective of trust. I actually think our first meeting is pretty illustrative. I was so excited to meet Carol. I had seen her CV and knew that she was graduating from a top PhD program where she had worked with scholars I cite regularly. Her mentors were some of my idols in critical race theory. I just knew we were going to be best friends.

But then we met. It was at a reception at our major annual conference that was being hosted by the school of education that had just hired us both. The dean who hired us introduced us to one another and I eagerly grabbed Carol and gave her a huge hug and told her, "You're my new best friend!" Appallingly, she didn't really hug me back. She also didn't respond to my statement. Where was her, "I know, right?" Honestly, as I look back at it all, I just have to laugh. God. I'm such a fucking Becky! My expectations of sorority-girl BFF bliss based on being hired into the same position at the same time with a Scholar of Color who also does critical race work was, well, *so Becky*!

Anyway, I realize now that Carol had no reason to trust or believe I would be someone she could work well with nor have any sort of relationship with. I also proved her right to keep her distance, particularly over the first year and a half of us working together and her getting shit on without me *even seeing* it. Once I did start to see it, I still managed to add to it. Even when I was very much trying not to.

So that's where I wonder. Can a Becky, even one like me who is sincerely trying to be an ally, an anti-racist accomplice, be trusted? At times I do feel that Carol really trusts me. For sure she does in ways that I know she can't trust other people we work with. But let's be honest. That's a pretty low bar. I want to be someone she can really trust. Like trust, trust. But truthfully because I'm so good at Beckying, I'm not sure I would even trust myself if I were Carol. Now that I write that, I realize I don't trust myself. It's not like I'm addicted to Beckying, it's more like I just don't know how to do different. Until I've done. Hmmmm. I think that is what Carol was alluding to. The Becky who fixes her mistakes and sincerely tries can't necessarily expect to not get caught up in whiteness and not Becky again. But maybe the Becky who realizes more and more frequently when she Beckys might be someone trust can be developed with? Is there hope for me?

50 SHADES OF BECKY

Dear Diary,

It breaks my heart. I have witnessed my Colleague of Color be denied courses, forced to meetings, silenced and belittled at those meetings, ridiculed for her research. She even had her pay docked one merit year just because she refused to go to meetings with the same people who were creating a hostile work environment for her. It was disgusting. She rarely asked anything of me and often provided important support to me. I sincerely tried to be an anti-racist accomplice, though I often failed and still sometimes contributed to her silencing and marginalization. But even when I really tried I actually managed to make her situation worse. But now she says she needs me. What am I supposed to do? I have to tell her the big news. Which is good news for me, but what will it mean for her? UGH.

Chapter Thirteen

"Aren't I Great!"

The Tale of a Self-Presumed Heroic Becky

Kelly E. Demers and Aubrey Scheopner Torres

Becky carefully maneuvered her SUV into the parking space at her daughter, Abigail's, school, the Jimenez Elementary Two-Way Bilingual School. Once she finished parking, she put on her hat and braced herself for the cold January air. Becky scanned the parking lot looking for any sign of Gigi. Soon, Gigi's Prius squeezed into the parking space next to Becky.

Gigi emerged from her car still wearing her medical scrubs from work. "Nice hat!"

"Thanks! You know how I hate getting any sun," Becky teased.

Gigi was used to Becky regularly making reference to Filipino mannerisms. She knew that Becky was referring to the near-obsession many of Gigi's family members had to keeping the sun off of them. While she was used to these comments, she sometimes found them off-putting. She was simply trying to pay her friend a compliment. If you had jet-black hair that soaked in the hot Filipino sun, you'd wear a hat, too.

Gigi and Becky had been friends since college. They had met during freshman year when both were taking a writing course called "Beat Poetry of New York, 1950–1965." Their friendship began when each one blurted out, at the exact same moment, "How is Allen Ginsberg going to help me be a better writer?" Ultimately, they both dropped the class, but from that moment forward, the two were inseparable.

"Are you ready for our favorite pastime?" Becky asked.

"Drinking?" mocked Gigi.

"Very funny!"

"Oh! You mean watching and judging people?" Gigi returned brightly.

"Yeah, but just to warn you, there might be a show tonight," Becky explained.

"Good thing I brought chocolate!" Gigi said taking out her box of chocolates.

175

"*Masarap*! *Salamat*!" Becky answered. Yum and thank you, two words Becky used often whenever accepting food from Gigi and her family. Leave it to Gigi to have sustenance, Becky thought. Filipinos always seemed to be concerned about food. Their first words were always, "have you eaten"?

Becky stopped Gigi before they opened the door. "I'm so glad that you decided to come. I know going to a PTA meeting right after work isn't the most relaxing evening activity, but Abbie loves it here and I think that the Jimenez School might be a great fit for Amelia. I'd love it if the girls could attend the same school."

"I really wanted to see if everything you said about the program is true," said Gigi as she gave Becky a quick hug and kiss on the cheek.

Becky was eager for Gigi to learn about the Jimenez, which Abbie had been attending since kindergarten. It was important to her that Gigi like the school, as Becky valued her opinion more than anyone else she knew—even more than her husband, Daniel, one of Gigi's distant cousins.

Becky was also nervous about having Gigi attend this particular PTA meeting because the focus was on whether the school should move to a new location across town in a Salvadoran community. This potential move had caused quite an uproar among some of the more privileged White mothers who considered the community "unsafe" and ridden with "MS-13 gang members," but, Becky thought, given her experiences as a White mother of a biracial child, she could navigate any drama that might come up. Even so, she wanted to make sure Gigi knew what she might encounter.

"Before we go in, just know that some of the families here are very privileged and you might hear some crazy suggestions."

"Like the mom who requested that a classroom be dedicated to meditation and the practice of yoga?"

"Namaste," answered Becky with a wink.

As the two women made their way into the school auditorium Becky asked, "How are Amelia and Kaloy?"

"They're doing well, although when I called Kaloy, I heard Amelia in the background refusing to take a bath . . . " Gigi's answer was stopped short by her surprise upon entering the room. "Oh, wow." She pushed out her lips toward the room in a sort of air kiss. Becky immediately recognized the gesture as the Filipino mouth-point. Gigi was referring to the clearly divided crowd they had walked into, with a throng of Anglo moms surrounding the superintendent on one side of the room and a small group of Latina moms at the opposite side.

"Is this typical?" Gigi asked.

Becky, embarrassed, nodded and looked down.

Gigi looked around the room with an uncertain smile. The room was dominated by trim, expensively-dressed White women. A few she recognized as Lulu-Lemon clad yoga instructors who resided in large McMansions in town. Gigi rolled her eyes and let out a deep sigh. With as much will as possible, she pushed down the sense of trepidation forming in the pit of her stomach. She didn't want to offend Becky. Becky was so excited that Gigi was interested in learning about the school. So, with a side look of friendly disapproval, she asked, "So, why would I send Amelia here again?"

Sensing Gigi's skepticism, Becky laughed nervously and shook her head as they approached the small group of Latina moms, which included Camila.

"Hi, Becky. I heard Abbie gave a perfect recitation of her Spanish poem today."

Becky nodded, smiling broadly. "Hola, Camila. Yes, she practiced a lot. Isabela was a great help, though. We can't help her with pronunciation the way your Isabela can! It's so great of you to come tonight."

Camila nodded and looked away. Becky wasn't sure, but Camila seemed uncomfortable. Gigi gave Becky a reproachful look. Becky wasn't sure what that was all about. But before Becky could ask Gigi, a group of White moms came over.

"Becky, we had to give up yoga tonight for *this*!"

"I know! I could've really used it, too," Becky answered. Recognizing that Gigi was getting quizzical looks from some of the group, Becky continued, "This is Graciella. She's considering sending her daughter to the Jimenez in the fall."

"Hola, Graciella! I couldn't help but notice the scrubs. Are you a nurse?" asked one of the moms.

Before Gigi had a chance to answer, Becky eagerly jumped in. "No, she's not one of those Filipina nurses. She's a well-regarded, highly-trained radiologist. I mean, I'm lucky to even be friends with her."

Gigi raised her eyebrows. Her head was still reeling from the exchange she had just witnessed between Camila and Becky. Gigi wondered if Becky even realized she was a bit patronizing to Camila. Why was Becky feeling the need to build Gigi up to these White women? She had the uneasy feeling that Becky was trying to paint her as one of the "good ones," an exception to the rule.

Becky continued, "Yes, and she works at Abbot-Mercy Hospital. You know, it's one of best hospitals in the entire country." Becky was now making Gigi feel very uncomfortable. She tried to get Becky to stop by gently putting her hand on Becky's elbow, but Becky wanted to be sure these women respected Gigi.

"You can't assume that she's a nurse just because of how she looks," snapped Becky. It came off more forceful than she had wanted. For some reason Becky felt determined that these overly-pampered White women learn a lesson.

The other moms stiffened, and Gigi sucked in her breath in shock. Gigi tried to save the conversation by quickly changing the subject, "Why did you decide to send your kids to the Jimenez?"

"Well my family values bilingualism. Our nanny speaks Spanish and we thought it would be best that our Amanda learned to speak it, too."

"Yes, I heard they can get higher paying jobs if they speak Spanish," another woman agreed.

"So . . . you're lucky in that respect, Doctor," joked one mom.

"I'm sorry. I don't understand," said Gigi.

"Isn't Graciella a Spanish name?"

Becky couldn't believe it. She had warned Gigi, but even this was something Becky hadn't anticipated. She interjected again. "Yes, it can be a Spanish name but Gigi isn't Latina; she's Filipina."

The women looked confused, so Becky continued, "The Philippines was colonized by Spain for 300 years and many were forced by missionaries to give their children Spanish names."

"I'm sorry," said one of the moms, "I didn't know."

Gigi had experienced episodes like this before, when people talk about you as though you are not there. It was maddening. Why was Becky giving a history lesson on Gigi's own culture and life?

Another White mom jumped in to try and save the conversation, "Oh, you're Filipino! I had a Filipino nanny once. My kids loved her! I think her name was Yaya. Do you know her? She lives on Madison, right near the Mobil station."

Although she was deeply offended by this woman's assumption, Gigi wasn't surprised. She'd heard it all before. Sometimes it was easier for her to let these types of behaviors go because bringing any attention to it sometimes made it worse. Her response really depended on the situation. Tonight, she decided to take a direct but polite approach, "Well, a 'yaya' is what all Filipino nannies are called," Gigi corrected.

Gigi looked over at Becky. She noticed that Becky's jaw was clenched. "Oh no, she's gonna explode again. Please don't," thought Gigi. She was annoyed. Why was it falling on her to keep this conversation civil? She should be the one on edge, not Becky. Gigi was concerned that Becky might add something about the way that yayas were exploited, but before she had a chance, another White mom asked, "Becky, how is Abbie?"

Becky's jaw relaxed as soon as she heard her daughter's name. "She just presented her Spanish poem today and did really well!"

"I love Abbie. She's so beautiful. I love her dark, russet skin! It just makes her look so exotic. You must be so proud of your little potato!" The woman scrunched up her face the way one would when admiring a baby.

Gigi shot Becky a wide-eyed look. Was this woman referring to Abbie as Brown on the outside and White on the inside? How was Becky standing for this?

Becky quickly inhaled and held her breath. The mom was making reference to a song she often sang to her son during pick-up, but she knew Gigi didn't know that and it certainly didn't excuse the exotic comment. Becky knew how unaware these White moms were, but it was in full force tonight. Or, was it always this way and Becky hadn't noticed? Becky tried to shake off that disturbing thought. She was really worried about the impression it was leaving on Gigi. To her relief, they both slowly stepped back and released themselves from the conversation as the other White moms started talking about the upcoming school fair.

"*Hay naku!*" Becky declared, her favorite Tagalog expression of "oh my!"

Gigi was surprised by how irritated it made her to hear Becky use a Tagalog phrase in this particular context. For Gigi it felt culturally appropriating and almost as if Becky were centering herself as the victim when she wasn't the victim at all. Gigi had the uneasy feeling that Becky was using the phrase to demonstrate how culturally enlightened she was compared to the other White moms. The sense of dread in the pit of her stomach started to grow stronger. Rather than push it completely down, she leaned in toward Becky and joked, "Did you know that I know every Filipino person living in this town? We're all great friends." Gigi paused and once again she asked, "*Why* am I thinking of sending Amelia here?"

"Well, at least if the school moves, it would be closer to you," Becky gently offered. Becky's comment, though, only further annoyed Gigi.

The meeting was called to order. Rows of chairs had been set out in front of two podiums, one for the superintendent and another for a Spanish translator. Becky watched as the Anglo moms all sat together and the Latino families sat opposite. Becky and Gigi sat together in the back, taking neither side, and distancing themselves far enough away so they could engage in their typical people-watching banter without disturbing anyone.

The superintendent, a tall White man in his late fifties, got up to the podium and thanked the families for coming. After each statement, the Spanish translator, a White teacher at the school, translated what he said into Spanish. The superintendent started by speaking about how Jimenez was a jewel in the district, attracting more students every year.

Just starting to feel the effect of the earlier racial microaggressions, Gigi asked under her breath, "Which students? White students, students of color, or *exotic* students with russet skin? By the way, you must be so proud of your little potato!" Gigi imitated the scrunched face. Her dread was turning into anger.

With the increasing enrollment, the superintendent went on, the building was lacking space for classrooms and family events. The district proposed moving the school to a new building across town that would not only meet their current needs, but also accommodate future growth, the superintendent explained. After his presentation, he opened the floor to comments and questions from the group.

"This should be interesting," Gigi said as they watched the Anglo moms immediately raise their hands.

"Interesting, or do you mean entertaining?" Becky asked, hoping to break the tension.

Gigi knew that Becky was being sarcastic. Normally, she would have been happy to play along, but something about the situation felt too serious and it rubbed her the wrong way. Perhaps, it was because she was making a decision about her daughter, who given everything that had just transpired, suddenly seemed all the more precious and very vulnerable.

The first Anglo mom reported, "I feel so marginalized by this decision."

More White moms spoke out. "This proposed location is too far from my house. I'm sending my son to another school."

"How can we encourage our children to embrace diversity when we're going to have to tell them to stay away from the dangerous people in that neighborhood?"

Gigi could not hold it in anymore. "They want to embrace diversity? Is that why they had a live-in nanny and didn't even know her name? How could they think her name was yaya?" Gigi exasperatedly asked Becky.

"Well, you go by Gigi. Daniel's cousins go by Dew Drop and Ging," Becky answered, immediately realizing that she shouldn't have said anything.

"What?" Gigi exclaimed. One-minute Becky was scolding these White women for their ignorance, the next she was making excuses for them.

"Come on, Gigi, I'm on your side. It's ridiculous, but they just don't know any better."

"There is a difference between not knowing and not caring, Becky."

Becky was taken aback. Usually she and Gigi were able to poke fun at the stupidity of White people. Maybe Gigi was mad that Becky hadn't said anything about the yaya comments. At least she said something about Gigi being a doctor. Then there were the looks Camila and Gigi gave her for thanking Isabela. Clearly Becky was missing something—and it had to do with her Whiteness. She took pride in realizing this.

Gigi, who was fluent in Spanish, listened carefully as the comments were being translated. She was now openly angry. No longer attempting to be polite, she told Becky, "They're not giving accurate translations. They're softening and editing what these White moms are saying. What the hell?"

"Maybe they're trying to spare them," Becky offered.

Gigi was stunned by Becky's comment. "Imagine moving the school, Becky, and how these White moms feel right now about this. Do you think that kids aren't going to pick up on this? I can only imagine how kids are going to start treating one another. These families have a right to know precisely what's being said!"

Gigi's heart was now pounding. She rose her hand and was given the floor. "I think it's important that these comments are translated accurately. I'm afraid they're not. Your Spanish-speaking families have a right to know that these White moms have a serious problem with sending their children into their Latino community."

The room went silent for a moment as Gigi's words sunk in. One of the Anglo moms stood up. "Why do you have to bring race into this? Are you accusing us of being racist?"

Gigi didn't back down. "Your comments are racist."

Another of the Anglo moms spoke up, "I don't see color. I was raised to respect everybody."

"I don't think it's fair to accuse us of being racist. We are *justified* in having these concerns," said another Anglo mother.

Gigi shook her head. She had no words she was so riled. Instead, she turned to translate to the Spanish-speaking side of the room.

One of the White moms demanded, "I deserve to have an accurate translation of what *she's* saying about *me*."

"Why are you being so divisive?" accused another of the White moms.

Becky had a visceral reaction to that last comment. She felt like she needed to save this situation. She stood up and spoke to the group. "I think tempers are flaring here." Becky paused. "I think it's important that we consider the impact this move is going to have on *all* of our children." Becky noticed shifting from both sides of the room. She continued, "We also need to consider how this move is going to change the educational experience at this school. Right now we ask for a lot of the native Spanish-speaking students. Not only do they help in teaching our kids Spanish and about the Latino culture, which I know is part of the model, but we also ask these children to travel every day to come to us. Look at how we are reacting to moving to their neighborhood. I think the point that Gigi is trying to make is that our kids are going to pick up on this. We need to be careful."

The air seemed to have been sucked out of the room. The Anglo moms were fuming. The Latino families were not making eye contact. Becky couldn't tell what that meant. Becky turned to Gigi who looked both appalled and infuriated. Becky was confused.

The superintendent thanked Gigi and Becky for their comments and for raising important issues. He then thanked everyone for coming and quickly adjourned the meeting. Becky was disheartened but at least she helped these moms face their Whiteness. Still, what was the point? They were all so defensive and still seemed blind to their privilege.

Gigi didn't move. She sat planted in her chair, furious. How could Becky interrupt her yet again? How on earth did Becky ever think that sending Amelia here—or even Abbie—was a good idea?

Becky noticed that the White moms wouldn't make eye contact with her as they filed out of the auditorium. Her mind raced with the possible comments she would see tomorrow on the mom's message board. None of the Latino moms would look at her either, especially Camila. Becky suddenly felt isolated and discouraged. She picked up her Longchamp designer handbag to find her keys. Gigi sighed and got up, making her way toward the door. Becky followed.

"Gigi, I'm sorry for what happened in there. That wasn't a good representation of this school community."

"I'm not sorry," Gigi said as they reached their cars. "They showed their true selves. That's important to see."

Becky sighed. "Look, Gigi, I know that was horrible, but I honestly think they mean well. They're looking out for their kids. They're protective and they have no idea what they are saying. We have to remember that they're good at heart, Gigi."

Gigi couldn't believe what she was hearing. How could Becky make excuses for such overtly racist behavior? Nearly shouting she said, "Ignorance doesn't make this shit okay, Becky. 'Good at heart' means nothing when there are real, severe consequences. You saw what I went through in there and all that I've gone through over the years. You stand by and watch Daniel and Abbie go through it. How can you say that they're good at heart?"

"I just don't think bludgeoning them with their racism is going to work. We need to be patient and lead the horse to water . . . "

Gigi was tired of being patient; only action would end the problem of racism. Gigi interrupted Becky. "How can you ask for patience? If you think *that* was bludgeoning, you should be glad I didn't tell them what I *really* thought. You need to ask yourself what you want: to be friends with them or to be an ally, because the truth is, they're not going to listen to what I have to say, but they *might* listen to you."

Gigi's voice was getting louder at each exchange. Becky felt the best thing to do was to calm her down. She spoke softly. "Gigi, I know I will never know what it's like to experience racism firsthand, but as a bystander seeing what you all go through, I have a pretty clear image . . . "

Refusing to be silenced, Gigi cut her off again and became even louder, "Not clear enough! You stand here defending them and *then* refer to your best friend and family as 'you all.' Becky, you're part of the problem. Wake up!"

Now it was Becky's turn to scream. "What? What do you mean?" Becky's head was spinning. She couldn't be part of the problem; she was one of the most "woke" White people she knew.

"You're using Isabela to help Abbie, just like all those other moms. You hold up a mirror to them, but do you even hold it up to yourself?"

Becky felt as though she had been punched in the stomach. "What the hell, Gigi?"

"Oh my God, Becky! Sometimes you have to face the truth. Every White mother who spoke at that meeting portrayed herself and her child as the victim. Not one of them considered what Latino families might need. Even you're worried about sending Abbie to school in that neighborhood. Admit it. And don't think you're a hero because you spoke up—stealing my words to make your 'point.' Don't think I didn't pick up on that. You sent Abbie to that school for the same reason as all of those other White moms: so your kid can learn about cultural differences on the backs of Brown children. I can't even imagine sending Amelia to this school."

Becky was devastated. "Gigi, you've known me for years. You were a bridesmaid at my wedding. You're Abbie's godmother. I'm married to Daniel. That has to mean something."

"Do you think that because you're married to a Brown man and have a Brown friend you deserve special credit?" Gigi was dumbfounded. How could Becky not see her own privileges?

Becky was shaking. "You think *I* haven't suffered at the hands of those White mothers as the wife of a Brown man and mother of a biracial child? Do you think it's easy to negotiate these two worlds? I worry constantly about whether Abbie will be accepted by either side. Maybe if you sent Amelia, then at least Abbie would have *someone*. What is so wrong about wanting what is best for my family? So I want to be a hero—so what. Look at you! You were doing the same thing tonight by participating in a debate that has *nothing* to do with you. Do you know how bad you have made things for me? Why do you think Brown people have a monopoly on suffering?"

As Gigi listened to this speech, she no longer saw her best friend of 15 years. Instead she saw just another progressive White woman who claimed a desire for racial harmony, but only as long as her needs came first. Why was

Becky so worried about what these White women thought and not about what Camila and the other Latino families were experiencing? She felt a powerful combination of emotions that included disbelief, sadness, anger, and hurt. She never thought this could happen to them.

They both stood staring at one another in silent shock.

"Oh, Becky," Gigi whispered. "I don't have the energy to explain this to one more White person, especially to you. Not tonight . . . maybe never." Gigi slowly got into her car, seemingly exhausted. As she pulled away, she saw Becky in her rearview mirror, standing alone in the cold darkness with her head in her hands. At the exit, Gigi took a moment to stop the car. She opened her window and deeply breathed in the chilly night air. With each inhale and exhale she felt an overwhelming sense of grief. Loss. She was alone yet again in defending her humanity and the humanity of other people of color. Her friendship with Becky would never be the same. Some wounds are just too deep.

Chapter Fourteen

White Lady

Myth or Fact?

Korina M. Jocson

Five o'clock. The skies had turned burnt orange toward the horizon.

Dusk represented a natural curfew, an internal clock that could only mean one thing. It was time to get home, at least for the children and preteens who were scurrying about and carelessly kicking up dirt into their stained socks. Their hair, cheeks and elbows marked with streaks of dust. The air so thick from diesel. And all around the sound of tricycle horn blowing.

But none of it mattered today.

It was the eve of another new year and Manang Pilar had invited all children in the neighborhood to stop by before the night's festivities began.

Manang Pilar is an elder, a storyteller, well-respected by both the young and the old; she held storytelling times on occasion to bring everyone together and to pass down a Filipino tradition common among many families and in many villages in the Philippines. "Kuwento-kuwentohan" is the event through which storytelling occurs. Manang Pilar's kuwentos (stories) offered lessons to last a lifetime. Some were real. Others were made up. The point was to inspire the young. Or maybe, to scare them, to give them something to think about. There were also times when kuwentos persuaded or willed a kind of behavior.

Manang Pilar sat in her rattan rocking chair and in the comfort of her home. A green coil of mosquito repellant had been smoldering in the corner. Its smoke had soared far out to reach the overgrown mango trees just outside the capiz-patterned windows. Children scrambled through the shadowy yard and climbed up the steep steps to the balcony where Manang Pilar awaited their arrival. They soon took their place on the wooden planked floor. Wide-eyed. Cross-legged. A mild breeze calmed their staccato heartbeats. The expansive windows had been opened just a few moments ago to let the swishing leaves create a slightly stronger breeze. The smoke swayed with it.

"Good evening, children," greeted Manang Pilar. "I am glad you are all here."

"Good evening, po." Each one responded in deference and graciously looked on, scuttling their bottoms only to make the wooden floors shine even more.

"I want to share something special with all of you. It is an important story. I know you will appreciate it. You need to hear it. My great grandparents told my grandparents—my Lolas and my Lolos—and they told my parents, and my parents told me. And now, I want to tell you." Manang Pilar impressed the need for stillness. "Do you want to hear it?"

All fourteen children maneuvered into a sitting posture, ready to hear this important story. What could be so important that it had traveled for generations? "It must be good," they thought.

"Has anyone ever told you about the White Lady?" asked Manang Pilar.

"No." Shaking their heads left and right, several of the children mumbled to each other the types of stories they had heard about folkloric apparitions, mythical creatures, and half-human spirited beings. Multo (ghost). Kapre (tree giant). Aswang (shapeshifting spirit). *They're the same. No, they're not. Yes, they are.* To their confusion, why had most adults in their lives not yet shared the story of the White Lady? They must have had their reasons—perhaps a psychological triggering, a haunting, from childhoods near and far. Some had probably stored away terrifying recollections of being swept away into oblivion, or being eaten alive with their youthful limbs falling prey to voracious appetites. Imagined or not, stories like these have affective dimensions that can be felt throughout one's lifetime. This, as part thrill of oral traditions, is kuwento at its best.

"Listen, when I tell you. The White Lady is one to be reckoned with," said Manang Pilar.

And for the next several minutes, time stood still as all fourteen children wrapped their minds around a fully-formed supernatural body. Indistinct. Eerie. Otherwordly. This ghostlike thing came into being with a blinding glow. It is synchronous with the semblance of manifest destiny common in American history books. The White Lady is dressed in a flowy fringe-like garb, reaching west with its racial logics to conquer minds and the material resources that often go with them. The White Lady's feet are in the air, yet it has no wings. How could that be?

Manang Pilar had the children's attention now.

It all started here, in this house, when my Apo (great grandparent) was about your age. She woke up in the middle of night to make her way to the bathroom. The White Lady appeared. Right here, behind this capiz window, next to the mango trees. The White Lady appeared out of nowhere. Yes, out of nowhere.

And just like that! Apo spotted the White Lady and couldn't believe what it was. She rubbed her eyes, inclined to deem the specter as a nocturnal illusion. Only it wasn't. She rubbed her eyes again.

Are you with me?

My Apo was not able to hold her pee in that moment. So, what happened? My Apo wet the floor. In shock, she let it all go because she just couldn't hold it. She started to cry but no one could hear her. Not one. Everyone was in deep sleep. It was dark. It was very, very dark. My Apo only had the beam of the full moon that night to guide her feet. And in that moment the floor was wet with the moonlight reflecting in the small puddle.

Apo looked down at the mess when she felt a touch on her arm.

The White Lady tried to reach for her hand, to take her away, away from her parents, away from her family, away from this place. In her frozen stance, Apo refused to surrender and instead just held her ground.

"Noooo. Go away. Please just go away!" begged Apo. She continued to look down, avoiding any eye contact.

Gasping for some desperate brown magic, Apo covered her eyes with the palms of her hand and wished for her limbs to stay intact. She had been warned that the White Lady turns children into a regular fare depending on appetite.

Then in one sweeping breath, the White Lady uttered what seemed to be kind words to Apo's surprise. Were they kind words to whisk away the fear? To gently woo Apo into her arms? Was the White Lady really not half as bad as people described? Was the White Lady really a saving grace in disguise? Apo could not quite make out the words.

"Come with me, come now. Never face darkness again." The White Lady was firm.

Surely, that was what every child desired. Those who were socialized to be afraid of the dark. Remnants of colonial education. The cost of benevolent assimilation. In the name of light. To be in the company of grace. Because to go with the White Lady is to be saved from savagery. Beastly imperfections of a people. Our people.

Apo closed her eyes and covered her ears this time.

"Noooo. Go away. Please just go away!" exclaimed Apo. She knew better than to be deceived in the night. "Go away. Go away. Go Away. Go away," she repeated.

In some inexplicable way, Apo's refusal took effect because all of a sudden the White Lady became weary from the jostle and its shape started to disappear. Until finally, its silhouette and lingering glow went away for good. But the White Lady's words stayed with Apo for many more moons, leaving an impression and wondering made her wonder she should have obliged to the demand or not.

That night, Apo returned to her slumber, kept her eyes shut, and let her dreams in. The small puddle on the wooden floor eventually dried up on its own.

Manang Pilar paused and let out a sigh. "So, you may ask, is the White Lady real or does it live only in the figment of our imagination?"

The truth is, Manang Pilar opened up an opportunity for a teachable moment. The White Lady, as had been told to her by elders, represented a way to generate a sense of fear among children. The spooky night experience was not unique to Apo, nor was it an isolated one. For generations, the White Lady had appealed to many children because behind the mango and acacia trees lived the spirited beings, and the like. Folklore meant stories. And sometimes parents and grandparents relied on kuwento to impart onto children how to be. Where and when to be, including getting home at dusk. Grimy or not after play.

"Is it real or imagined?" posed Apo.

The children looked puzzled. This was the first time they had heard the story and the question from Manang Pilar did not seem fair. On the one hand, the fear had been instilled in them, just like in previous generations. A means of social control. To act in a manner consistent with cultural norms such as obedience and deference. A respect for elders that without tradition would dismantle family structure, chosen and blood. On the other hand, the ritual of kuwento about the White Lady on this new year's eve served as a perfect example to ring in a new perspective, a new mode of understanding the world, a new sense of seeing or believing in the otherwise.

By now, all of the children had bid their goodbyes to Manang Pilar, on their way to light up the sky at midnight and partake in delicious puto bumbong. Because steamed purple rice caked topped with freshly grated coconut was made only on special occasions. The crowd in the marketplace filled the air with spectacle. People danced in the streets. Loud booms from canons on the ground. Raining fireworks in the sky. Watusi sticks and firecrackers in hand. It is new year's eve after all.

That night, the festivities carried on like usual. Something grand, something bedazzled. But when it was time to walk home from the marketplace, the children centered on the hazy moon in sight. Watusi still lit and crackling in one hand.

Maybe the White Lady might choose to appear. Maybe not.

It was time for bed . . .

Six o'clock. Sunrays had made their way through the morning mist. And the children still in their dream-like state. Who is ready to take on the day, sprung from the dirt beyond some mango and acacia trees?

Section Six

Guiding Questions

1. In "The Guilt of a Becky" how does this Becky fall short from being an ally? In what ways has she been supportive? What are some things she needs to consider before assuming she is an ally? How could she have better supported Carol? Have you seen this kind of relationship in your own environment? Describe its impact on you.
2. Why is it important to understand that although a white woman seeks to be an ally she must constantly reflect on her behaviors, lest turn into a Becky?
3. In "Aren't I Great!" how do the behaviors of Becky impact her friendship with Gigi? Why does Gigi get so frustrated with Becky? How has this impacted their friendship? Have you seen this play out in your environment? How has it impacted you?
4. In "White Lady: Myth or Fact?" the author metaphorically describes why one should be skeptical of the white lady's intentions. How does this relate to the behaviors of Becky(s)? Why would people of color, particularly, women of color, be wary of the white lady?
5. If you are a white women, notice as to whether or not you have friends of color who speak about things, like race, that at times make you feel uncomfortable or is the friendship always about the friend of color not bringing up topics of race? How does this kind of relationship speak directly to your white sensibilities? And, in turn, what does this mean with regards to how you see yourself as an ally? What does it mean to be an ally?

Section Seven

Becky(s) as Violent

On September 4, 1957, photographer Ira "Will" Counts Jr. shot one of the top one hundred photos of the twentieth century, according to the Associated Press. The image is called, "The Scream Image." The picture depicts racial desegregation at Little Rock Central High School where Elizabeth Eckford, one of the Little Rock Nine, is foregrounded, behind her a sea of hateful white faces. One face in particular was that of the screaming imager herself, Hazel Bryan, a very angry young white woman. Though the picture is just a stand-point in time, articles have since been written about how these white women treated Eckford (Blakemore, 2018). From continuous racial taunts to physical violence, Eckford was so traumatized that she suffered mental health conditions as an adult and to this day, cannot reconcile with Bryan despite Bryan's said effort in civil rights. Sadly, the same vehement violence can be seen when white women teachers teaching in schools that have predominantly Mexican American students yell "'English! English! You're in America! Go back to Mexico!" (Valenzuela, 1999, p. 131). It is precisely these kinds of behaviors that make students of color, to steal from hooks' (1993) words, "lose [their] love of school" (p. 3). Clearly, the violence of white women leave horrifying lasting impacts on those they victimize. However, before delving into how people of color, moreover women of color, experience the violence of white women, a more thorough understanding of the violence of white women must be had. Furthermore, by masking the violence behind the façade of innocence so inscribed in the stereotypes of white women, the violence becomes even more vehement.

That white women occupy a unique space in white supremacy, both privileged because of their whiteness and marginalized due to their gender, makes the study of white women so compelling. Daniels (1997) reiterates this in her analysis of white supremacist discourse in mainstream America.

She asserts, "white women have historically been—and continue to be—situated within a complex nexus of race, and often class, privilege combined with gender oppression" (p. 56). And, in this complex web situated between white supremacy and patriarchy, white women have developed unique attachments to folks of color, particularly, women of color; for in doing so, it better solidifies their status. For example, Daniels (1997) argues that "images of white women, either as mothers or as sexual beings, are constructed in opposition to images of subordinated women, that is, to Black women" (p. 56). If Black women are defined as sexual deviants who are just welfare moms then white women are portrayed as "chaste, pure, asexual, good mothers, and exemplars of femininity" (p. 56). What defines white women then is their juxtaposition to women of color, particularly Black women. Meaning, they need an opposite in order to define themselves. This is a curious phenomenon that needs further exploration.

Psychoanalysis is warranted to more deeply investigate why white women must identify their standing, identity, or image only when attached to the ideal of another. Fortuitous is this approach in that it delves more deeply into one's psyche: one's desires, attachments, motivations, etc. Cheng (2001) corroborates this stating, "what has been missing in much of the critical analysis of race relations and representations has been a willingness to confront the psychic implications of the haunting negativity that has not only been attached to but has also helped to constitute the very category of 'the racialized'" (p. 25). Then to investigate more deeply as to why one must have an unhealthy attachment to another to make meaning of themselves is a worthy endeavor, especially when the attachment requires the denigration of the other.

Although not often discussed as such, this phenomenon is a fetish; though not as sexual attachment, but rather in an excessive form of attachment. In one of my articles "White Skin, Black Friend" and in my book, *Feeling White*, I discuss how trying to achieve the ideals of whiteness (e.g., all moral, pure, innocent, etc.), like any other ideal (e.g., body image), will nonetheless leave folks feeling empty, shallow, inadequate, and melancholic because it is impossible for any human to fully achieve an ideal. In this state then, fetishization can be psychoanalytically interpreted as a performance of whiteness that facilitates one's narcissistic need to feel humanly fulfilled as a process of atonement for white racialization" (Matias, 2016, p. 92). Therefore, white women feel racially inept because achieving whiteness is an ideal one can never achieve. As such, they create unhealthy attachments to people of color, moreover, to women of color in order to make sense of themselves. However, in order for them to identify as pure, innocent, and moral, they must characterize their counterparts with the opposite. And by identifying themselves as pure and innocent, it then masks the types of violent behaviors they enact onto people of color.

In fact, despite popular stereotypes of white women being innocent of some of the most atrocious racist acts, they, too were complicit, at times even main aggressors, of it. As Jones-Rogers (2019) reveals, white women were not innocent bystanders of slavery, they were indeed "mistresses of the market" (p. xiv) "who stood to personally and directly benefit from the commodification and enslavement of African Americans" (p. 205). There is an entire litany of literature that captures the violence white women have enacted onto people of color. In fact, for this book alone, I had over one hundred national submissions painfully describing their traumas with white women. Later, many authors divulged to me how hard it was to relive these violent experiences. I feel responsible. I feel pained. To hear of the many folks, many of whom were women of color, deal with these violent behaviors of Becky(s) was gut-wrenching. Clearly, as bell hooks (1995) states, "the racism of white women should be militantly challenged" (p. 100) and this book is an attempt not only to challenge Becky(s) but to stop the violence.

In fact, just as hooks describes the vehemence of white feminists toward Black feminists, the same can be true about the violence altogether. Although people of color experience the violence of white women writ large, women of color in particular, undergo a more directly aggressive form of violence from them. Meaning, not couched under the guise of needing protection. Needless to say, Miss Ann engaged in violence against her Black male slaves by ordering whippings, but engaged in violence to Black women slaves by directly throwing at her cast irons pots (as dramatized in the movie *12 Years a Slave*). In the same manner, Miss Becky engages in violence toward men of color through operations of sexual fetish (much like how white men sexually fetishize women of color) but unlike men, Miss Becky engages in violence toward women of color more directly. Since women of color, particularly Black women, are the pinnacles of her fetish of attachment that give her meaning—though men of color are the pinnacle of her sexual fetish—Becky(s) as Violent then preoccupies herself with enjoying the power and privilege to demean, defame, and dehumanize them. Frankly, Becky(s) of this type are violent to all people of color but engage in inhumane degradations more so with women of color.

Therefore, Becky(s) as Violent are white women who vehemently project their psychoanalytic issues onto people of color simply because they feel inept in their own lives. They have no remorse. They believe themselves absolved of their wrongdoings simply because they self-characterize themselves as innocent. And they do this by mischaracterizing women of color as perpetrators. This is why these Becky(s) take great pains to mischaracterize women of color as angry, not collaborative, or as the problem. They nitpick a women of color's character. They must control the narrative of women of color in ways that paint her so negatively because they know they are defined by its opposite. The more heinous she paints the woman of color, the more angelic she appears. Whether yielding their power as a teacher over a student or an administrator over faculty, Becky(s) as Violent use their power in whiteness to traumatize women of color, never taking responsibility, let alone ever recognizing the responsibility, they have in enacting that violent behavior. In the end, they enact violence with a smile.

The stories in this section deal with Becky(s) as Violent in different ways. Though violence is often understood in terms of physical violence, these stories show how the violence of these Becky(s) morphs into spirit murder; one that triggers the posttraumatic stress that many folks of color experience with regards to racism. Becky(s) as Violent pretend that all the stress and trauma felt by people of color are unwarranted. She does this by relying on her innocence. Yet, truth be told, the history of violence from white women is recognized, persistent, and deadly (as aforementioned in other section introductions) and present themselves in different ways from men of color to women of color. In fact, when asked about writing the chapter, one author, a Black man, writes,

> In many ways, I see this story as connected to my personal experience working with white women in education. While I don't see myself as the central character, Imani, I have been on the receiving end of white women's vitriol and chronic anti-Blackness, which has been in the drag of care, concern, or personal ambition.

When asked what she wants readers to come away with the other author, a Black non-binary womyn, writes a lengthy painful response.

> I want readers to come away with knowing that violence enacted by humans is not limited to the weapons we take up as individuals. It includes the legacies of violence individuals represent in society. Humans are the primary interface any individual has with society, and as a result, we unknowingly weaponize people's trauma when we remind them of previous injustices. As a person racialized as a black, I do not have the luxury of herd immunity to [whiteness] as a container. If people different from me are to know anything about my truth as represented by this parable, it is that you cannot know my truth unless you know me. Building authentic relationships courageously is how I seek to overcome the violence I cannot escape alone.

The other author, a man of color, discussed with me the need to incorporate a spiritual element that better captures how spiritually murdering these violent behaviors are. When asked about his goal for writing the chapter, he writes the following:

> A goal is to have readers leave understanding the perpetual haunting of gendered white dominance and more specifically white women's acquiesce and culpability in reproducing Black suffering, spirit murdering, and white dominance. In many ways, I hope this story challenges a narrative of 'with time comes progress' and aims to illuminate how even well meaning, "liberal" white women can be accomplices in larger, historically based, yet presently manifested systems of oppression.

In fact, both authors talked at length of the impacts of these violent expressions. But the authors did not stay there. In writing this chapter, one author further describes the harm she has endured from these Becky(s) as follows:

> I also found myself healing and acknowledging the extent of the mental harm I've endured at the hands of Beckys. I learned that this harm is ongoing and healing; for one wound does not mean I am healing from others or not continuing to be injured.

Many authors from the book discussed how traumatic it was to relive these violent experiences, but in their vulnerability and bravery, they also express how cathartic it was to let it out. In my own scholarship, I found writing to be a catalyst for healing. This is essentially what I wanted to offer my authors. There were times I reached out to contributing authors to listen to their experiences. In offering my ear, I listened to their humanity. Although Becky(s) as Violent attempt to take away our spirits, mental health, physical strength, confidence, they will never take away our humanity because the biggest thing I learned from editing this book is that we always have each other.

REFERENCES

Blakemore, E. (2018). "The Story Behind the Famous Little Rock Nine 'Scream Image' It didn't end when Central High School was integrated" Taken from http://webapp1.dlib.indiana.edu/archivesphotos/results/item.do?itemId=P0026600.

Cheng, A. (2001). *The Melancholy of Race: Psychoanalysis, Assimilation, and Hidden Grief.* New York: Oxford University Press.

Daniels, J. (1997). *White Lies: Race, Class, Gender and Sexuality in White Supremacist Discourse.* New York: Routledge.

hooks, b. (1994). *Teaching to Transgress: Education as the Practice of Freedom.* New York: Routledge.

hooks, b. (1995). *Killing Rage: Ending Racism.* New York: Owl Books.

Jones-Rogers, S. (2019). *They Were Her Property: White Women as Slave Owners in the American South.* New Haven, CT: Yale University Press.

Matias, C. E. (2016). *Feeling White: Whiteness, Emotionality, and Education.* The Netherlands: Sense Publishers.

Valenzuela, A. (1999). *Subtractive Schooling: U.S.-Mexican Youth and the Politics of Caring.* Albany: State University of New York Press.

Chapter Fifteen

Present Tense

A Southern Gothic of Schooling

Kevin Lawrence Henry Jr.

It had been two years. 2007. The air never quite felt the same after "The Storm." Maybe it was death that lingered in it; gave it its weight. Maybe history had never settled in her tomb, finding atmospheric expansiveness more desirable than gilded crypts. All of it seemed to be unfazing to the Horsemen who patrolled the city at night. They initiated a curfew. "For your safety, looters and criminals," they said. Signifiers without a sign. Classifications with different meanings. Is that not what unnatural disasters do? Unsettle things. Break them up a bit. Fracture peaceful illusions. That's what the hurricane did to the air. And some say that's what it did to Time. People literally stared talking about their lives—as not a continuum, but as "pre" and "post." Some say Imani had fallen victim to Time's undoing. She couldn't get with the times. Some speculate it was airborne. That's how she had gone mad.

The sun adored Imani; it sunk into the plushness of her rich, dark skin; it found sustenance in her glistening locks which smelled of a divine, sweet ambrosia. Imani would awake before the sun could start its day. She preferred witnessing its rise from her newly renovated shotgun house. She lived in the house that her mother had lived before her and her mother before her. It was the family house. And it had an abundance of memories—laughter, joy, pain, struggle, hope. A house of dreams, despair, and desire; it was sturdy. 426 North Tonti Street survived The Storm. It had 12 feet of water and enough mold that the walls refused to talk. When Imani took over the renovation process, she decided the house would be a bright chartreuse. After all, she would think, "it's the color for lovers and dreamers." Much like her thoughts, Imani was a dreamer. She had such hopes for the rebuilding of New Orleans. That was one of the reasons she returned to the city after the great storm. She wanted to change it. Make things right. She left for college three years before the hurricane decimated the city. Everyone in her family was thrilled that Imani would attend one of the nation's most prestigious schools, Hayek University located in Massachusetts. They were even more thrilled when she returned to teach. According to the nation's mythology some of the greatest minds attended Hayek. The veracity of the statement could never be truly ascertained. Whatever the case, Hayek was the citadel of elite social networks, old money, you know . . . whiteness and with that comes power and prestige and exclusivity. And you know . . . oppression, suffering, and death.

Imani's eyes are open. It's 5:10 in the morning and she allows the covers to envelop her before the alarm trumpets Hot 8 Brass Band's *Get Up.* She listens for the birds, but not a chirp in ear. The city is still resting and clinging to the remaining minutes of slumber. It's one of those mornings where everything is peaceful, serene. She pulls the stack of index cards on her nightstand and shuffles them. She pulls the Toni Morrison, quote from *Beloved* and voices it gently, "I used to think it was my rememory. You know. Some things you forget. Other things you never do. But it's not. Places, places are still there. If a house burns down, it's gone, but the place—the picture of it—stays, and not just in my rememory, but out there, in the world." "Ashe" she says after reading the quote.

Imani glances at the art on her wall—she made most of it. One particular piece stands out, however. It was a reprint of one of Basquiat's pieces. The one of the head. A friend from college had given it to her on her 21st birthday. She always admired how Basquiat's work forced us to look at ourselves. And maybe more specifically our interior qualities. The stuff that really structures us, undergirds us.

By now the sun was beginning to rise. It peaked through the trees outside, hugging the space that existed. New Orleans could be most beautiful in the morning. This was one of those mornings. Time had seemed to pass quickly as Imani loitered in her deep mahogany bed admiring the cultivated beauty around her. It dawned upon her that she would need to begin getting ready for work. She did her morning ritual—prayed, played some music, showered and all its accompanying acts, dressed, and ate a light breakfast. Her attire for the day: a marigold loose turtleneck top with gold-hooped earrings, blue tapered slacks, and multicolored flats. She took one last glimpse into the ivory bone mirror to make sure everything was alright; Imani looked fly, of course. She dropped everything and nearly collapsed. The face behind her back and within the mirror said to her, "You need to open your eyes, girl!" It was gone before she could breathe again. Heavy was her heartbeat, pounding more precisely. The skin of her heart stretched covering the fear that hollowed it. It was like a drum whose beat was not of her own. A possession she knew not of.

Hurrying into the car, Imani couldn't understand what just took place. She was educated, beyond bright by conventional and unconventional standards. Therefore, there was a reason. It was a hallucination, right? Something in her morning tea? An accident from the herbalist? Perhaps, a mix up of sorts. A concoction for a cocktail not meant for her. Imani relegated the encounter to some far-off recess of her mind.

She pulled up within minutes to the stately school in uptown New Orleans. It was a few blocks off of St. Charles Avenue where old money—sugar money, cotton money, inherited money— homes aligned the street of purple, green, and gold beaded oak trees. A sight to behold. Mardi Gras festivities, for sure, had transformed the trees into some other species of oak. Imani walked into what could only be conceived of as a palatial school.

It had such a plush architecture. Vaulted ceilings, seemingly always polished hard wood floors, elegant staircases, large windows that opened students' daydreaming fantasies to new heights. The school, Blanchard Beauregard, built shortly after Reconstruction, had educated many of the elite white New Orleanian families—that was the past. There was no real need for private schools until much later in Time. Schooling was understood, then, as a public necessity, one of the responsibilities of government; public schooling had yet to be abandoned and contorted into a privatized plaything. Although, to be clear, schooling did map onto racist, capitalist, and patriarchal desires. Schooling was for seduction. That's how vulgar power relations are created, sustained, conserved, and ultimately camouflaged. Seduction. The glory of Beauregard had been restored following the great storm. However, for much of Beauregard's modern history it was in ruins. After the desegregation orders the building was allowed to become moribund. Nobody really there to live for. And so, neglected by the state. Life certainly coursed through the building, with the Black inhabitants who populated the school. Oddly, it took The Storm to restore it to its prior glory. That was only after the school was converted to a charter. Money and resources seemed to flow freely and without hesitation into the hands of the white charter leaders.

Imani zipped into the side entrance of the school hoping she would be unnoticed, hoping the copy machine wouldn't be occupied. Impossible.

"Hey, Ms. Morrison!" a student exclaimed.

Imani took off her glasses, "Hey, my dawlin'. Good morning. How was your night?"

Will was excited to be talking to Imani. She was one of his favorite teachers. "You know. Same old. Same old. Had to work last night. But I'm gon' cop these Jays this weekend." Imani smiled and laughed at Will as he started dancing—the jigg—toward the end of his sentence. "I hope you're picking up a pair for your Math teacher!?"

"I gotchu, Ms. Morrison," Will said with a smirk.

"You also got your homework?" Imani quizzed.

"See Ms. Morrison. You starting already. I'll see you in 6th." They both laughed as they each went their separate ways.

Imani entered the teachers' lounge and rushed to the copier. Her plan was aborted before she could make it. Becky Kate pulled her aside. "Imani, I'm going to do it." The level of glee in Becky Kate's voice was overwhelming for Imani. It was only 7:30 am. "Do what, Becky Kate? Other than not sneak up on me like that!" They both laughed. Becky Kate was Imani's friend from college and her School For Them cohort member, SFT for short. SFT was an alternative teaching program designed to place "well meaning," but inadequately prepared recent college grads in the neediest of urban schools. Despite the pronouncements from politicians from both the left and right of how wonderful and successful these teachers were, no middle or upper middle-class white parents desired them or horded them for their own children. This was the first time in recorded history such a thing occurred. Becky Kate was a young, white recent grad of Walton University in Connecticut. Becky Kate and Imani's alma maters were rivals; not only were their respective schools two of the most prestigious and oldest schools in the U.S., but they hosted an annual football game, which cemented the rivalry. Becky Kate's parents were judges in New York and they awaited Becky Kate's ascension into the legal field. Becky Kate, however, was unsure about the law. She figured she could buy some time with SFT before applying to law school. Plus, she felt like she was doing something good; she was saving these kids from themselves and from the backwardness of New Orleans—though she did love the cuisine and Mardi Gras.

"I'm going to apply for the Social Studies Department Head position!" Becky Kate said excitedly. "Wow. That's really awesome, Becky Kate. Have you spoken with anyone from SFT about it?" Imani asked. "Of course, I have" Becky Kate said emphatically, "Everyone there is encouraging it. And think it would be great to have a SFTer in leadership. You know how terrible the old guard was before the hurricane." Imani wasn't too sure how terrible the old guard was. "A lot of the teachers Becky Kate were really strong Black women educators. How do you think I got to Hayek?" Imani quizzed.

"Girl, you're different. You're not like most of the people from here. And I'm sure as hell those teachers had little to do with anything" Becky Kate said. Imani was angered.

"How could you say that, Becky Kate?" Becky Kate fumbled around the characterless lounge—it was actually quite dull—rolling her eyes before she turned to Imani. "Calm down, Imani! You always get so ghetto with me. Let me stop before you throw the race card again. And ruin my day." Imani was over the conversation. "Keep me posted on things, Becky Kate," she said as she walked out the lounge.

As Imani finished making her copies, she wondered what it would mean to have Becky Kate serve as department chair. Would Becky Kate be able to handle the demands of such a position and have the experience to support other teachers? As Imani walked to her classroom, she passed Linda. Linda Moore was the woman Becky Kate would be going up against for the position. Ms. Moore was a native of New Orleans. She served as department chair prior to the great storm. Linda was one of the many Black teachers who were summarily dismissed after The Storm and required to reapply for their jobs. It was, perhaps, the largest displacement of Black educators since *Brown v. Board of Education.* Never mind that. Time, apparently, had settled the past. In a post-Civil Rights Era world, firing Black teachers to usher in a new reform is standard operating procedure, so what happened after The Storm need not be uttered or considered for what it was—normal. Linda was one of the lucky teachers. She was rehired. That was not the case for everyone. Many of her colleagues did not return to their schools. They were surplus bodies, not needed for the "new" vision of charter schooling in the aftermath of The Storm.

Imani looked into Linda's classroom, as Linda was writing on the board. "Hi Ms. Linda!" Imani cheerfully said. "Oh hey, Imani!!! Come on in here, girl!" Imani quickly obliged, moving toward Linda to give her a quick kiss on the cheek. "Well, how's it going? Ready for the day?" Linda asked. "Yeah, but I just don't know. It seems I've been off this morning, Ms. Linda." Imani responded. "Baby, sometimes we all have days like that. I'm sure everything will fall right into place."

"Thank you, Ms. Linda. Let me get myself to my class. You know they're already waiting to get in," Imani said.

Linda chuckled, "Alright, my baby. And I see you're teaching about Marie Laveau today." Imani was confused. "Huh?" she said, "Marie Laveau? The voodoo lady?"

"No," Linda corrected. "Child, she's the Voodoo Queen of New Orleans. Get it right." Imani smiled and remarked, "I'm not teaching about her Ms. Linda."

"Then why" Linda asked, "do you have her picture in your copies?" Imani looked down and it was as if artic waters were pulsating throughout her body. It was her. The woman in the mirror. Atop her copies." Imani was frightened. How? Just how?

Linda instinctively grabbed Imani and hugged her tight. She could see something was wrong with Imani. "What's wrong, baby?" Linda asked.

"It's just . . . It's not right. Something's not right, Ms. Linda" Imani said with hesitation. The bell rang and she knew she'd need to hurry to class. She felt a familiar warmth as Linda let go. It reminded her of a point in Time, of her past and some of the Black women educators who cared for her. Where had Ms. DeCuire gone? Or Ms. Doucet? Or Ms. Robertson?

The hours seemed to fly by that day. Imani ran into Richard, the principal of the school, as she checked her mailbox in the main office. Richard, a nondescript white man in his mid-to-late twenties, was an alumnus of SFT. He started teaching after college and soon became well admired in educational reform circles after The Storm. He had a simple philosophy—there should be no excuses for student learning. Individual merit was the only thing that stopped children from learning and educational competition and charter schools were the superior reform method. As Imani saw Richard, she could smell the remnants of whiskey on his breath, faint but traceable. She turned around and grabbed the mail from her box, reading pensively a sheet of paper about nothing. Only thoughts in her head were safe. "Please don't let this man speak to me." As she turned around, there he was edging toward breaching personal space.

"Armani! Nice to see you in here." Imani stared and provided a smile made of haphazard and over it. "Hi, Richard. It's Imani," she said, emphasizing the pronunciation.

"My apologies. I'm not used to saying exotic names" he said dismissively. "Anyhow, I'll be sending you an email this evening. We need to go over your classroom observation. I read over Steve's notes. And he mentioned you handled a discipline issue with a circle process?" Richard looked both puzzled and disturbed. "You know these kids need consistent discipline policy. At Beauregard we're zero-tolerance. After the hurricane, they need order." The level of disgust accumulated in Imani's stomach. "Sure, Richard. I await your email."

"Thanks, Imani." Richard said with a false smile. As Imani walked out the office, Richard ran up to her. "Aren't you happy Becky Kate's gonna get the position as Social Studies chair?!" Imani looked puzzled as the announcement was only sent yesterday and teachers would apply. Imani inquired, "I didn't know it was already settled, Richard." Richard seemed to almost whisper as he said, "It's not, but . . . she's one of us, Imani. If we want to change this school and the culture of laziness among the students and those veteran teachers, we've got to get our people in leadership." Imani returned Richard's false smile and headed toward the social studies corridor. She overheard Linda and Becky Kate in Becky Kate's classroom. "I personally am offended, Linda. I am a good teacher and have my own teaching practices that I employ. I'm about results and not edutainment!"

Linda looked Becky Kate in the eye and said, "There is no need for offense, when there are facts. Becky Kate, it is not okay to kick students out of your classroom . . . " before Linda could finish her sentence, Becky Kate burst into tears. "I felt attacked and genuinely scared for my life. So, I did what I needed to do." Linda looked at Becky Kate with incredulity. Linda thought, "I know Becky ain't about to try to use these old crocodile tears on me."

"Becky Kate, I was in the classroom with you. I observed everything. One, the disagreement was over how we historicize things. The student merely said ironically that the Civil War was about state's rights to enslave Black people. Not some abstracted notion of state rights. You began to raise your voice and embarrass the student. Secondly, do you really think the student was trying to hurt you, Becky Kate? C'mon. I was there and he simply disagreed with you." Realizing her tears had no purchase in the conversation, Becky Kate quipped, "Well, Linda, it doesn't matter what I think, clearly. Of course, you're going to side with him."

Taken aback, Linda probed, "What exactly does that mean, Becky Kate?"

"You know exactly what it means, Linda. Ever since we reopened this school after the hurricane you people have been making it about race. I'm not a racist and you know it! But according to the students and some of you, I am. I hold them accountable. That's what I do. I believe they need to have grit. And, yes, I have tough love. But for y'all," she says mockingly in a southern accent, "That's racist. What am I supposed to do when all everyone does here is play the race card! I'm doing all I can for those children."

Imani was outraged overhearing the things Becky Kate had said. As she walked closer to the room a student tapped Imani on the shoulder. Before Imani could turn around she collapsed.

What a strange thing Imani thought. Today was definitely bizarre. As she opened her eyes, she first saw the narrow hallway with the immaculate hard-wood floors. She quickly lifted herself assuming the student who tapped her would assist. However, there was no student in sight. Imani was puzzled. The student was just there. Maybe the student went off to get help. As Imani walked down the corridor she noticed the lockers were of a different color. Purple. Odd, Imani thought. The lockers at Beauregard were blue. A flash of nervousness struck Imani. Maybe she had fallen harder than she assumed. Walking in the hallway she stumbled upon a metal case enclosed in glass. That is when it dawned upon her. Something is very wrong. AGAIN. She looked at the pictures of graduating classes. They were all white and stopped at 1963! "What in the hell?" Imani whispered. "1963." Everything said Beauregard in the casing, but this wasn't the Beauregard she was most familiar. With her heart nearly beating out of her chest, Imani hastens her walk. She hears talking. Finally, help she thinks. Nearing the classroom, she hears voices that sound like Becky Kate and Ms. Linda.

"No, Bernice. We will not put those children in the same classroom as Beauregard pupils. You coloreds have already gotten so much over the last few years. What more do you want us to do? I am diligently working with you, trying to lessen fights and other disturbances. Most of which, your colored children are doing. But the social order, as we know it, has been undone. So, naturally, the Beauregard pupils will respond in kind."

"Margaret . . . "

`"Please call me, Mrs. Rimanelli, I prefer that, in fact."

"Mrs. Rimanelli, our children. All the children of Beauregard, White or Black, need teachers who care about them and don't ship them off into the basement of this school. Or, throw them into classrooms with teachers who don't even try to teach them."

"Bernice—Mrs. Bradford. You are being insubordinate! How dare you make such an assertion about me or anyone else in this school. As head teacher of the English Department and now having to deal with this miasma of court mandated desegregation edict, I am doing everything in my power to make you and your colored children feel comfortable in this place. You all refuse to follow any semblance of rule, of conduct, or of order. This is most assuredly why many of you colored teachers were fired, as well. You all create a hostile working environment for us."

Imani couldn't believe her ears. Where was she? Walking closer to the classroom she began to peer inside the room. She saw the two women talking, their body types resembled Kate and Linda, but they clearly weren't. Imani was horrified at what she heard and saw. She pulled out her iPhone to attempt to make a call or text or send a tweet. Something. Anything. Alas, nothing. Her phone wouldn't work. Imani attempted to reset her phone, but she dropped it. "Shit." The women pause from their conversation, as they too heard the thud. Petrified Imani folds into a ball. As Margaret walks to her door to look outside, she looks directly at Imani. As Imani opens her eyes she notices Margaret is faceless. Imani gently waves and says, "Hello." Margaret never notices or hears and walks back into the room. Imani stands, noticing Bernice is faceless as well.

Unbeknownst to Imani, Marie Laveau stands beside her. As the two faceless women continue to talk, Marie whispers in her ear startling her, "Mon chérie. Open your eyes, girl. Use your magic. Divine. Be a Seer." Imani turned around and there Marie was. Only to vanish. The fear had now dissipated and she was left with questions. What the hell is going on? Would she ever return to the present? How could such similar conversations be happening nearly sixty years prior? Why had she been transported to another time? Why had Marie Laveau chosen her? What was a diviner? A seer?

As Imani contemplated these questions, she felt gentle hands on her. She awakened. It was Linda, Becky Kate, Richard, and the student. Linda asked, "Are you okay? What happened, my dear?"

Too afraid to fully explain, Imani said, "I passed out."

"Well, we know that." Richard quipped.

"Becky Kate," Imani asked, "Would you be willing to drive me home tonight?"

"Of course" Becky Kate emphatically said. "But first we're going to the hospital."

"No, no. No hospital. I think I need a little rest and some hydration."

Becky Kate started her car and they were well on their way to Imani's house. Imani turned the music down. "Becky Kate, let me ask you something."

"Sure. Ask away."

"Why do you want to be department chair?"

Becky Kate replied with laughter, "Simple. It's mine to have and I get a little more say and money."

Imani interrupted, "But you actually don't have much experience at all and really don't know the children or their communities."

Becky Kate looked puzzled by Imani's comments. "Why would you say such a thing? You've never told me that before. And that really hurts. And you don't know much either."

"Becky Kate, I'm not trying to be department chair."

"Well, I know enough" Becky Kate said increasing the acceleration.

Not leaving it as is, Imani pressed further, "I mean, we're all just starting out, Becky Kate. Wouldn't it make sense for Ms. Linda to serve as chair? She's a phenomenal teacher. The parents love her and she has the experience. Plus, wasn't she the chair before The Storm?"

"I don't know or care what she was Imani. What is wrong with you? Why aren't you supporting me?"

Frustrated, Imani remarks, "Becky Kate, it's not about you actually. It's about the kind of leadership the children need and who can guide your department."

"Imani," Becky Kate said firmly, "it's been my dream to be department chair and I really think I can change these children's lives. We went to the same summer training. We went to the top schools in the nation. We deserve to be leaders. I deserve to be a leader. And those children are fortunate to have us."

Becky Kate kept her soliloquy going and Imani began to feel lightheaded. She closed her eyes for all of a second and she once again was transported, this time, however, into the future. Imani was back at Beauregard. She thought "not this shit again." As she walked the hall, she heard Becky Kate's voice. She peaked into the room to see a significantly older Becky Kate with other social studies teachers. It happened. Becky Kate was chair and she was discussing some draconian approach to teaching. The room of all white teachers disbursed, moving like robots. They all moved swiftly to the elevator. Fearing them, Imani ran to the foyer of the school; it was still beautiful. Vaulted ceilings, elegant staircases. But as Imani looked closer there was fresh blood dripping onto the otherwise pristine hardwood floors. "What is this?" thought Imani as she reached down to touch the blood. As she crouched down staring at the pool of blood she saw the reflection of Marie Laveau. Imani jumped up. "What do you want?!" she cried, panic sweeping over her soul. Marie Laveau smiled and repeated, "You need to open your eyes, girl." At this, Marie Laveau slowly pointed upward. Almost frozen of fear, Imani peered up to see the strange fruit, which hung from the top floor. There, she saw the body of a young looking Black woman. At first Imani did not recognize who the woman was. Her locks were hung beautifully much like Imani's. Almost entranced, Imani started up the stairs to get a better look. With each step her heart pounded. Oddly, as much as she wanted to know who the woman was, she was afraid to know. Finally, Imani noticed Becky Kate was leading a lynching of this woman. Imani was horrified. She pushed through the crowd at the top of the stairs. They didn't even notice she was there. Once at the top, Imani moved to raise the head of the hanging woman. There before her was a reflection of herself. This cannot be the future. This cannot be my future. The immense pain Imani felt ripped through Time and returned her to the present. Becky Kate was still talking. "These kids need order and rules. I can give them that, Imani."

Looking back at Becky Kate, Imani somberly responded, "I see now." Imani jumped out of the car weighted by the past, confused about the present, and perturbed about the future. Imani was provoked by Time and she knew this time she'd have to do something. Time had chosen Imani to be a guardian of it. For seeing Time's false chronology, Imani became Time's wound worker. Drifting in the hereafter of the past and lurking in the future of the now. Whatever was left was to be undone. And there is where she found her magic.

Chapter Sixteen

Slow Death by Becky

Cause, Asphyxiation

shelby "xhey" dawkins-law evans-el

I'm holding my breath. The wind whistles louder than my thoughts on this southern state day. Underneath closed lids I can feel the weather shift as clouds break. The sun streams through the trees, warming the darkened melanin of my face, shoulders, and hands. I feel heavy air around me stir and hot fumes almost lift me up as the smog dissipates. Rustling leaves sound something like applause, cheering for the sun coming out. I exhale and open my eyes to a scene of the thick, onetime permanent fog lifting. The ground swells full of promise rising above a sea of heavy pollution as the stench of civil war battles past clears the field. I am almost relieved—I want to be. All of a sudden the University banners crack in the wind as the weather shifts.

The battle isn't over. It's still happening.

After enjoying the warmth all of a sudden everything freezes. I am over- come by cold creeping into my toes and up my fingertips. I feel the iciness in my blood as it reaches to chill my spine . . . my stance is firm, but deep in the stillness something shifts beneath my feet. Steadfastness doesn't prepare me for what's coming. I squint, looking past the last few trees still standing on the horizon. I realize I am in the present day at my university that just had a white nationalist rally over a confederate statue in the quad. Confirming that the university quad was clear of the pedestal that contained the confederate monument, I surveyed the perimeter to make sure there were no more white nationalist rally members. Nothing. Even the white Becky who stood near the statue as a protective guard abandoned her post. The gates looked ragged from being shaken on both sides, stemming from the days of marches, rallies, and protests from white nationalists. The air was almost clear of its pepperi- ness now, but something still lingered.

Realizing all this white mayhem I am all of a sudden riddled with pain. I crack a hoarse cry as I choke on something I can't see. The pain quickly spreads through my nerves and my fingers twitch. My legs collapse from underneath me. On my knees, the palms of my hands blister. Something was holding me down.

The fog didn't lift, it was pushed.

As I try to pry myself back on my feet I hear a woman's cries in the distance. The smoky substance creeps into my ears as Her screams return. I can hear the horsewhip crack across Her back. I weep with Her. The tears sting too. Unable to lift myself, I crawl to the familiar stone table that rests upon the backs of my ancestors. My gaze softly narrows on the figurines of those enslaved on campus. They're still as sturdy as ever. Locking eyes, I lift myself up high enough to see the words etched on the stone tablet's surface but something is missing. I hear the crack of the whip again. "People bond and . . ."

nothing.

Someone removed the revisionist history from the only marker we have of my ancestral life. Black life. The slavers' pedestal is gone, but so is our only record that we built each seat at that table. The wind picks up again as I lock eyes with the figures I kneel before. Although their features are faded I can still see their purpose.

I startled awake from a nightmare I barely remembered. This happens a lot. Even when I take pills to sleep, I somehow never escape nightmares, only the panicked feeling which scares me too much to fall asleep on my own. It's in those moments of the late nights and early mornings that I am most afraid of my mind. Afraid with the spirits of ancestors who haunt me most when my mind thinks it is alone. Maybe it's this fear that poisons my sleep. Rather than reconciling the feeling, I let doctors' concoctions lull me into a sense of security that proves itself false when I wake up sweating. A drug that calms you down will only take you to a sunken place.

"It's supposed to be over now. This bullshit has got to stop"

I go to Confederate University. I know, it's ridiculous for a Black femme to go to a school with obvious enslaving roots, but the brochures ten years ago advertised a very different climate than is present today. I was coerced with promises of opportunities that I knew I couldn't afford, literally. That's how they did all of us Black "college bound" kids. Recruit, retain, release. You see, CU is one of those *public* ivies. All that means is the crimes against humanity on which the institution was founded were done for the benefit of all the "people" rather than only richest of the colonizers. Well, all white people.

I came to CU a decade ago to get an undergraduate degree. The weight of the debt accrued under false pretenses scared me into committing for graduate school. Now the amount is so staggering, I have no choice but to finish my "sentence" and hope for forgiveness. I'm 28 years old now and I have no idea where that $285,000 went. At CU, all you had to do was pass the exam at the end of each semester and boom, you get a check. In this case the check was an unfathomable amount of cash, far more than any teenager should be trusted with. In others, it was a check on a list of requirements that earned you a degree you could supposedly cash in for a job at the end. With a Bachelor of Arts in psychology that promise was tantamount to fraud.

But this university was wrought with errors. Recently, it made national news over the debates as to whether the confederate statue that prominently stood in the middle of the campus quad should be removed. It was also the site where white nationalist marches took place whereby students debated free speech versus hate speech. Contentious? It was. So despite having been a university built by the enslaved generations ago, the remnants of racial oppression lingers today.

Because of all this I enter this campus in a dialectical state. I mean, after all I am getting a graduate education here, right? But as I step foot on campus my breathing is both shallow and heavy now, struggling with the embodiment of racial tension. I carry all of my post-slavery stress that emanates from this university on my shoulders. This is precisely why Classmate Becky's bullshit pisses me off as much as it does. I made progress on my path to critical consciousness, having been raised by a single, middle-class mother who taught me that I was special; not like those other Black kids. Writing my life story through prose, poetry and paint had helped me reach a new level of racial consciousness. It took all of my might to suppress the anger boiling inside me that day. Becky's denial, her blame, her self-victimization . . . to think that her rights were somehow infringed upon by us asserting our humanity. Who was she to determine what is or is not racism? To deny its very existence. To try to gaslight me to a dark place. Let me explain below.

It was the last day of my last semester of classes for the PhD when Classmate Becky really tried my soul. After 20 semesters of dealing with shit from other Becky(s) like her from undergrad til now, I swear last week this Becky becked at me for the last time. After all the white nationalist rallies, the rhetoric of hate, and the support to keep confederate statues up, she had the nerve to argue against me in class, claiming white nationalist marches are simply free speech and I had to learn to be more tolerant. She argued this to me, a Black womyn from the south!! For generations we, Black folx, have had to live under the scrutiny of whiteness. I was tired of it. It was not right. My rage lost all eloquence and descended into anger and I don't even remember what I said to her but I'm sure there were some very choice words. I must've shown this anger in class because another Becky, Professor Becky, quickly disciplined me to behave. I was done. Checked out. Exhausted. So during our last class, instead of engaging in our last session on social justice in higher education (*the irony*) I chose to dig deeper into the latest book added to my inter library loan list. My laptop is open on google: "Geneva Crenshaw." I was deep in my rabbit hole when Classmate Becky broke my attention. She was hovering over me, clearly wanting to talk. *Fuck.*

A shiny figure draws closer, golden locks gently billowing in the smoke rising around her disturbing presence.

"Hi.. umm," says Classmate Becky.

I snap my laptop shut, rolling my eyes under closed lids. *What does she want?*

"So, I just wanted to apologize . . . "

I blink.

"Like . . . ya know, with everything thing that's happened I feel—," Becky's voice broke off.

"You mean the Klan rally?" I can tell I'm scowling at her now. My poker face gone.

"Yeah, that," Becky sighs.

"Look, I don't need your—"

"I just want to say sorry. I'm struggling to understand my whiteness and . . . it's just hard okay. And you're just so . . . " Becky struggles to find the right word to continue.

"Angry?" I offer.

" . . . intense. Like, and you know so much and when you share stuff it's like. Well yeah, she's smart, but that's pretty extreme," Becky continued struggling with her words.

"It's *they*," I correct her.

"Right, sorry."

Becky looks down at her hands, fingernails nearly bitten off til bleeding. *How long has she been freaking out . . . ?* I noticed her when she came in but deliberately ignored her after last week. I start packing my backpack, trying to cram my ultra-slim laptop between nearly ten different texts I had yet to finish.

"I just didn't realize racism was still, a thing," pleads Becky.

"A thing?" I asked with a raised eyebrow.

"Yeah, like. We don't get taught that in school so I just . . . I didn't know."

"Where are you from?" I ask.

"Huh? Like, oh—I'm from Lee County," Becky says almost shamefully.

"Lee?" *She would be from there.*

"Yeah . . . I know who it's named for . . . now," Becky says proudly.

"Did you know that's where those 'Klansmen' met up before coming here to rally on campus?"

Now her eyes were welling up with tears. I could feel it even though I wasn't making eye contact. *Don't comfort her. Don't be complicit.*

"I just—I'm learning. I know I shouldn't cry," starts Becky.

You haven't been given anything to cry about.

"White tears. I get it. I just, I mean . . . I just shouldn't even lead with this. I'm sorry. I'm working on being less white and—"

I cackled. I couldn't hold it in this time. "Let me stop you right there . . ." Before I could get the words out a loud snapping noise jars me out of my dissociation. I realize the noise came from me as I slammed my own laptop closed and blinked back to reality.

"Still there," Becky says.

I don't look at her so she slides a small envelope across the table. I can feel her attempt to have eye contact but the intensity fades quickly as she turns her gaze away. I can feel the shame wafting off of her. I continue packing my things as she looks down at my hands that have yet to welcome her gesture.

"No need to even open it," she stammers. The crackling inflection of her voice is gone. "I get it. Even throwing this away is emotional labor for you," she sighs. "Just know I'm sorry." She bows the slightest bit, intruding further upon my space, to which I finally glare in her direction, seeing through her. She quickly bolts out of the room. No more tears are in sight.

With her gone I hadn't noticed I was holding my breath the whole time she stood over me.

1 . . . 2 . . . 3 . . . 4 . . .

I exhale. I feel my jaw unclench and the blood return to my jaw and my face. I'd been holding in so much with her. Ruminating since last week's class where she proclaimed that all protests matter . . . not her exact words but the idea of the Klan coming to campus prompted her to invoke her 1st amendment rights rather than my inalienable rights to life. I guess the pepper spray and riot gear used on students, not terrorists as the campus tried to label them, had brought her into the light. Her pompous self-righteous air deflated when she saw white kids acting as a human shield against our own campus' newly-militarized cohort of top-flight security officers. But the hot air flowing from her punctuate ego polluted the atmosphere. Meaning, when she finally realized her insistence to support freedom of speech was nonetheless supporting hate speech the damage was already done. We're always left with the wreckage of their self-destruction.

I'd imagined dozens of scenarios since last week of how I would approach her in our last class. The preoccupation had exhausted me though. After nearly a week of ruminating I had to swallow my self-doubt to ask my professor for an extension provided in my accommodations. The psychic energy spent had reached full blown racial battle fatigue. Post-traumatic stress disorder is what I have an accommodation for, but that's because academic science hasn't caught up with what we know about the post-traumatic symptoms of being descendant of enslaved peoples.

Leaving the classroom, I check my phone. 27 notifications! Someone tagged me on Twitter post and it's been retweeted several times. Notifications keep rolling in as I open the app. It's Journalist Becky. She was well-meaning, at one point. Her retweets in support of removing the confederate statue got me a lot of followers early in the campaign to remove the statue. To support the cause, she interviewed me for a piece. I was hoping the administration would actually pay attention to it since it was a national outlet. Given the bring the statue down rally's wild success they probably rushed it to print. I scrolled through my mentions.

@JournalistBecky: "Check out my latest piece on the controversy at @ConfederateU Interviews include activist @thegradvocate board member @ChadChaddington

Though I was suspicious of sharing my story with her, I knew we, the campaign, initially needed visibility. But at this point we had plenty of that. Tweets were coming in. National publications were publishing articles about it. So when Journalist Becky kept coming back to me I felt her constant questions and needs were always emotionally draining. In fact, it became more about her than the movement. I couldn't take it anymore so I took to calling her out on Twitter. I tweeted, "You should probably do more homework" and "You are only focusing on the shallow facts and not deeper history." As more retweets rolled in, I got a notification for a DM from her. I know she was pissed. She loved to be viewed as an ally but when challenged she went back to plain old Becky. So, I ignored it.

My phone vibrated yet again, this time with an email. I rolled my eyes before the banner finished scrolling through . . . *From the Office of the Chancellor Official Communication*

what now?

As I scanned yet another official communication from the Chancellor Becky's office I was overcome with disgust at the latest episode in the saga. There was a time that I really admired her, back when my Black skin was used as a symbol of progress for the university. Back when I was "well-behaved" like a "good" little Black girl. During those times I had earned a seat at the table. They boasted about their invitation to me because I wore my Blackness so visibly yet not boisterously enough to be perceived as more threatening than my nearly 6ft frame already was. I used to negotiate my Blackness behind closed doors with only the certain students elected to highest office. However, the discussion of our university's monument to murder was off limits then. Plantation politics of respectability didn't allow for that conversation. Mounting evidence wasn't enough. It had to come from their own records. But they were scared now. I could read between the lines of their bullshit. I could codeswitch.

Protests had swept the nation in the wake of what university administrators referred to as "racial bias incidents." Our local Becky in Chief was no different in her casual and obligatory recognition of our protests. These emails have gotten pretty regular and even more mundane. In the past they spoke of racism as if it were new. For example, they spoke of the confederate statute as if they'd only just learned its meaning. Free speech as if we were all always afforded that right. The ahistorical approach to naming the problem was always at the crux of what was wrong with their solution. Today would be no different.

I remembered Chancellor Becky's smile as she gazed down at us during our direct action that past fall. Her performance was so on purpose then. Her lavender pantsuit made her stand out from the stage full of men behind her. She didn't flinch when we burst through the doors of the hall emblazoned with names of soldiers who fought and died for slavery. The Board was present but stoic. They shifted nervously in their seats clearly uncomfortable being encircled by Black bodies. Chancellor Becky continued to smile politely, waiting for us to finish. She was clearly not caught off guard. In that moment I wondered if someone had tipped her off.

Seething anger hissed between my teeth as I scrolled back to read each word in detail. Hot with anger, I snapped another screen shot and edited it with a circle drawn around the most offensive remarks. I opened my twitter app to fire off yet another angry thread of mentions.

@ConfederacyUniversity #ChancellorBecky is at it again. Our demonstration was not "an opening for productive dialogue." We're done talking. We're DE-MANDING! Remove the monument now or . . .

Pausing at my words the cursor impatiently flashed waiting for me to finish my thought. Reconsidering how to best phrase the tweet so as not to implicate myself in future acts. Writing and rewriting the tweet I copy and pasted drafts between my notetaking app and additional tweets to add to the thread. Exasperated, I walked to my car and reviewed each phrase, making sure to tag the relevant stakeholders. I'd learned that an op-ed was not nearly as effective as a carefully timed string of tweets. I tagged the student newspaper and a few local and national media outlets that'd all began following me months ago when the protests started. That's when Journalist Becky reached out to my DMs to interview me. I'd played this game before. Maybe this time the administrators would acknowledge the voice they'd been so initially happy to welcome as their "tokens" to tables; one in which I'd since been disinvited from.

The ding of another notification drew my attention back to the screen. I hadn't actually opened her email yet. I was dissociating again. I opened the app and tapped her name, nearly dropped my phone in shock.

Dear CU Family,

After careful consideration I have decided to resign from my position as Chancellor Effective June 30th. In my time here I've learned that both sides are not always to blame when ideological conflicts result in violence. This is true when the southern states seceded and it is true now. Though I knew this intellectually, it is only through the pain I witnessed here this weekend that I realized how my actions perpetuated a culture of hate-motivated violence. It is for these reasons that I have decided to step down from my position. CU needs someone with ethical ambition. Who will courageously take risks with humility, motivated by love. I have not done that in my tenure here and you need someone who can and will. While I like to think I could improve, I clearly have much more learning to do and it would be irresponsible of me to continue to learn on your time. I thank all of our community members, particularly our anti-racists activist leaders for the emotional labor to make this university a sacred, safe and loving space. We are not there yet, but in my last act as Chancellor I will follow their lead and remove the statue tonight. To the Black and Indigenous members of our community, I pray you may one day forgive me for my mistakes and outright willful ignorance. Nothing I can say or do will undo the harm I've caused. I can only do this one last act to demonstrate I know I was wrong and set a tone for my successor who will inevitably be responsible for not inciting another riot by outsiders. Thank you for your unwavering honesty and eloquent rage.

Sincerely,

Chancellor Becky

My heart felt like it wasn't beating. Ringing filled my ears and the drums popped with a force painful enough to make me shrink into the fetal position. My nose got that stinging sensation it gets right before it starts to run uncontrollably accompanied by tears that never seem to stop. I cried with my whole body, shaking, yelling. I should be happy but I'm not. I knew this wasn't the end and that it was about to get worse. As insidiously racist as she was, Chancellor Becky passive aggressiveness was our last line of defense from an overtly white supremacist state government that would unleash backlash that could result in another lynching on campus. The last six months of police surveillance was only the beginning.

Tired, I looked at the time on my phone. After all of this rumination I was still on campus, sitting in my car after 9:00PM. I could've cooked dinner by now, but feeding myself is a fugitive act and I was still on campus. I was about to finally drive off when another email arrived. It's Professor Becky from the class I just left. The subject line reads, "Last Week's Class." This time I can feel myself hold my breath. I click anyway.

Dear shelby,

I am writing to you about the incident in class last week between you and Becky. I understand that you were upset by her words. After spending time reflecting on how I could have been more of an ally to you, I want to apologize. It was not my intent to isolate you from your peers with my silence. I understand my intent does not negate impact. I am working to interrogate my privilege as a white woman and professor who holds the power in our classroom space. Thank you for your grace as we all continue to learn from you and our experiences being vulnerable with one another. I hope you can forgive me. I understand if you do not. I cannot ever be in your shoes, I can only make sure I'm not making it harder for you to move through life and do what I can to make it easier. I'm sorry.

Sincerely,
Professor Becky

Though the words are written almost perfectly, I don't trust her. Professor Becky and her kin wear flowy skirts and blouses that show their too many tattoos worn like a badge of otherness. The overly rehearsed earthiness is only trumped by her timely radical politics. Her only knowledge of oppression is extracted from womyn of color's work naming their trauma. She pimps it. She is among many but stands with none. Harnessing the power of the others' steadfastness, she regurgitates their race talk without an analysis of power or violence that goes beyond the corporeal. Which is why she's still committed to the state.

crack, Crack, CRACK!

My tear-filled eyes are blinded by sudden burst of accusatory red flashing light. I freeze. The cops! I hear blood pumping through my already ringing ears. My hands fumble with my phone searching for the shortcut to record video. I hear a muffled hello coming from an aryan assassin. None of my comrades in sight, all I can imagine was the hashtags and speculation that is unlikely to make it to the national news cycle. They'd blame me.

I'm in a parked car.

"Miss?" The voice said. "Are you okay?"

I stare blankly.

"Could you roll down the window?"

I fumble my keys into ignition to turn the power windows on.

FUCK! She's gonna think I'm running.

I turn the ignition off. My head aches with each pump of blood ringing through my ears dehydrated from draining all the tears I could cry in one day.

"Miss, it's okay," she says through the glass. Can you hear me?"

I nod.

"I just saw you crying and I wanted to make sure you're okay to drive. Do you need me to call someone?"

I shake my no. I'm holding the steering wheel so tight my knuckles reveal the traitor's hue within me.

"Okay, can I give you a number to call in case you feel panic?" she says in a deliberately human tone.

I nod.

"Here." she pulls the card out of her pocket, careful not to brush her firearm.

It's loaded.

"I'm just going to leave this under your windshield wiper okay? Please don't hesitate to call." I can finally see her soft sympathetic gaze but my eyes are too focused on surviving. As she walks away, I stay frozen there for what feels like hours. I finally exhale, I roll down the window but choke on clean air. The cold night air shocks my system. I continue to cry tearlessly until exhaustion overtakes me as I slump in my seat.

> *"Yea though I walk [in] the shadow of death I fear no evil. For thou art with me."*
>
>   *Psalm 23:4*

Though she'd long-since left the church, the verse—or what she remembered of it—echoed in her mind as she approached. As she meditated upon the counter narrative she constructed from oral histories of ancestors and peers, she closed her eyes and imagined. She imagined the scene of the day the others bragged about. A Black womyn's body writhing in pain, skirt in tatters . . . the crack of the horsewhip seemed to reverberate through her toes from the roots of the tree behind it. She let her fingertips graze the surface of that evidence the other planted. She could no longer muster the saliva required to spit upon their altar. Her mouth long-since grew dry from her hoarse screams. She looked at her hand, the hue of her skin, and revolted at the light-ness. Though her body was Brown, her Blackness was diluted. Diluted with each drop of white blood the other forced inside her foremothers. She wanted to claw at the Brown skin to remove the memory but knew that would only reveal more pale flesh underneath. Melanin was no longer enough to shield the burning light of day. She came prepared.

As she slid her fingertips into her back pocket she recoiled slightly as she felt cold steel. Pulling out the blade, her hand began to shake. The pale flesh of her palms began to sweat, as if knowing danger was upon them. The blade almost slipped from her sweaty fingers as they shook with every beat of her heart. Poetic. She felt the cold steel blade press against her right palm and a drop of hot, red blood escape from her body. As she dragged the blade further across her lifeline, blood gushed with the force of thousands of teardrops she'd cried upon the hallowed ground on which she stood. A steady stream began to form as she clenched her fist around the wound, as if she was trying to wring out the blood that stained the hands of her one-time masters. The blood dripped on the grass, seeping into the already blood-soaked earth. She no longer feared the pain she'd felt before. She feared the pain she'd feel if things went unsaid. Undemonstrated. She clenched her fist tighter, squeezing blood onto the steps of the monument the other built to their original sins. She must have nicked an artery because when the first drop touched the marble steps the blood began to flow like the river. It splashed, splattering the façade of the stone altar. Finally, the theatre looked like the crime scene it had always been. In the distance, the unsung stood from their kneeling position, lifting the weight of the world that once pressed upon their backs as they climbed from the depths of graves marked by idolatrous arrogance. "It's happening." She need not speak a whisper for her ancestors to hear. Her prayer was louder than her spirit. She was PhinisheD.

Section Seven

Guiding Questions

1. In "Present Tense" how does Becky Kate act in violent ways toward Imani and others? Imani continues to have dizzy and headaches that indicate a story shift, however, how can her headaches be a metaphor for how people of color deal with the violent ways of Becky(s)? Have you had experiences where you physically or mentally got ill because of the behaviors of Becky(s) in your life? Describe the circumstances that made you ill.
2. How is understanding the violence behind the behaviors of Becky(s) instructive? What can be said about this kind of violence? How does it differ from more masculinized ideas about violence? How can we better protect ourselves?
3. In "Slow Death by Becky" the main character encounters several Becky(s) throughout her day. How does this impact her state of mind? Her sense of self? Her relation to her education? Her interaction with the officer?
4. Why is it more dangerous to presume the innocence of Becky(s)? How does this characterization further complexify the violence? Have you experience violent behaviors from a Becky before? How has it impacted you?
5. If you are a white woman, in what ways are you ensuring your rhetoric, behaviors, and emotions are not violent? Are you willing to be told when they are violent? Consider how you might respond.

Section Eight

Becky(s) as Manipulators and Gaslighters

The 1944 film, *Gaslight*, depicts a couple in which the man (played by Charles Boyer) manipulates the surroundings to such an extent that the lead woman (played by Ingrid Bergman) ostensibly feels like she is going crazy. From moving house items and pretending he did not do it to lowering the gas to flicker the lights, the man is able to convince the woman that she is not only going crazy, but that because of her delirium, she should give him complete control of her estate. Spoiler alert. Although caught in the end of his wrongdoings, the viewer comes to find out the man is none other than a con man trying to mask his own criminal activity.

This same manipulative theme was replicated in the 2016 movie, *Girl on the Train*. In this film actor, Emily Blunt, is made to believe that she is nothing but an alcoholic, and that her alcoholism ruins her family and marriage. As the film goes on, she comes to understand that her entire marriage was wrought with psychological, sexual, and physical abuse so much so that she blocked out reality. She realizes her husband cheated on her with several women, murdered one, and so twisted reality with physical and psychological abuse that Emily was unsure of what was true anymore.

This twisted type of manipulation is what constitutes gaslighting; a form of psychological manipulation where an abuser abuses her power to engage in tactics that denigrate, confuse, and disorient the abused. In fact, racism writ large is a gaslighting tactic whereby people of color are made to believe—by the white racially privileged—that race is not a thing when they experience race everyday. Denying the racial realities of people of color thus leaves them to wonder, "Was it me, but was that racist?" Some even go as far to explain a racially microaggressive experience and then say "but that's not about race." It is almost as if dominant society has gaslighted people of color to a point where they begin to question their own experiences, truths, and realities.

This is of grave importance because in K–12 education rarely is anything negatively said about the relationships between teacher and K–12 student. Movies depict white saviors coming into urban jungles complete with ungodly students of color. Books about care, love, and empathy in teaching glitter our teacher education libraries. Even the teacher education students themselves are quick to engage the term love when asked why they want to become a teacher. In my own college courses, one by one, teacher candidates share aloud that the reason they want to become a teacher is for the simple fact of loving kids. I find this a unique rationale because, sadly, so do pedophiles. Though I am not making light of the situation, in fact, I think quite the opposite.

What preoccupies me most is exactly what kind of love is being felt or expressed such that my pre-service teachers believe themselves to be giving it out when the literature by many scholars of color demonstrate that students of color are not feeling the love. Or, per Valenzuela (1999), if teachers are already caring for their students then why is Valenzuela demanding an authentic care? Furthermore, if empathy is already a given in the teaching profession, then why are scholars of color like Duncan (2002a) articulating the presence of false empathy in his own experiences with teacher candidates? Duncan (2002b) even discusses the sentiment of love, more precisely the lack thereof, for African American male students, claiming, "As a consequence, the black male students at CHS have little chance for appealing to those who hold these institutional views of them. They, in short, are 'beyond love'" (p. 136). Clearly, students of color are experiencing a loveless state of education. Coates (2015), for instance, describes his schooling as follows:

> To be educated in my Baltimore mostly meant always packing an extra number 2 pencil and working quietly. Educated children walked in single file on the right side of the hallway, raised their hand to use the lavatory, and carried the lavatory pass when en route. Educated children never offered excuses—certainly not childhood itself. The world had no time for the childhoods of black boys and girls. [So] How could the schools?" (p. 25)

Clearly, he does not have favorable memories of schools. The point here is that although there are pontifications of loving kids, caring about students, or empathizing with the students' lives, students themselves say that ain't true. Yet, because K–12 students (as children themselves) do not have the power to attest or directly challenge the narrative of how white women teachers simply love their students, they are gaslighted to believe that they are. Herein lies the gross manipulation—as teachers mistreat their students, they first twist reality of their mistreatment by never owning up to it and second, they pretend to care and love them. And in this twisted relationship, the students are gaslighted.

This same manipulation qua gaslighting is seen when the majority of white administrators in academia pretend that they are instituting something to "help a faculty grow" when in the end, all they are trying to do is control the faculty member by issuing erroneous suspensions or exacting their power by curbing their annual merit pay. Particularly for women of color academics, white female administrators who are Becky(s) as Manipulators and Gaslighters grossly abuse their power through these manipulative and gaslighting tactics. They do this by ensuring that they control the narrative of the woman of color, as if the woman of color herself does not know what she is experiencing. Then, they try to convince the woman of color and all her colleagues that she is the problem as a way to isolate her and that the woman of color faculty member simply needs to "take responsibility" for actions that are not her own. These Becky(s) wield their power to ensure that the woman of color's background, her side of the story, or even her humanity is never heard, seen, or recognized. Instead, she focuses her energies in creating a narrative that so denigrates the woman of color faculty member that the woman of color eventually pulls away, disconnects, or self-isolates.

And when this happens, this Becky will pounce on the woman of color blaming her for her protective state—one which she had to develop to withstand all the hostile manipulations. To be clear, this protective state is no different than K–12 students of color who are constantly mislabeled the bad student and, in doing so, retreat from school. Similarly, faculty of color, particularly women faculty of color, retreat from the departments, faculty meetings, schools, or universities because, frankly speaking, they are done with the manipulation and abuse and have found life, success, and happiness beyond the control of these Becky(s). Of course, this will further anger Becky(s) as Manipulators and Gaslighters precisely because they feed off their manipulation of others. Just as the perpetrators described in the films above, Becky(s) as Manipulators and Gaslighters have no remorse. In fact, they engage in these manipulative tactics criminally. Their goal is to so demoralize a person such that the person has no other choice than to accept the state of abuse. As such, these types of Becky(s) are highly dangerous to folks of color. Since they are already masters, more precisely, mistresses of deception, these Becky(s) will not only gaslight everyone; she will then turn around and feign the façade of a righteous human being. These Becky(s) are the ones who boast how great they are in equity or diversity, claiming they help everyone, when, in fact, what they do is wreak havoc in the lives of people of color.

Although one may find it easier to believe a male narcissist would engage in gaslighting behaviors to control his reality and manipulate women, realizing that same gaslighting and manipulative powers of a Becky is another. Because of whiteness and how white women are stereotyped as innocent, the mere thought of her insidiousness is, at times, unfathomable. As such, be careful, for as these women smile a seemingly innocent smile, they do so under the guise of deceit. The stories in this section explore Becky(s) as Manipulators and Gaslighters in metaphoric ways. Whether by assuming bodies of color in a science fiction realm or creating Black women to do the biddings of white women, the stories nonetheless fixate on the mechanisms of manipulations that Becky(s) employ. For one author, a man of color, the process of manipulation and gaslighting was particularly personal within his experiences in academia such that he wrote his story to be a warning to others. He writes the following:

> I hope that students of Color will read this chapter and feel validated about listening to their cultural intuition when they sense something is off. Academia can be a isolating, challenging, and at times an outright bizarre place. Beckys contribute to this isolation then capitalize on it by gaslighting us into believing that they are our one and only ally. They create a false sense of security and dependence in order to exploit our labor and intelligence for their own professional gain. That is why when pursuing lofty educational goals, C. Gambino reminds us that "if you want it . . . You can have it . . . But stay woke"

The authors of another story write a similar cautionary remark. They write, "Readers should recognize the manipulative motives of some Becky(s) though cloaked in concern and the false sense of alliance and partnership." These authors then talked about the dangers of dealing with Becky(s) as Manipulators and Gaslighters by writing, "When confronted with the truth, these manipulators have been known to blame Black women, attempting to build themselves up by tearing down the Black women in their proximity in an attempt to destroy them and discredit their being and relevance." As aforementioned above, these Becky(s) are highly manipulative and have lived their lives discrediting folks of color, particularly women of color, precisely because they see women of color, Black women mostly, as their arch nemesis.

However, one of the stories' authors wanted to warn her readers not only of white women exhibiting these Becky traits. Instead, she offers a caution to folks of color who are so lured by whiteness that sadly engage in Becky-like behaviors themselves. She writes the following:

> Whiteness can be seductive. I am certainly not exempt from that—from the clothes I wear, to what I eat, much of what we do, even when we are being more critical and conscious of our decisions, has some connection to whiteness. When I was thinking about this particular story, I was thinking primarily about my transition into a faculty role at a university of higher education. As faculty, students, or employees of the university, we are rewarded when we enact whiteness. Though I myself make every effort I can to not give into whiteness, I have

witnessed first hand how people have done it and in turn receive benefits. This story was written with those thoughts in mind—what does it mean to continue to exist in a world where whiteness attempts to seduce you whenever/wherever it can? How do we as folks of color who are critically consciousness of whiteness and white supremacy continue to fight against whiteness even when it can mean we lose tangible benefits?

Just as I have written about whiteness internalizing into people of color in my book, *Feeling White,* so too can the behaviors of Becky(s). In fact, in private discussions with women faculty of color around the nation, many divulged how their most treacherous betrayals came from other folks of color (students and faculty alike) who found ways to work whiteness in the academy to their benefit at the expense of another. That whiteness can be so alluring is a painful reality. And these individuals who use whiteness to their benefit to enact harm on women faculty of color do so without remorse because in the end, they know that by using it (qua feigning victimhood, pointing the finger at the power hungry Brown faculty member, not taking responsibility for their own aggressive behaviors that led to a faculty member trying to protect herself, even feeling self-righteous for enacting harm, etc.) they were offered some twisted form of protection. Worse yet, some believe they had to use whiteness as some perverted sense of social justice, much like how one might utilize Derrick Bell's interest convergence to get ahead. Clearly, these individuals are not social justice warriors. They and their behaviors are, as one author writes, "not ok, it was not just, it was not equitable." But knowing these types of Becky(s), they will never own up to their wrongdoings even though I hold out hope that they will.

REFERENCES

Coates, T. (2015). *Between Me and the World.* New York: Spiegel & Grau.

Duncan, G. A. (2002a). Critical race theory and method: Rendering race in urban ethnographic research. *Qualitative Inquiry, 8*(1), 85–104.

Duncan, G. A. (2002b). Beyond love: A critical race ethnography of the schooling of adolescent Black males. *Equity & excellence in education, 35*(2), 131–43.

Valenzuela, A. (1999). *Subtractive Schooling: U.S.-Mexican Youth and the Politics of Caring.* Albany: State University of New York Press.

Chapter Seventeen

Facing the Becky Within[1]

Socorro Morales

About 120 years ago, sleeving was only in its infancy stages. And back then, to a much higher degree than now, it was only available to the select rich and white elite. Sleeving, the process of physically moving your consciousness into a body you were not born with, revolutionized how we thought about and perceived death. Specifically, sleeving allows the mind to exist in a realm of its own, known as a cortical stack, until ready to be inserted into the neck of a new body. Though a stack can survive a body's physical destruction and death, stacks are ultimately not indestructible themselves—a person's consciousness can be killed permanently if their stack is destroyed.

Human history has always been perceived to move linearly in a natural progression (i.e., savage to civilized), even though Indigenous ways of knowing have come to understand time as cyclical and reoccurring in waves (i.e., rebirth). Because so much of how the world functions revolves around white supremacist ideologies, little regard has been given to the interaction and relationship between the Earth and its inhabitants, most notably humans. As a result of the realities of global warming, the polar ice caps have melted, pollination had to be genetically engineered because bees have died off, and face masks are a regular part of one's attire because of the high concentration of pollutants in the air. And in the midst of the Earth dying a slow death, we managed to find a way to extend the life of the same elitists who have killed it—thus the birth of sleeving.

Though the technology tied to sleeving has shifted over time, those who can have access to it have largely not changed. For the rich white elite—it has provided an avenue to live forever. Some of the most poor people of color may never have the funds or be approved for the credit to get a new sleeve, thus, their lives have largely been unaffected and as a consequence, often have the shortest life span. There are of course underground ways to obtain sleeves, but often those are laced with diseases in hopes that the poor who buy them will be killed off faster.

My name is Esperanza Ramirez. Reclaiming Identities in School for Empowerment (R.I.S.E.) is the agency that I work for. I have been with the agency since its inception. Conceptually, I believe in what I do. And I am also damn good at it. I am a highly skilled and trained Decolonizing of the Mind Agent, or DMA. I, like my colleagues who are both white and of color, am charged with the task of uncovering white supremacist ideologies lodged deep into the psyches of both white and folks of color. Though we work together as a whole, we are each separated into different units or squads based on skills, expertise, and training. I am specifically tasked in working with Latinx and Chicanx communities because of my own background as a Chicana and my lived experiences, but also because of the training that I have received in understanding educational issues pertaining to these particular communities. All DMAs are responsible for continually engaging in this de-colonizing of the mind process—we are expected to read, reflect, discuss, and assess ourselves every month. We do this within our own ethnic and racial group, but also across racial and ethnic lines.

I take my face mask off as soon as I enter the Moore Building, R.I.S.E. headquarters in Downtown Los Angeles. I place it, dirty and dusty, into the face mask sanitizer machine located near the entrance. In five seconds, my face mask is good as new. I fold it into my jacket pocket as I enter the elevator—4th floor, Mateo's office, director of this location. He has a new assignment for me.

"Well damn! I knew we didn't fuck up when we recruited you!" Mateo shouts in between swigs of water. He claps his hands loudly as he stands up. On his desk are scattered files, a tall nameless bottle with two shot glasses next to it, and the artificial light that we all use in our cubicles to mimic the sun.

"You really don't have to stand every time I do something right, otherwise you won't ever sit," I say with a slight smile as I sit in front of his desk.

"I always liked your confidence," Mateo says as he pours whatever is in said nameless bottle into each of the two glasses. "Plus, it gives me an excuse to bring out the good stuff. Home brewed," he says as he hands me a shot glass. "Don't even ask me what's in it because I actually don't know this time. Cheers."

I take the shot glass, clank it against his desk, smile at Mateo and chug it. It's actually smoother than I was expecting, even though it burned all the way down.

"You identifying that whole school out there in Fontana was really impres-sive. Rather than taking them out to a DS, we just brought it to them. Teachers, staff, some of the students and parents that you identified. We got them all. Great work."

DS. Disinfect Site. Where we run everyone who needs to decolonize their mind and consciousness through a set of procedures that can help them start that process. Some continue that decolonization process after they leave. Some need multiple treatments to even see why their participation in a DS is necessary. And some never recover and remain locked in a colonial abyss, refusing to find their way out. Mateo seems hopeful about everyone recovering from this one.

"As always, your work is impressive. Which is why I'm going to direct your expertise and skills to a slightly different but as you know related project. You received the memo I'm sure from main headquarters about 'double stacking'? And this whole 'Bequis' (pronounced Beckies) situation?"

"I did get the report, yes. Double stackers—those who have embedded two consciousnesses into one body. In our case, most often referencing a white consciousness that has infiltrated a body of color. I know that with the rise of the number of white stacks infecting bodies of color, we are working toward understanding this phenomenon within our respective units in more depth. What's taking center stage now within the Latinx unit are the Bequis that you mentioned—Latinas who embody whiteness."

"That's right. And as you already know, double stacking means that whiteness has a spectrum. Initial reports coming from your colleagues across the nation have shown that there are people of color who believe in social justice, and even embody it in terms of what they dedicate their life to. But buried deep down, they have internalized whiteness. And those forms of consciousness, remained locked together-intertwined."

R.I.S.E. realized long ago that the issue of white supremacy is everyone's issue, and that white people have a specific role. White DMAs target white teachers, white administrators, and white schools who perpetuate white supremacy. They send them to DS' that provide tools for the white mind to decolonize itself. We have always known that white supremacy would need white people as a part of the fight to combat it. But what has become perverse and insidious in this day and age is the way that people of color, to their own detriment, believe in whiteness. Targeting the sleeves of people of color with white stacks is crucial to undermining this project of internalized racism.

"I know that this is a natural progression of where R.I.S.E. is going but I'm actually a little surprised that it took you so long to cue me in on this, Mateo," I say as I cross my right leg over my left. My right boot scrapes across Mateo's desk slightly as I move my foot.

"Esperanza, you're smart enough to know that you would be involved eventually," Mateo says as he leans back in his chair. "But I wanted to get the initial reports first before sending you in. You're my best agent. We both know this. But I hope that you understand this is a dangerous time for people like you. Even though they are hiding themselves, these Bequis are out here in droves—serving as undercover agents for the Daughters of American Values (D.A.V.). The white women at D.A.V. are using their resources to have white stacks infiltrate Latinx bodies and serve as 'role models' for 'good' Latinx folk. They then use their economic power to reward these Bequis so that Latinx peoples can see that if they change their behavior and absorb whiteness, it will lead them to greater economic and social prosperity. Essentially, they *want* Latinx to want to be white, like the racial category they were given on past census data."

"Spare me the details, Mateo, you already know who you're talking to. I've been here since the beginning of R.I.S.E. I know how whiteness works. I break it down every time I take on a new apprentice for R.I.S.E., which by the way, you have yet to give me the info for this new one I'm meeting today. I've mentored and graduated 70 agents over the years. I can identify the traits of the Bequis because I understand whiteness so well. I know that she can use her identity to deny that racism exists. For example, she uses her financial mobility or success to promote the idea of, 'well I did it, so can every other Brown person' type of deal. If she was/is an immigrant or has parents who were/are immigrants, she says stuff like 'well they [and I] got their [our] papers the right way,' completely ignoring how immigration law works and changes over time. She can also be anti-Black, which has many dimensions to it, but in particular it can relate to the idea that she doesn't want to be in the sun because she will 'get too dark.' Or she might not want to have children with a Black person because their children will 'be dark.' And while she may espouse all of this rhetoric, she may herself be dark-skinned or someone who would not be perceived as white. She also says that Latinx students do poorly in education because their parents 'just don't care' and therefore, their status on the economic ladder comes from their own lack of individual effort, not systems of oppression. In an effort to distance herself from first generation immigrants, even if she herself is one, she may express shame or embarrassment around the Spanish language. She may, for example, decide to respond to her Spanish speaking family members in English even when they are speaking Spanish, or say that at least she's not like 'those paisas' who don't speak English. In effect, she hates herself. And the worse part of it is that she doesn't realize how her actions of self hate are rooted in white supremacy."

"Well done. I know that you have been around long enough to understand how white supremacy manifests itself and how it has adapted over time. But I do want you to heed my warnings on this one porque a veces eres muy terca. You're good at what you do. But these Bequis spare no one—they will take you down if they get the chance. Trust that the D.A.V. has information on our most high profile agents, and that includes you."

"Alright, Mateo, I'm hearing you. I really am. I'm just pumped. You gotta trust me on this one. Just hand me the next assignment you got. I'm ready to go full force."

Mateo sits in silence as he looks at me for what feels like a long time, but in reality is probably only ten seconds. I can almost read what he is saying to himself in his head, "terca, terca, terca," but we have been through this back and forth before on other assignments. I'm not sure why he thinks this time will be different.

"Ok, well here's the folder on Project Bequi Extraction" Mateo says as he hands me a clasped binder folder, with no identifiers on the outside, but a number of divider tabs on the inside. "It has everything you need including briefs from around the nation, common Bequi phrases reported by R.I.S.E. agents, and your next target who is a Latina superintendent in the Rolling Heights School District. Also, the name of your new apprentice is Ixchel Hernandez. Her info is on the first page. Real promising, former school teacher in San Diego. She's really looking forward to meeting you."

I stand up from my seat, place the folder into my brown messenger bag, and pour another shot from Mateo's nameless bottle into my shot glass. I pick it up and drink it swiftly. "Thanks for this. I won't let you down," I say as I take the face mask out of my jacket. I turn and head for the door—I'm supposed to be meeting with Ixchel soon.

"Esperanza, remember what I said about this project. Your name says it all. You give us hope for the future of undoing white supremacy. Please take care of yourself because we need you," Mateo says.

I don't turn my body, but I nod my head when I hear Mateo's comment. "I know you do," I say as I open the door to exit his office.

I stare down at my watch—it's almost time to meet with Ixchel. She had already come into town a few hours prior.

The walk from the Downtown metro station to Grant Rea Park is only about ten minutes. Overshadowing the tall skyscrapers iconic of LA is a thick cloud of dark smog—it hasn't rained in who knows how long now. I honestly don't even remember. Honking can be heard from the bustling evening commute and cars practically on top of each other. The demolition of a building is also heard faintly in the distance. Probably some new lofts, I thought. My phone beeps twice—it's Ixchel:

"Here. See you in a few."

"On my way," I reply, and shove the phone back in my jacket pocket. A dog barks and growls at me as I speed past it. Ixchel wanted us to meet at a public park, which I used to enjoy long ago when the sun would still emerge regularly. Now, most parks are just deserted pieces of dirt, which is why I found it interesting that Ixchel chose a park to meet up.

I enter Grant Rea Park through the main entrance, walking through the old, algae covered gate that hangs on by a small hinge on the right corner where I see Ixchel sitting at a lone table bench. I can only see the top half of her face since the bottom is covered by her face mask.

"This place is pretty empty as I was expecting," are the first words that come out of my mouth as I sit across from Ixchel. The bench seat, which is made of stone, feels cold on my body as I sit.

"I guess, I sometimes reminisce about the days when people would actually come to parks to socialize," Ixchel says. Her dark brown hair sits at her shoulders, covering her ears. Her eyes match the color of her hair.

"Well you know those days are long gone," I say with a sigh, fixing my face mask with my left hand and adjusting my messenger bag with my right.

Ixchel utters a slight laugh. "Consider me old school."

"Will do," I say. "So, shall we get down to business? I'm sure you have quite a bit of questions. Everyone always does."

Ixchel blinks her eyes a few times before responding. "Of course I do. But let me start by saying that I'm happy to finally be meeting you. I've read and heard so much about you."

I smile under my face mask. "Well, you can't always believe the hype. We all have to come to our own conclusions. But thank you, I appreciate that."

"With that said, I do have some questions. I'm trying to make sure that I fully understand what I learned in training. You know, to be honest, I had a hard time believing some of the concepts. Uh, let me take that back. Not necessarily *believing*, but maybe putting the concepts in a context is more what I mean."

Hmm, I think to myself. Believing? "Can you tell me more about what concepts specifically? That would help me out."

"Yeah ok. Um, let's see . . . I'm not sure that I fully get why there would be investments from white people to have DMAs? What would they gain from that?"

I feel a sense of relief when Ixchel asks her question. For a moment there, her use of the word 'believe' gave me some concern, given that it reminds me of the many times that the white elites say they don't believe that racism can exist because they have never experienced it themselves. Believing the stories of those on the margins, is one of the first lessons that agents learn. "I could see how those answers are not as spelled out as they should be. The real answer is almost impossible to believe. You see, back before the emergence of sleeves and stacks, whites and, I suppose, people of color as well, but whites in larger proportions, managed to elect a white supremacist to the presidency. White supremacy had already existed, of course, in every walk of life from institutions to everyday microaggressions. But the election of a white supremacist president who so blatantly represented whiteness openly and without remorse, was unprecedented. So much so, that white people actually scared themselves. Neo-nazis who had remained primarily clandestine, rose up and were no longer afraid to show themselves. White folks had never considered so seriously the question of what would happen if their own whiteness went unchecked—they were too used to marginalized groups and people of color keeping them in line. But that year, it went too far. And they realized that even though they were white, they had finally engaged in a process that would lead to their own demise."

"But how did that process lead to their own demise? I don't think that I've ever considered *myself* what it would mean for white people to be afraid of whiteness."

"Well," I said and paused slightly to shake my right leg, which had a fly on it, "believe it or not, even white folks have limits to their whiteness. It got to the point where white people were trying to 'out white' each other. The poor white folks became increasingly restless and angry that they were losing medical benefits, jobs, and the supposed privilege they felt they had. Part of the reason was that people of color rose up, but they also created their own autonomous communities. They began banding together in enclaves and leaving the white folks to their own devices. They created independent, underground trading systems among themselves that were able to sustain everyone. They created and developed communities where they were accountable to one another, and not the 'white master.' They educated themselves and their people in the ways of being that were not grounded in Eurocentric ways of knowing. Without a clear scapegoat, white folks were scapegoating themselves."

Ixchel furrows her eyebrows. "Ok, so then there is where I get stuck. How were people of color organized enough to create their, I mean, our own communities? I feel like they, I mean we, are super disorganized, even lazy. Like Latinos for instance, you know we always be running late to everything. When I used to be a teacher, my Latino parents always showed up late or didn't show up at all to school hosted events. I always thought to myself 'but this is your kid that we are talking about here, don't you care!' Like come on, now! How are we supposed to get anyone to pay attention to us if we keep slipping up and looking lazy?"

Her comment puts me on alert. Something's not right.

"Ixchel, those sound like stereotypes about Latinx communities to me. No te parece?"

Ixchel laughs loudly. "That sounds so paisa. You know what I'm saying. If Latinos just worked harder, then they could get to where they want to be in life. They could stop blaming white people for all their problems you know? White people have it hard too. They experience reverse racism and no one believes them! I feel like I'm trying hard to bring up my Latinos but I can't do it alone! Latinos need to put in the work instead of thinking the system is against them."

It is in this moment that I realize I'm knee deep in shit. Ixchel is a damn Bequi! She's staring me right in the face, a Latina, claiming that Latinos need to get over their problems without considering how structures impact those issues. Everything she has been sharing with me, including her indignant tone, confirms this. There's no nuance to her understanding of structural racism and white supremacy. These thoughts continue to race through my head as I think of a game plan. This is not good. I keep my eyes fixated on Ixchel, but I use my right hand to reach into my pocket. I have to use my tranquilizer to stop her. All I need to do is keep her talking and stab it into her arm as fast as possible.

"You know what, now that I think of it, you are making some good points. Like you're right, Latinos need to rise up together and not be lazy. Like how are we going to change the narrative if we don't own up to our own deficiencies?"

"Exactly! You get me," Ixchel says. "That's why the R.I.S.E. training was such a joke. Like hello, of course white people have all the . . . "

I didn't let her finish. I knew I had to act before she became too suspicious. As quick as a glimmer of light, I reached across the table and stabbed her left arm with the tranquilizer. It activated instantly. I could see Ixchel's eyes widen as I reached over, but I was too fast for her reaction. Once stabbed, she was out cold, face lying down on the table. I breathe a sigh of relief. Damn, Mateo wasn't kidding. No wonder he was so worried. Fuck. I have to call this in.

"You didn't think we would let her come alone did you?" I hear from behind me. I try quickly to turn my head to see who it was, but I'm too late. Everything goes black.

"Hey Esperanza, I've been waiting for you to come into the office to try this new batch of drink. You know how Jimmy loves to make new concoctions. That's one of the reasons why I married him. He's such a creative person and a damn good cook!"

Esperanza flirtatiously places her bag down on her desk before turning to look at Mateo, batting her eyelashes. "Mateo, you silly. You know I hate the taste of alcohol. Or, did you forget that I turned you down the last time you offered?"

Mateo stares at Esperanza with a confused look on his face. "Um, well . . ." he starts but is unable to finish his sentence because Esperanza cuts him off.

"And you know I've been meaning to talk to you about this whole Bequis thing. I think we have it all wrong. I feel like Latinos need the elite whites to help give them the tools for success. Don't you think?" Esperanza slowly tilts her head to the side and smiles a patronizing smile to Mateo.

Then, everything goes white.

NOTE

1. The following narrative is a fan fiction account using the premise of the dystopian world put forth by the 2002 novel and 2018 Netflix series *Altered Carbon*.

Chapter Eighteen

The Case of Becky the Mad Beckologist and Dejanae the Humanoid

Leta Hooper and Wyletta Gamble-Lomax

In the year 2235, the Critically Conscious Afro Diaspora ancestral ghosts communed and organized their spiritual energy to gather billions of galaxies together to create a mid-size planet called Sankofa. Sankofa was 2458.42 million miles away from the following Earth and Mars. The ancestral ghosts created Sankofa to be a planet that delivered the long legacy promise of Afrodiasporic liberation for Indigenous people and people of color. In essence, Sankofa was a safe haven; a liberated, and radical healing space that responded to the multiple centuries of violence and traumas that are rooted in whiteness, toxic masculinity, capitalism, imperialism, and colonization found on Earth. The lush green terrain and untainted natural resources preserved the livelihood of animals and people.

Sankofa sparked the interests of government officials, scientists, and citizens who resided in the colonized territories of planet Earth and Mars. It emerged interests and curiosity of explorations by so many people. Because the ancestral ghosts were well-equipped and too familiar about the workings of colonization and whiteness, they created an invisible force known as the Mahogonyites that delivered a strong nuclear reaction that severely affected people's physical and mental conditions.

Operating effectively, Sankofa functioned and thrived independently without the economic, social, and political structures of white supremacy. The Mahogonyites delivered a visceral reaction to specific populations who were clueless about the negative impact of Western ideologies and opted to maintain their societal privileges of race, class, religion, gender, body function and image, and sexuality.

By the mid-year of 2235, the Black Feminystas were the first group of people to inhabit Sankofa. They collectively organized and created spaceships that easily transported them back and forth between their homelands and Sankofa. By the end of 2235, 1.5 billion of Indigenous and people of African descent lived productively in Sankofa.

It did not take an extensive period of time for officials of the Gallatic Whiteness Council, which was comprised of liberals, conservatives, Evangelicals, Republicans, and members from prominent alt-right and right wing organizations to be aware about the fast-paced shift of the racial and ethnic demographic of people on planet Earth. Because of the swift and uncontrollable tracking, mass exodus of African descent people on planet Earth, the Gallatic Whiteness Council started to be concerned about the demographic shift that would no longer be sustainable to maintain the long legacies of myths and lies centered on inferiority about people of the African Diaspora. Instead, living on a "White Only" planet will expose the fallacies of rhetoric regarding people of color and revoke the privileges from people of color who identify as white.

People who were talented and known as organic intellectuals occupied Sankofa. The collective Black excellence intellectuals led to the development of a liberated post-secondary institution in 2240. The post-secondary institution is known as Afrodiasporic University. Afrodiasporic University was known for producing high tech goods or resources. It did not take long for the colonized planets, Earth and Mars, to depend on the goods of Sankofa.

Sankofa attracted the interests of many outsiders, especially white people. The founders of Afrodiasporic University followed the legacy and mission of the Critically Conscious ancestral ghosts and decided to make the admittance process restrictive. Admittance to Afrodiasporic University was a multi-layered critical screening procedure. The transformation of the application process was in response to both students of color and White students who were able to emigrate to Afrodiasporic University but experienced severe migraines, hallucinations, challenges of breathing, negative interactions with local people, and an inability to access goods in Sankofa. While these students' ideologies appeared to align with the university's mission during the application process, the faculty, students, staff, and citizens of Sankofa drew upon their intuition and found that these type of prospective students' ideologies remained to uphold Whiteness. The students acted in ways that went contrary to the mission and ended up returning back to their home planets.

Regardless of the program at Afrodiasporic University, it was required for the prospective student to complete an in-depth application that requires a submission of a digital essay that searches for critical consciousness on socio-political issues affecting communities that are vulnerable in society. The application process also involved a three-dimensional video conference call interview with existing students and faculty. This device was unique as it inspired other post-secondary public and private institutions because its biometric data includes a magnetism that screened and verified the prospective student's history of interactions, levels of engagements, and activism with Black people and people of color. The data of the 3D video call stores the prospective student's demographic information and responses of interview questions for one year. The device consists of software that included a mixture of historical and contemporary workings by Black liberated scholars such as W. E. B. DuBois, Carter G. Woodson, Malcolm X, Martin Luther King Jr., Derrick Bell, Paulo Freire, Kimberle Crenshaw, Patricia Hill Collins, Audre Lorde, James Baldwin, and Ta-Nehisi Coates. Additional screenings were also required for students to participate during different phases of the programs in order to fit the mission of Afrodiasporic University.

IF BECKY THE MAD BECKOLOGIST CAN'T, DEJANAE CAN!

Becky is an American white woman who grew up in a small town in the northeastern region of the United States. Her upbringing fit the "all-American girl trope"—raised in a middle-class, Christian, educated, and moderate political community by a mother and father. Becky's mother precisely fit the standards of Eurocentric beauty and Becky equally reflected her mother's image. However, over time Becky struggled with reckoning the following of her mother's trajectory and legacy of beliefs. She wanted to cause disruption instead of being silent on issues that affect women and people of color. Her mother was a high-ranking member of the organization For Empowered Liberated Ladies Only (FELLO). This organization merely comprised of white affluent and middle-class cis gender women. Since her teenage years, Becky frequently found herself puzzled about her mother's political views and decisions for men and women in high-ranking positions. When Becky attended Knowledge is Power University, she pursued and completed a program in innovative computer programming. Prior to completion, Becky applied and got accepted to work at Women Are Scientists Too (WAST) organization in North Carolina.

A few weeks before Becky was about to depart for North Carolina to work for WAST, she overheard her father and mother talking in the kitchen. In an soft tone manner, Becky's mother said, "Honey, I guess this is just a little phase she is going through. I don't think she will do this science thing for long."

Becky's father uttered in frustration, "I'm not sure how I feel about her being in science. It's not the field for her. She just needs to know her place in the world and science is not it. I mean the few women that I work with struggle. Becky just needs to know her place, meaning what profession is for her and what is not."

Although Becky was eavesdropping, she realized that they disapproved her goals. But nevertheless, she decided to persist.

While living in North Carolina, Becky esteemed herself as being anti-racist and intentionally surrounded herself among communities that comprised mostly of people of color. She was often on the frontlines as an ally to work with people of color tackling various injustices across employment, housing, healthcare, education, and most passionately, women of color in STEM fields.

For years, Becky heard so much about Afrodiasporic University and wanted to complete a certificate program that would mobilize her to be the owner of any science organization and have access to the knowledge of nationwide science organizations to dominate the computer software and programs on Earth. Being the owner of the best privately-owned science organization in the world was something Becky dreamed of since childhood. It was not surprising because Becky's father was Dr. Richard Bradley, the founder of Life Changers Incorporated. This science organization had changed the way people travel. With high tech air droids, long flights were no longer necessary and world travel had changed forever. A once 17-hour flight now took 17 minutes with an air droid. This great technological advancement was only accessible to extremely wealthy people. Dr. Bradley changed the future and would undoubtedly be inducted into the International Science Hall of Fame.

With this family connection, one would think Becky had it made in the science field, but Dr. Bradley believed that because he earned everything by "pulling himself up by his bootstraps" and working hard, Becky should do the same. Dr. Bradley refused to be a professional connection for Becky. He wanted her to figure it out on her own and see if she has what it takes and can manage being in the field.

THE UNDENIABLE AND PRICELESS
VALUE OF BLACK WOMAN'S WORK

Dr. Washington is an intellectual Black liberated progressive woman, who is a mother and wife of a loving husband who is an intersectional feminist. One would expect that raising a child in a home that is filled with Black liberation, the child would be proud of who he/she is and constantly question and challenge whiteness. This was not the case for Alonzo. Since middle-school, Alonzo struggled with the idea of masculinity and his father's role in the household. Although his father did not possess the same educational attainment and professional accomplishments as his mother, he struggled with his father and mother having an equitable voice about issues that concerned their family.

Alonzo believed that society has disadvantaged the Black man since the beginning of time. According to Alonzo, the Black community must liberate Black boys and men first, then Black girls and women. His feelings of shame for his father's perceived roles in the household led to intense disdain for the image of his family. When Alonzo attended college, he legally and officially changed his name to Tarik during his sophomore year. The decision to change his name to Tarik came after reading the book "Pan-Africanism for Woke Black Men." Although his parents were disappointed with his decision and could not grapple with his beliefs, they hoped that he would come to reality about Black liberation. They ultimately still loved him.

Dr. Washington served as a manager of the galactic astronomical division for Life Changers, Inc. Dr. Bradley often vocalized his admiration of Dr. Washington's excellence. He constantly used her ideas and labor to create innovative projects but never gave her credit.

Infuriated with the restriction of navigating in discriminatory economic society on planet Earth, Dr. Washington became informed about the works of Sankofa and pursued her interests in a contractor position for Afrodiasporic University's Science and Technology department. Dr. Washington was very familiar with Dr. Bradley's misogynistic and patriarchal views of science and similar science organizations that limited or dismissed girls' and women's interests and contributions. With the support of Afrodiasporic University and organizations in Sankofa, Dr. Washington established a mentoring service.

Dr. Washington's labor and contributions for Afrodiasporic University exceeded the annual salary she received at Life Changers Inc. She received numerous awards from government agencies, professional organizations and companies. The countless recognitions led Dr. Washington to resign from Life Changers, Inc. Dr. Washington as well as her family were showered abundantly with public assistance that covered the health, economic, and social needs.

Although Dr. Bradley was disappointed with Dr. Washington's decision, without his control, he instantly granted her access to do research or work on any projects at his lab. Dr. Bradley became dependent on Dr. Washington's name and presence. Because Tarik struggled to find a job after college, Dr. Washington persuaded Dr. Bradley to hire Tarik as a security guard for Life Changers Inc. Dr. Washington and her husband desperately wanted to relocate to Sankofa, but they knew their son's limited views on Black liberation would serve as a hindrance.

Whenever Becky went to see her father, Dr. Bradley at his job, she admired Dr. Washington. She noticed the absence of Dr. Washington at Life Changers

Inc. and inquired about it to her father. When her father informed her that she left the organization but still has access to it, Becky immediately searched for Dr. Washington on the internet and emailed her to inquire about mentorship.

When Dr. Washington received Becky's notice, she immediately responded and established a plan to meet and mentor Becky on computer programming at the Life Changers Inc. lab in North Carolina. This mentorship was fruitful for Becky as she prepared to work and navigated through WAST.

Becky had something to prove. She worked hard. The demographic landscape of the workforce for Life Changers, Inc. contradicted with the representation of scientists and workers at WAST. She knew that getting access to Afrodiasporic University would be the key to change her life and lead her to leave an even greater impact than her father. Becky also knew that her impact would mean much more because it was about change for the marginalized members of community and not solely for the one percent of the universe. Dr. Bradley changed world travel, but could not change prejudice and injustice. Frankly, Becky became fixated on this goal and was willing to do anything to enroll in the university.

While working at WAST for several months, Becky befriended women of color who were astronauts. Although the women of color were cordial toward Becky, they made it obvious that they had boundaries that Becky could not cross. Becky was fully aware of this, but whenever she saw the women of color who were scientists, astronauts, or administrative assistants talking collectively in the workspace she passed by slowly to eavesdrop their conversations.

One day, Tameka, an administrative assistant, was talking to Sherri, a scientist at WAST, about the "My Black is Beautiful" organization tuition-free and one-year program at Afrodiasporic University. Becky overheard this conversation and was highly interested. She recalled her last experience of attempting to travel to Sankofa to attend a conference at Afrodiasporic University, which left her having severe migraines for two weeks.

While she did not want to make attempts to go back to Sankofa, she decided to use her tech savviness to create a humanoid in an image of a Black woman who could recite the excerpts from the workings of Angela Davis, W. E. B. DuBois, and James Baldwin. Becky then created a software that included the workings of black liberated scholars. She used such information to operate as a sensor to control the mental and oral process of what she called, Dejanae.

Becky knew that it was not sustainable for her to visit Sankofa without experiencing extreme migraines, so attending Afrodiasporic University for a year was impossible. What was possible was the use of Dejanae, the humanoid in the image of a Black woman. Dejanae mirrored the aesthetics of the beautiful women of color Becky worked with daily. Dark brown skin, kinky curls, unmatched confidence and undeniable intellect were Dejanae's main ingredients. After months of mastering Dejanae's look, responses, and personality, Becky was confident that Dejanae would thrive in Sankofa.

Becky was noticeably nervous the day of Dejanae's 3D video interview. Although her colleagues were unaware of Becky's creation, they could tell that something was troubling her and impacting her work. Tardiness and inaccurate responses were Becky's reality as she wondered about the video call. What if the admissions board figured out that Dejanae was a humanoid? What if Dejanae's responses were insufficient and did not align with the overall mission of Afrodiasporic University? Why was she willing to take such a huge risk to access Sankofa and Afrodiasporic University?

Becky knew that her extensive research and vast knowledge of scientific programming was limited and ultimately invalid without her connection to the expertise and resources provided in Sankofa. She needed it. She HAD to have it. Whatever the risk, she was willing to go through it.

After receiving her notice of acceptance into the "My Black is Beautiful" program, Becky was thrilled and looking forward to the privileged information she would access through Dejanae.

Dejanae traveled to Sankofa and arrived to the most beautiful campus Becky had ever seen. Warm sunshine, green hills, talking monuments that honored prominent figures, who were people of color in the fields of education, engineering, medicine, and politics caused Becky to lose her breath. Becky gawked and scrambled to figure out who these prominent figures were since she had never seen or heard of them before. With all of this among the beautiful faculty, staff and students on campus, Becky was simply overwhelmed. She glowed as she viewed Dejanae's every move at Afrodiasporic University and prematurely celebrated the success of her creation.

WHEN BECKY GETS A TASTE OF DEJANAE'S WORLD BUT REALIZES IT'S NOT SWEET

During her first few days in Sankofa, Dejanae quickly became noticed for her beauty, intellect, and arrogance. She was highly admired and inspired by the political and social terrain in Sankofa and Afrodiasporic University. While she attended classes regularly and met the workload of requirements for courses in the "My Black is Beautiful" program, Dejanae also found herself doing outreach work virtually that assisted vulnerable communities on planet Earth and Mars who could not afford to relocate to Sankofa.

Dejanae's presence, minimal participation, and immediate desire to be recognized and idealized was noticeable to residents of Sankofa, as well as students, faculty, and staff of Afrodiasporic University. Becky was baffled by this error in her programming for it did not fit the traits of the Black scholars in the software. Becky wondered, "Where was the sense of entitlement and superiority coming from?" She knew she did not program these traits into Dejanae's makeup, but they were gradually appearing on a daily basis.

As she viewed Dejanae's interactions with faculty, students, and community members, Becky began to worry. With all of her intellect and knowledge about the future of scientific methods and approaches, Dejanae seemed very opinionated and judgmental, while simultaneously very mediocre and lackadaisical in her own efforts.

Becky's premature celebration was over and now she was worried. Becky had worked so hard to create the perfect humanoid to access a space in which she could not dwell. Becky manufactured the perfect being, or so she thought. Where did things go wrong? This surprise in Dejanae's personality baffled her and as a result, Becky worked night after night on upgrades and revisions to the programming, but nothing seemed to work.

After eight days in Sankofa, Dejanae began to have a slight headache. She complained of feelings of queasiness and confusion. When seeking medication to feel better, Dejanae insulted the medical community, by stating, "With all of your technological advancements, you can't even cure a simple headache. I'm going to file a complaint and forward my concerns to the head physicians of this university!" Dejanae quickly scheduled an appointment to see the top University physicians the next day. Community members, university faculty and classmates all knew what was wrong.

Becky refused to believe what she was witnessing. Quite puzzled, she said to herself, "I accomplished this unthinkable and miraculous challenge by getting into Sankofa, didn't I? There can be no way that now the Mahogonyites are having an impact on Dejanae. Why is this happening? What can I do?"

Once examined by top university physicians, it was clear that Dejanae had to leave Sankofa and return home in order to be alleviated of all the symptoms connected to the Mahogonyites. She was so close, yet so far away. With all of her knowledge of communities of colors, Indigenous tribes, community activism, and civil rights movements around the world, she still was unable to access Sankofa. Even after the perfect crafting of Dejanae, she still could not crack the code of Sankofa. What would it take? Why was this happening to her?

Becky had never faced such a barrier in her life. She was used to making one simple move and things would immediately change to her favor. Unfortunately, that did not work this time. Dejanae was given the discharge documents to immediately board the "Wanna-Be-But Can't" rocket ship.

Both Becky and Dejanae remained perturbed and insulted by the entire medical community's decision. Becky knew if Dejanae remained in Sankofa for one additional night, Dejanae would eventually die. Becky also knew that if Dejanae died in Sankofa, the technological devices underneath Dejanae's body would be exposed.

Becky became infuriated. As Becky was pacing back in forth in her apartment, she started to cry and shout simultaneously saying, "You got to be fucking kidding me! This is bullshit! I literally had access to this planet for days and this so called top university and they can't even cure a fucking migraine. And after all the community service I have done on behalf of the Afrodiasporic University!"

Becky stopped and went to her computer and started sending notifications to commentators and editors of major mainstream news platforms such as CNN, MSNBC, Fox, *Washington Post*, *New York Times*, and *USA Today*. The subject of her email was *"Conscious Black Girl Almost Died in Sankofa: Can Humans Really Trust This Planet?"* Becky figured that if the people on planet Earth will see that if Dejanae, this type of Black woman, cannot survive in Sankofa, then who can survive this planet? Becky knew she would have access to Dejanae and her discharge papers, as she planned to use both sources as forms of evidence when she arrived back in North Carolina.

When Dejanae arrived home, Becky immediately went to the WAST lab and examined her programming. Externally, she found that Dejanae was in great condition. Becky found that Dejanae's skin and hair were still perfect. It precisely reflected the aesthetic features of the women of color at WAST. Now out of the range of the Mahogonyites, Dejanae appeared to function normally, she no longer experienced the same physical or mental symptoms when she was in Sankofa. However, the powerful force of Mahogonyites caused memory loss for humans who were rejected from Sankofa and had to return to their retrospective planet. Without the headaches and queasiness, Dejanae seemed back to her normal self.

News platforms contacted Becky to inquire additional information about her email in regards to the conscious black girl almost dying in Sankofa. Unfavorable to Becky, the news platforms wanted to hear the actual experience from Dejanae instead of Becky talking for her.

With frustration, Becky knew this would be a damn near impossible challenge. She couldn't grapple with the idea of why she couldn't talk for Dejanae. Afterall, she created her. She knows how she thinks.

Upon further examination, Becky was shocked at what she found. Dejanae had dark, ugly, irreversible scaring on her heart and her prefrontal cortex. "Where did these scars come from? How did they appear? Was it exposure to the Mahogonyites that caused this or was it something else?"

Becky stayed up for days with an undying determination to discover what was going on with Dejanae. This was such a serious dilemma that Becky asked her father, if she could use one of his local labs. Much to her surprise, he granted her permission.

Over the next couple of weeks, an exhausted Becky ran multiple tests to assess Dejanae's heart and brain condition. She was stumped and completely confused about these findings. The test results showed that upon immediate creation, Dejanae ascertained these scars on her heart and prefrontal cortex. The cause was not Sankofa. The cause was not exposure to the Mahogony-ites. Becky, herself, was the cause.

But how? Becky thought to herself. As an ally of people of color and a lover of all that is Indigenous, how could this be the case?

While watching the news one evening, it was announced that Dr. Bradley would continue his world tour in the city Becky resides. Knowing that her father would be in town made Becky both uncomfortable and excited. She was uncomfortable because being in the presence of her father always made her feel small, but excited, because maybe, just maybe, he would have some insight on Dejanae's condition.

Becky knew that she was taking a huge risk by sharing the creation of Dejanae with Dr. Bradley, but at this point, she felt there was nothing to lose. If she could just fix Dejanae, change some of her physical features and an ethnic sounding name, she thought maybe the board members and student recruitment committee at Afrodiasporic University would readmit her into the "My Black is Beautiful" program. The brief exposure she had to that wealth of knowledge was simply a tease and Becky needed more. It was like a drug for her and again, she was willing to do whatever it took to access Sankofa through Dejanae.

At 9:17 p.m. on Thursday night, Dr. Bradley made his way into the one of the Life Changers Inc. local labs he permitted Becky to use. After hearing Becky's explanation of Dejanae and her access to Sankofa, Dr. Bradley burst into uncontrollable laughter.

Dr. Bradley shared that she should not waste her time trying to access a space that is not meant for her. He also had long been one of the many people to ignore and undermine the contributions and advancements of Sankofa and Afrodiasporic University. After giving her one final glance, Dr. Bradley shrugged his shoulders and left the lab.

Becky sat uttering to herself, "At least I'm nothing like him. What a racist," she mutters confidently.

THE MOMENT OF TRUTH

At approximately 8 a.m. the next morning, Becky awoke to Dr. Washington, her mentor, standing over her. Dr. Washington inquired about Becky's presence in the lab.

Becky figured that hiding Dejanae from everyone had not served her well, so instead, through her tears, she shared the entire story with Dr. Washington, hoping that she could provide some insight into why all of this had occurred.

Dr. Washington shared, "And you're stumped by this? Really? The founders of Sankofa are no fools. Your activism and 'care' for communities of color does not remove you from who you are. No matter how many marches you attend, rallies you plan, and marginalized people you help, the condition of your heart and mind remains the same. You felt that Dejanae's mere Black phenotypes were enough. You felt that giving her some quotes from scholars of color would change who you are internally.

"Keep in mind that Dejanae is you and you are her. It is your heart that is the issue. It is your brain that is the issue. There is an ugliness that remains there and you need to be honest about this before you ever again attempt to move forward in your endeavors. Your attitude of simply being there is not enough. For white mediocrity will always simplify, undervalue, question, and even become combative whenever it sees or is met with Black excellence. Black excellence is worthy of intellect and grace. There must be a heart change in order to make a difference. There has to be genuine care, but also the acknowledgment of your own privilege—you are a straight, white, educated, able-bodied woman who has access to immense wealth, yet you think you should just access the world's wealthiest and most advanced space because you feel like it?

"This is all rooted in deception and you question the condition of Dejanae's heart?! Being an ally is not enough. How about starting with honesty, plain and simple. Self-reflection, plain and simple. You know why you cannot access Sankofa? Because you do not deserve to be in that space. It is that simple."

Upon hearing this, Becky began to cry and shout at Dr. Washington saying, "I worked hard to get where I am! Your people have never been satisfied with the folks who are white allies. Your people continuously isolate us when we do show up to help. Prove to me that being a white ally has been wrong in history."

Dr. Washington stared at her for a long time and remained silent. As Dr. Washington turned around to walk away and her footsteps began to fade into the distance, Becky's cry grew louder.

Becky's screaming and crying captured the attention of Tarik. Tarik barged into the lab and immediately looked at his mother and Becky. Crying and wailing from the airs of her belly, Becky immediately spoke as she simultaneously pointed to Dr. Washington saying, "She is the problem. She is attacking me. Arrest her!"

Tarik barks with accusing eyes toward his mom and said, "Ma, what's going on? What's the problem?"

Dr. Washington gave a puzzled and passionate look to her son said, "I have no problem. Perhaps you should ask Becky and her so called Black humanoid."

Becky squinted her eyes at Dr. Washington. She refused to be belittled by this Black female scientist who only volunteers a few days on Earth to help women and girls in science. Feeling the rage inside her she stands up, wipes her tears, points the finger at Dr. Washington and yelled, "Arrest her now! She created this humanoid to secretly infiltrate my father's lab."

Becky, almost empowered in her privilege says, "Yes, that's right. I'm Becky Bradley and my father owns this lab. Arrest her now."

Tarik shakes his head and moves toward his mom. "Son, what are you doing? I know you are not arresting me. I am your mother. I have always taught you the right knowledge. You know that I am innocent. I would never lie to you."

With a few tears rolling down his face, Tarik cuffs her and scoffs, "No, you're wrong. I have never seen Becky cry before. You must have done something." Tarik begins to escort his mother out of the room. Becky was so consumed with her own emotions that she even smiled at overhearing the officer.

Now in the lab alone, Becky stands over Dejanae. She begins to feel guilty. She looks deeply at Dejanae's beautiful black face. Becky seems to have hope in herself. She begins to regain her composure as an antiracist. She realizes her wrong but continues to stare intently at Dejanae. "I am you. I am you," she whispers. "I am you."

Just then Becky sees a flicker of light reflecting from a mirror next to her. Becky lifts her head up and stares at the flickering light and sees her own white face and in the back of her mind hears Dejanae say, "No, you are you."

TWO MONTHS LATER . . .

As Becky walks to her new job at the right-wing organization, White Women Know Science (WWKS), she receives a notification about a new groundbreaking scientific discovery coming out of Afrodiasporic University. Angrily she asserts, "This is bull——" but her inattentiveness and anger blinds her to the oncoming traffic. As such, a newly created speed bus that travels at record-breaking strikes Becky. Aghast, onlookers whisper and watch as the advertisement on the side of the bus about a new skin care product continuously slides across the electronic screen. It simply reads: "Love the Skin You're in from Within."

Chapter Nineteen

Who is Dr. Farsa?

Luis Fernando Macías

INTRODUCTION

In 2015, a chapter president of the NAACP resigned after she was found to be misrepresenting herself as a Black Woman. She defended herself by saying that while she grew up white, as an adult she came to identify as Black. While her story garnered national attention, it is far from unique. In academia, scholars often misrepresent themselves in order to gain credibility or conflate their affinity for a group as membership.

The following counterstory takes a Sci-Fi, thriller approach to comment on the lengths some scholars will go to in order to pass themselves as kin to the marginalized communities they research, the various "Becky Behaviors" they exhibit in their performance, and the role that institutions play that promote this behavior. Told entirely by the composite characters' digital communication[1] (i.e. emails, texts, social media posts, documents), the story follows Alejandro's experiences in his first year as a graduate student at Westward University, a predominately white institution (PWI).

Dr. Rebeca Farsa, an acclaimed professor in Westward's Department of Critical Education, recruited Alejandro to work with her on a research project with Mexican migrant families. Alejandro moved from his hometown on the US-Mexico Border to attend Westward. Alejandro is excited about continuing his education but is having a difficult time in his new environment and people around him. As the only Latinx, student of color, in his program he feels isolated and faces various racial microaggressions and other challenges. Alejandro relies heavily on his family and friends back home for support and guidance but even with their help there are certain situations that confound him. Specifically, Alejandro begins to experience increasingly bizarre occurrences while working with Dr. Farsa. These seemingly inexplicable events unsettle him and raise his

247

concern about Dr. Farsa's research, her authenticity, as well as his own safety.
The story begins on Alejandro's first day on the Westward campus.

Date: August 20
[Text message between Alejandro and his mother]

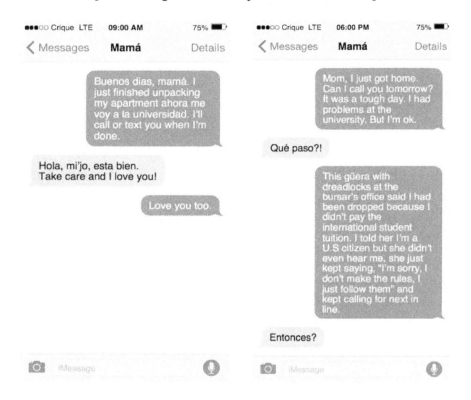

●●●○○ Crique LTE   06:05 PM   75% 🔋

< Messages   **Mamá**   Details

> I heard your voice in my head while it was happening telling me to stay calm and not raise my voice. So after the third time I said "ok" then I went home to get my passport.

Y luego?

> That's when the campus police stopped me for "jaywalking". They asked me for my student ID. I told them I was new and showed them my TX license instead. They said they needed verify the ID and also asked me for my green card! They had me on the curb in front of all these people while they ran my ID. It took forever, everyone saw, it was terrible but they finally let me go.

Call me now! I need to hear your voice.

📷   Message   🎤

Date: August 21
[Text message between Alejandro and his sister, Camila]

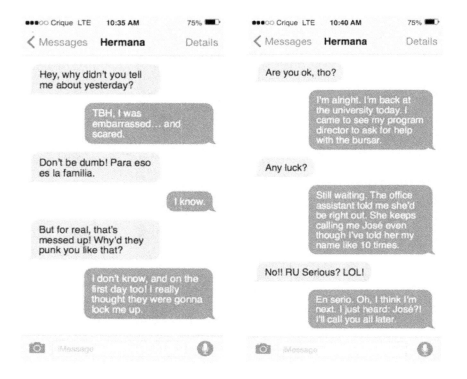

●●●○○ Crique LTE   07:30 PM   75% ▬▭

< Messages   **Hermana**   Details

> Sis, I just got home. The rest of the day went much better. The director walked me over to Dr. Farsa's office. She's the prof I'll be working and studying with. Farsa went with me to the Bursar's office. Los regaño! She was like "This is my new research assistant, we have a lot of important work to do and you're holding us back. You are discriminating against him!" She totally had my back.

Que Bueno! Is everything resolved?

> I think so. I just need to wait on some paperwork. The problem was that they processed me as international student because of my name. SMH. Farsa said if I had any more trouble she'd come with me again though. She's super cool. She gave me a quick campus tour afterwards.

Awesome!

 iMessage   🎤

●●●○○ Crique LTE   07:35 PM   75% ■□

‹ Messages   **Hermana**   Details

> Yeah, we talked almost the whole time in Spanish, which was nice because I haven't heard any since I got here. Then, she took me out to dinner to make up for the bad first impression.

She seems to really be looking out for you.

> I think so. She said 'people like us have to stick together'.

Orale! Es Latina?

> She said something about Ecuador. Her Spanish is a bit funny, like she slipped in and out of a few accents when she spoke.

Like Drake?

> LOL. Yeah, maybe that's how folks from there speak or maybe it's from all her travels? Who knows but yeah I'm sure she's Latina.

Yeah, that'd be weird if she was just pretending. Bueno, thank her for us and text me tomorrow. Mom is super worried about you

◻ iMessage   🎤

Date: September 1
[Dr. Farsa's email to Alejandro regarding research methods class]

Hola Alejandro,

Thank you for your contributions to class discussion, they were very productive. To answer your question from yesterday's class: you may use your field notes from your research assistantship for a grade in our methods class assignments. Which brings me to this: please meet me tomorrow at 4:30 pm outside of my office. I will drive us to the "tomate" migrant campsite. I'll drive us the first time but you will have to quickly learn how to get there by yourself. It's about an hour's drive on unmarked country roads and there's no formal address to the campsite. Cell phone/GPS is not of much help because it's so remote so please bring a notepad to take notes on how to get there. Once you know how to get there though it's pretty easy to remember. Also, don't wear anything too formal or professional tomorrow. You want to make sure you blend in with the families, most of them families I know from previous years did not come this year but there are new families I recently met who are interested in the research. I'll introduce you when we get there.

Lastly, I will show you how to properly transport, use, and store the recording equipment tomorrow. This is one-of-a-kind equipment, which means it is very expensive, so we have to be very careful. Do not worry though; it will all make sense when you start using it.

Saludos,

Rebeca (seriously, please call me Rebeca, Dr. Farsa is far too formal)

Date: September 5
[Alejandro's field notes from his first Tomate camp visit]
Project: A Bilingual Understanding of Siblings and Adolescent Reading
            skills: (USAR Latinos)
Legend: *FN:* Field Notes *PN:* Personal Notes

PN: We arrived at "tomate" around 6:00 pm. Rebeca was not exaggerating, it's far and all I saw the entire time along the side of bumpy roads were huge stalks of corn. I hope to never get lost out there. It'd be impossible to find me.

FN: When we pulled into "tomate," Rebeca got out first and walked over to the families who were sitting under a big tree. I stood by the car until she waved me over. She introduced me to the families by telling them "Miren, Alejandro también es Mexicano, pueden tenerle confianza." I introduced myself and talked to the families in Spanish for a while.

FN: After introductions, Rebeca and I toured some of the families' temp homes, they are really small. The Sánchez family let us use their tiny living room for a tutorial on setting up the recording equipment. The video cameras were self-explanatory, but the headsets took a bit longer to set up my first time.

PN (description/impression of headset): The headsets are the one-of-a-kind equipment. They are not too complicated to operate but I was hesitant to handle them at first. They look almost exactly like the soft, padded helmets some soccer players wear to prevent head injuries. They slide on over the person's head and are secured by a chinstrap that has a small microphone. Inside of the headset are hundreds of small electrodes that register brain waves. Rebeca said headsets are totally safe, normally they are used for neuroscience research, but hers have been modified to capture specific brain activity found in bilingual speakers. I had no idea this project was going to be this high-tech!

FN: Rebeca first put the headset on the Sánchez parents (so that the children remember to not be afraid of it), then on their children. After we turned on the headsets and checked that the mics were synced to the cameras, there wasn't much else to do but to take observational notes as the family went about their evening.

FN (headset use): Rebeca stressed that the families need to wear the headsets during all recordings and because they need constant recalibration, participants should wear them to sleep at least twice a week. She said not to worry, they're so soft that you hardly know you're wearing it. She also suggested that I wear one also because it would provide additional, comparative data.

FN: The family went about their regular routine for the most part. They were fidgeting a bit with the headsets and us being there was a bit weird. Rebeca said something to them about this project helping their children with school somehow. I didn't catch exactly what was said but that really piqued their interest in the research.

FN: (Data Storage). When we got back to campus late that night, Rebeca took me to her office to show me how to download the data from the headsets. In a locked storage locker, there are a series of very large, clunky, hard drives that connect to the headsets. She gave me the keypad combination and very seriously said that it's of the utmost importance that I connect the headsets right after an observation because "the data needs to stay fresh."

PN: This educational research terminology sounds odd but I'm sure I'll get used to it. I guess I just never realized how scientific and mechanical qualitative research sounded.

Date: September 16
[Text message between Alejandro and his mother]

Left screen (Crique LTE, 11:00 PM, 75%, Messages — Mamá — Details):

Mi'jo cómo estás?

Hola mama, estoy bien gracias. Sorry I'm just now responding. I was in class then went to do observations the rest of the day. I barely got home from the camps.

Estás bien? Are you eating?

I'm eating, but miss your food. I think I'm getting the flu though. I have a headache and feel sluggish. I have so much work to do though and I don't want to miss class.

You have to take care of yourself! I wish I was there to help you. Have you asked for a day off from work?

Right screen (Crique LTE, 11:05 PM, 75%, Messages — Mamá — Details):

No.

Porqué? Your profesora is looking out for you, no? I'm sure she'd give you the day.

I tried but I don't think she heard me. She talked over me to tell me that her research is partly funded by the government so it's important all the work gets completed on time. So, I really don't want to miss work.

Yo sé como es tener que trabajar enfermo! But at least take the weekend to just rest, ok?

I'll try but Rebeca asked me to organize some boxes in her office suite on Saturday.

It's not mandatory but she said that if our work together goes well she'd recommend me for a summer position and even connect me with important scholars to find a job after graduating. So, I want to make a good impression by helping with these kinds of things.

Ay Mi'jo!

Date: October 10
[Prof. Biely's email to Alejandro]

Subject: Apologies for class
From: Alejandro@westward.edu
To: Biely@westward.edu

Dear Prof. Biely,

I just wanted to follow up via email to once again apologize for nodding off during lecture yesterday. I felt light-headed during class so that's why you saw me put my head down. I understand your need to reprimand me in class but I meant no disrespect. I have made a doctor's appointment but regardless, I assure you it won't happen again.

My sincerest apologies,

—Alejandro

———

Subject: re: Apologies for class
From: Biely@westward.edu Alejandro@westward.edu
To: Alejandro@westward.edu

Jose,

I appreciate your email. They don't call Westward "the public Ivy League of the region" for nothing. It can be very demanding, especially for someone from a background like yours. Normally, this would cost you a letter grade. However, I am making an exception because Dr. Farsa speaks well of you, and I trust her judgment. I expect you to be fully prepared and engaged for next class period.

Best,

Dr. Biely
. . .
Theodore Biely
Professor
Department of Critical Education
Westward University

Date: October 12
[Text message between Alejandro & his friend ,Veronica]

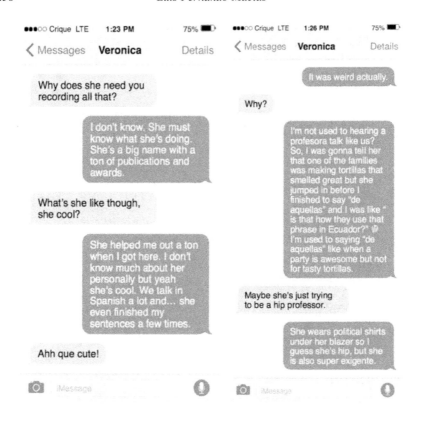

●●●○○ Crique LTE   1:33 PM   75% ▬▭

❮ Messages   **Veronica**   Details

That's not bad though,
why do you mention it?
Did she chew you out or
something?

Kinda. There was a
problem with one of the
headsets during a
recording and I didn't
catch it.

Was it a big deal?

I didn't think so but she
was not happy about it.
She told me what I did
wrong and said "don't
repeat these mistakes,
they are not indicative of
grad-school material"
then smiled.

Oh, I thought she called
you a pendejo or
something! LOL.

Might as well have, it
was a low-key burn but
the smile tripped me out.
It was exactly the smile
gringos gave me at the
restaurant right after
saying "I'd like with
speak your manager".

 iMessage

●●●○○ Crique LTE   1:35 PM   75% ▬▬▷

‹ Messages   **Veronica**   Details

Ugh! I hate that mean
smile. Is everything
straight now?

> Yeah. She just said that
> to make up for that lost
> data I have to wear a
> headset to sleep for a
> week.

What?!!!!

> It's because I'm bilingual.
> It doesn't hurt to wear it
> but it's not really
> comfortable either.
> They're safe though. She
> got all these university
> permissions to use them.

Jano, you're supposed to
be the smart one.
Remember what
happened to my tía at
the county hospital? The
docs said the new
procedure they wanted
to do was safe and they
even said she signed off
on it but she only said
she'd think about it. Y
ahora cómo está?!

> But this is different! It's
> educational research on
> bilingual families.

 iMessage   🎤

●●●○○ Crique LTE   1:39 PM   75% ▬▭

< Messages   **Veronica**   Details

Whatever, but what
you're telling me is weird.
Maybe it's because I'm
not a bookworm but
none of this recording
and swim caps stuff
sounds right, even if she
is a mera-mera with
awards. I wouldn't be
surprised if those caps
are causing your
headaches. Do the
paisas you record also
feel sick?

I don't know.

You haven't asked?! Ya
ni la chingas!

She's my professor, I
work for her, AND she's
already talked to the
dean about wanting to be
my advisor. I want to
make a good impression
and definitely don't want
to cause problems for
myself. Plus, if the
headsets were
dangerous how come no
one has complained
about them?

No one that you know.

What do you mean by
that?

Now you're making my
head hurt. I'll let you
figure that out by yourself

📷   iMessage   🎤

Date: November 1
[Dr. Farsa's email to Alejandro regarding conference]

Subject: Conference Invitation
From: Farsa@westward.edu
To: Alejandro@westward.edu

Hola Alejandro,

Just a quick note on a few things. I am still waiting for the data that we lost because of your oversight with the Sánchez family headset. Please make sure to finish wearing the headset and have the data downloaded no later than Friday. The reason for this particular rush is that I need some of the newest data because I was invited to speak at a research conference in NYC in two weeks. It's somewhat short notice but I would like you to come with me. This would be a good introduction to academic conferences for you and a chance to meet important scholars in our field. If you're interested, the university will cover your expenses, all you need to do is arrange any makeup assignments from your other professors. Let me know by the end of the day so that I can plan accordingly.

Saludos,

—Rebeca

Date: November 3
[Text message between Alejandro and his sister]

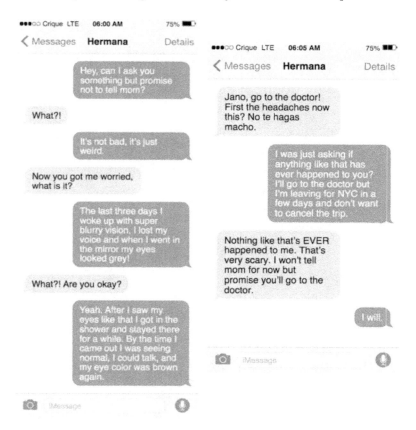

●●●○○ Crique LTE 06:00 AM 75% ▬▭

‹ Messages **Hermana** Details

> Hey, can I ask you something but promise not to tell mom?

What?!

> It's not bad, it's just weird.

Now you got me worried, what is it?

> The last three days I woke up with super blurry vision, I lost my voice and when I went in the mirror my eyes looked grey!

What?! Are you okay?

> Yeah. After I saw my eyes like that I got in the shower and stayed there for a while. By the time I came out I was seeing normal, I could talk, and my eye color was brown again.

○ iMessage ●

●●●○○ Crique LTE 06:05 AM 75% ▬▭

‹ Messages **Hermana** Details

Jano, go to the doctor! First the headaches now this? No te hagas macho.

> I was just asking if anything like that has ever happened to you? I'll go to the doctor but I'm leaving for NYC in a few days and don't want to cancel the trip.

Nothing like that's EVER happened to me. That's very scary. I won't tell mom for now but promise you'll go to the doctor.

> I will.

○ iMessage ●

Date: November 5
[Text message between Alejandro and Veronica]

●●●○○ Crique LTE   2:13 PM   75% ▬▬❙▷

< Messages   **Veronica**   Details

> No! Want me to tell you or not?

Of course, tell me.

> Can I call you?

Text it, kids are napping in here.

> Ok, so last night, I was leaving my closet office and passed by her office suite. The door to the small room outside her office is normally closed but this time it was slightly open. I looked inside because I heard these super weird mechanical noises. It sounded like a tape being rewound and I heard what sounded like these robotic voices talking in Spanish.

That's fucking weird! Are they wire taps from her ICE spying?!

 iMessage

●●●○○ Crique LTE   2:15 PM   75% ▬▮

❮ Messages   **Veronica**   Details

> No. Esperate

> So, I walk in to the room and the noises I heard are coming from inside Farsa's office. I stand there for a bit and then knock on her door. Nothing. So then I 'barrio knocked' and heard her yelling "Ocupado! I told you to go away, no need cleaning, vete!" but she said it like in a robotic, almost auto-tuned voice.

What. The. Hell?

> She must have thought that I was the custodian por eso me large, she sounded super pissed.

Who talks to the custodians like that?! And, what the hell with that robot voice stuff, does she have audio equipment in there or something?

  iMessage

●●●○○ Crique LTE   2:19 PM   75% 🔋

< Messages   **Veronica**   Details

> Not that I know of. Her office is big but minimalist. There's nothing in there but a standing desk, her computer, some books and that tower where she keeps her big hard drives for the research.

Jano, I'm telling you this is now confirmed super creepy.

> Yeah, it is weirding me out more and more. She was so cool in the beginning but has been gradually been more exigente and meaner, and now I'm straight tripping out.

You still wearing that scary swim cap?

> I am but it's because she told me I had to for the conference in NYC. I'm going to stop wearing it when I get back though. I'm thinking wearing it to sleep messed with my eyes because they were hurting.

You wore it to sleep? Jano! Ok. I'm not saying anything anymore but I told you! And you should really tell the families to stop using it, too.

📷   iMessage   🎤

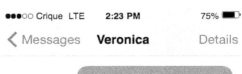

●●●○○ Crique LTE   2:23 PM   75% ▬▬

‹ Messages   **Veronica**   Details

> I know. I'll talk to them. I
> just really want to go to
> NYC and don't want
> more drama. I know it's
> work but I'm hoping to
> treat it like a mini
> vacation. I need it. Grad
> school's been kicking my
> ass.

Bueno, pero ponte
trucha while there. Nada
es gratis en esta vida.

 iMessage

Date: November 13
[Alejandro's email to his sister]

Subject: Odd Email

Hey sis, this is the email I was just talking to you about. I'm at the airport, sending "nice to meet you" emails to people I met at the conference when this one came in. Tell me what you see; it just looks like a blurry photo of an old college newspaper article. In the email, the person just wrote "Alejandro, nice job presenting. FYI: Careful with the transfusions." What's that supposed to mean?! I'm thinking it was someone at the conference but what are transfusions and why the anonymous email? And . . . what's up why attach an old article from the Carmona College Gazette about a sophomore who "falls in love with Latin America" during her study abroad? I'm guessing she's the blonde in the picture wearing the obnoxious sombrero, holding the maracas. But I have no idea who this student Rebekah Lazelod is. I'm tripping out. This is odd, right?

[Attachment]

Date: November 13
[Text message between Alejandro and Veronica]

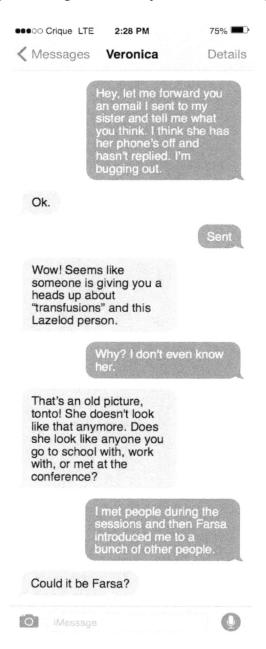

●●●○○ Crique LTE   2:28 PM   75% ■■▷

❮ Messages   **Veronica**   Details

Hey, let me forward you an email I sent to my sister and tell me what you think. I think she has her phone's off and hasn't replied. I'm bugging out.

Ok.

Sent

Wow! Seems like someone is giving you a heads up about "transfusions" and this Lazelod person.

Why? I don't even know her.

That's an old picture, tonto! She doesn't look like that anymore. Does she look like anyone you go to school with, work with, or met at the conference?

I met people during the sessions and then Farsa introduced me to a bunch of other people.

Could it be Farsa?

🎙 iMessage   🎤

●●●○○ Crique LTE   4:28 PM   75% 🔋

‹ Messages   **Veronica**   Details

She looks way different.
She's got dark skin,
eyes, and hair. Her face
looks different too.

People age, wear
contacts, tan, dye their
hair, and get facelifts all
the time. Just look at the
Kardashians. Is Farsa
her married name?

Not that I know of, but
she doesn't really talk
about personal stuff.

Esto me da mala espina.
Then again, someone
might just be messing
with you. What about
José, who is he?

No idea. This is an odd
way of messing with me
though. What are they
talking about with
transfusions?

You really better find out.

 iMessage

Date: November 20
[Alejandro's email to Veronica and Camila]

Subject: What is this?
From: Jano@gmail.com
To: Vero@gmail.com, Camila@gmail.com

Vero, Camila:

   I'm sending you all this from my personal email, don't accidentally reply to my university email. After NYC I got really freaked out so I told Farsa that I wasn't feeling well and asked for a few days off. She said:

   Of course! Don't worry. You can make up the work hours later. I'll try and move my schedule to go to the camps this week. For now, just continue wearing the headset while you rest and come to download the data so we don't get too behind.

   So after reading this I'm thinking something is really up with the headsets, if even while sick she wants me to wear them, right? So, I stayed at my apartment trying to rest but I just kept replaying all this stuff in my head then I remembered something. Do you remember how I told you that people in my program kept calling me José? Well, I was thinking they were just being racist jerks but then I started thinking, "Could they have been confusing me with someone else?" (Still racist now that I think about it.) Anyways, I didn't want to go to the university and start asking for José, especially if I'm supposed to be at home sick so I started looking online for terms like "José + Westward University + Department of Critical Education + Farsa" and on like the 7th page of search results I found a link to an old school directory that had him listed as a student in the program. I emailed him but the email bounced back.

   At that point I felt like I was onto something. So I get an idea. I wait until evening classes are over and go to the university. I walked into my closet-office and again go through those old boxes that Farsa had me sifting through when I first got here. Nothing. Then I started taking out all of the drawers in that old desk. Nothing. At this point I'm sitting on the dirty carpet todo agüitado thinking I had just made a mess for nothing and that's when I saw it: a tiny thumb-drive taped to the inside of the desk. I tore it out and plugged the flash-drive into my computer and you won't believe me, but it was José's flash-drive! He was Farsa's student. He must have taped it there for someone to find. It's full of documents, videos, recordings, emails that he kept on Farsa and her research, I think he was going to expose her lies. Look at the screenshot of all these files! What he found out is all kinds of messed up. It makes a lot of sense but it doesn't make any sense at the same time. So you'll have to follow me on this and I can explain more over the phone. Here it goes:

Rebekah Lazelod, the blonde student in the newspaper article that mystery person sent me, is actually Rebeca Farsa! Farsa went by Rebekah Lazelod when she attended that small liberal arts college. She majored in Latin American Studies and got all those recognitions for her Spring Break service trips work to Yula, a town in, you guessed it . . . Ecuador.

So, she then went on to an Ivy League for grad school and it was there that she changed her name to Farsa and got this big national award to do her dissertation on transnational families in Yula. I know what you're thinking, so what? She loves Ecuador and maybe married someone from there and changed the spelling of her name to sound more local. No big deal, I mean look at Beto from Texas running for president, right? Well, this is where things get super weird. Yula is not just some hidden gem tourist town. It's actually a failed hippie settlement that is now know for medical tourism. Specifically, the town has several clinics that specialize in something called a Racial Procurement Procedure (RPP). The wiki page for RPP says that this "highly controversial procedure is touted as allowing people to align with the heritage they choose, not the one that society imposes upon them." A screenshot of one of the clinic's webpages says:

RPP begins by making the desired surgical modifications. Ongoing intellectual, linguistic, and cultural transfusions are required for conservation. For improved results, RPP should be accompanied by observations and periodic social interaction with desired host population. For maximum effect: intimate encounters and if possible procreation with target group members is encouraged.

If you remember, in that strange email that person mentioned "transfusions." This is what they were talking about! Farsa had the RPP done to masquerade as a Latina and needs those "transfusions" to keep up the charade. Y aun peor . . . she's using her research as a front to get the transfusions she needs.

Vero, you were totally right about the headsets! José recorded these video diaries about what the headsets were doing to him and the families. They were making them sick, too, in the same way I was feeling sick. That's because the headsets don't measure bilingual brainwaves! What they actually do is connect to our brain, mining our idioma, expressions, memories y no sé que más. That's why she needs them connected to those big hard drives in her office. She takes OUR knowledge and keeps it under lock and key in her office. Whenever she needs a transfusion, she just hooks herself up to it and uploads the information that she needs to try to talk and behave like a Latina. She's never had any of the experiences and struggles that shape us pero así de fácil she pretends to being one of us, makes a career out of it, and gets awards for it.

I know this is totally bizarre but you gotta believe me. José has a ton of documents to back this up and it explains a lot of what I've been going through. She's using me to gain trust with the paisas and mine our thoughts! I don't know what to do now. Who should I contact? The police, what will I tell them? My professor is not really who she says she is, she is stealing my thoughts with this swim cap, check out this flash-drive, it explains it all. No way! They'll laugh at me then lock me up. I think I'm going to go to HR first but still no one's gonna believe me! I think that's why José kept this file. Worse yet, I can't find anything about his whereabouts to ask him. The last document in the flash is a .pdf of an email he got from Farsa about a meeting at a new camp. Let me forward it to you so you can read it in full. I don't know what happened to him after that meeting. He seems to have just disappeared. Party line call me after you read this. I gotta talk it out.

—Jano

<Attachment: Dr. Farsa's email to José>
Subject: Conference Invitation
From: Farsa@westward.edu
To: Jose@westward.edu

José,

    A few minutes ago I got off the phone with the foreman at the tomate camp and he is very upset. He informed me that this morning all of the families that were taking part in my research have left the camp saying that they were leaving because they did not want to continue getting sick from the headsets. Why would they think that?! Quite honestly, I am shocked. At no point during our work together did you ever communicate any participant's hesitation about the equipment. At best you failed to address any of their concerns and at worst you misinformed them behind my back!

I have never been part of a work environment in which someone felt they had the authority to make such important decisions about a project that is not theirs. By not informing me about the participants' concerns you have not only jeopardized this important research project but also the tomato harvest at that camp, and you may have also done potentially irreparable damage to the university. This is egregious! After a relatively productive year working with you this is how you thank me for my mentorship? By posing a serious threat to my reputation as a scholar and researcher?

I am in the middle of doing serious damage control and as your supervisor I require you to help rectify this. I need you to meet me at tomate today at 5:00 pm to talk to the foreman and the grower. This email serves as official record but I will call your phone shortly also. I expect you to be at tomate and depending on how it goes we may have to then go to another camp to recruit other participants so I do not know what time we will return.

—Dr. Farsa

. . . .

Rebeca Farsa
Professor
Department of Critical Education
Westward University
Fiat Distinguished Scholar

Date: November 25
[Group text message with Alejandro, his sister, and Veronica]

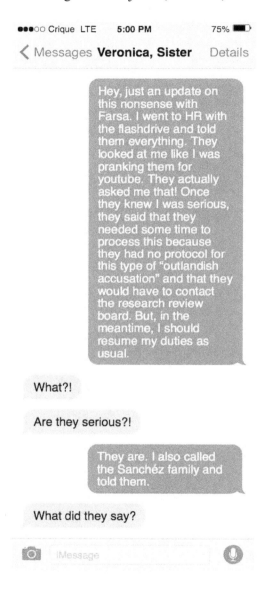

> They were super scared. I told them I reported it and that I was waiting on the university for next steps but that I would not put the headsets on them again. I asked them not to tell anyone about this for now.

Ten mucho cuidado, Jano. You gotta play this very smart.

> I know. To avoid going to work I told Farsa that I couldn't drive out to the camps because I still wasn't feeling well, I told her my dizziness hadn't gone away. And you know what she did?!

Qué?

> She came to my apartment to "check up on me". She (all of a sudden) is worried about me. But in reality she came to grill me with a ton of questions. I think she's on to me.

En serio?! Llámale a la policia pero ya!

> And tell them what? My professor came to check up on me because I called in sick to work?

io iMessage   🎤

●●●○○ Crique LTE   5:05 PM   75% ▬▭

‹ Messages **Veronica, Sister**   Details

Ay Jano! This woman is legit dangerous.

I agree. Can you do anything to avoid her for the rest of the year? Ask for another work assignment, then maybe take classes online next semester so you don't have to see her?

Even if I did that, the only reason I can afford to be here is because I'm getting paid to work on her project. I'm just hoping HR has my back.

It's like they trapped you.

Exactly, and to make me even more paranoid, I'm thinking HR talked to Farsa. All of a sudden she was asking me about how long I've felt sick and asking if I had talked to anyone at the university about it. She even asked if I had talked to the families about it. That's not subtle, right?

 iMessage

●●●○○ Crique LTE   5:08 PM   75% ▬▶

< Messages **Veronica, Sister**   Details

No la chingues! They
really are protecting one
another and not you.
Jano, I don't want you to
be alone with her again!
Imagine what she'll do to
you if she finds out you
reported her. Activate the
location tracking on your
phone and just call/text
us more regularly.
Estamos asustadas.

That's not a bad idea. I'll
just wait and see what
HR does. I hope I'm
wrong and they actually
do have my back.

 iMessage

Date: December 1
[Human Resources' email response to Alejandro]

Subject: Resolution
From:Waterhouse@westward.edu
To: Alejandro@westward.edu

Dear Alexander,

This email is in response to our unconventional conversation regarding your concerns about Dr. Farsa. Westward takes any and all concerns about the safety of the research conducted by our faculty very seriously. Considering the serious nature of this accusation, we expedited the investigation by calling an emergency meeting with the university's research review board and convened an internal search team to look into the whereabouts of Mr. Jose Martir.

The results of our investigation should put you at ease and even provide you with a bit of a laugh. The research review board found absolutely no ethical, medical, or procedural issues with the headsets used in Dr. Farsa's USAR Latinos research. Any headaches that participants experience may very well be from their constant exposure to chemicals or their harsh working conditions in the field. They are definitely not related to the research equipment. It is top-of-the-line equipment that is regularly checked for safety. Additionally, USAR Latinos has been recognized by many professional organizations for its exemplary methodology and has even been used in professional development courses on the subject. This indicates that Dr. Farsa's methods are in this case, literally, textbook perfect.

In regards to Mr. Martir, let me assure you that he is absolutely fine. Our search team located him and I spoke with him myself a few days ago via Skype. He has not been seen on campus or even readily available because he is conducting his own dissertation research in a remote village in Latin America and thus difficult to reach. I was not able to see him because of the poor internet connection but from the sound of his voice and his own admission he's doing very well. He explained, rather embarrassed, that the flash-drive you found was part of a science fiction assignment in a performing arts elective that he took. He apologized for the trouble it caused. He asked me to send him the flash-drive and delete any copies that may exist to prevent any future misunderstandings. I shared your request to speak with him but unfortunately our call dropped before I could get his consent to share his contact information with you. Nevertheless, please be assured that he is fine. I do however ask that you please honor his request and delete any copies of the document that you may still have in your possession.

In closing, we appreciate your vigilance but please move forward with your work and study without any concerns. This email serves to recognize that this matter is now formally closed.

Sincerely,
Cara

. . . .
Cara Waterhouse
Human Resources Officer
Westward University

Date: December 11
[Dr. Farsa's email to Alejandro]

Subject: Contract Termination
From: Farsa@westward.edu
To: Alejandro@westward.edu

Alejandro,

I know the first semester can be difficult. Your time thus far at Westward has shown promise but it has been marred by difficulties both personal and professional. I do not wish to add to your difficulties but after much thought and reflection I am afraid that I can no longer have you work on the USAR Latinos project. I know how hard it is to find Latinx mentors in academia, that's why I tried very hard to be a mentor to you but I cannot work with someone who does not believe in the work.

I was willing to work with your ongoing, undiagnosed, health issues but the fact is that your work was inconsistent. Additionally, I had a frankly appalling conversation with Westward's Human Resources department and IRB Board about claims that I endangered my participants and even harmed one of my most illustrious former students, José. The combined poor performance plus the fact you without so much as having spoken with me, made damaging claims about the safety of my work and my authenticity as a researcher, scholar, and person leaves me no choice but to terminate your work contract. As I'm sure you know from having read the student/employee contract you signed, grad student work assignments are on a semester-to-semester basis. They are contingent on funding, performance and at the research supervisor's executive discretion. I will be exercising my right as the research supervisor by not renewing your contract. You will receive a check for the last weeks of the semester, even though you will not be working on the project. Consider this my way of taking your economic situation into account as you find a new way to secure your future here at Westward.

With regards to your grade in my methods class, rest assured that I hold myself to the highest ethical standards and that I will grade your final paper objectively. Moreover, I have also spoken to the Dean and removed my petition requesting to be your academic advisor. You are welcome to choose other qualified faculty members in our program for that role.

This unfortunate situation has taught me a valuable lesson moving forward. I am often driven by my passion to help the next generation of Latinx scholars but perhaps now I will learn to also be guided by that person's acumen.

—Dr. Farsa

. . . .

Rebeca Farsa
Professor
Department of Critical Education
Westward University
Fiat Distinguished Scholar

Date: December 12
[Alejandro's text message to his mom]

●●●○○ Crique LTE   5:09 PM   75% ■■▷

❮ Messages   **Mamá**   Details

> Mamá, the university didn't believe me about Farsa. They said José's documents were all part of a play he was writing or something. I don't believe them though! Why did they do an internal investigation instead of going to the police? They didn't even let me talk to him to confirm he's okay. They just said all is fine, the matter is closed and that I should keep working.

Ay mi'jo. I'm sorry. That does not surprise me to be honest. Places like universities are built by people like us, not built for us. Are you okay though?

> No, mamá, I'm not. I just got an email from Farsa. She fired me! She accused me of faking illness, being a bad worker, and attempting to ruin her reputation. How could this happen?!

  iMessage

< Messages   **Mamá**   Details

Esa mujer!!! Are you safe?

I am, but should I still go to the police? This isn't right.

We all believe you corazón but I don't know if that's a good idea. I do not think the police will do anything. It sounds like the university is protecting her. Protegete tu mismo! Sabes que, let me see if I can buy you a ticket to come home. I don't want you there alone.

I don't want to go home a failure. I don't know what to do… is it over for me? I can't afford to be here without this assistantship. I should have just kept quiet and wore the damn headsets. Maybe that's the price I needed to pay for this opportunity.

No eres un fracaso, me entiendes! You stood up for what is right. I'm proud of you! Together, we'll figure something out. No more text. Ándale, háblame I want to hear your voice.

📷 iMessage   🎤

NOTE

1. The digital communication narrative is inspired in large part by the 2018 motion picture *Searching* directed by Aneesh Chaganty.

Section Eight

Guiding Questions

1. The issue of manipulation and gaslighting is gravely important. Why do they play a role in the behaviors of Becky(s)? Have you experienced these behaviors before? How does it impact you? How is engaging with these behaviors not healthy for people of color? How can you recognize it is happening to you?
2. In "Facing the Becky Within" Esperanza encounters a unique kind of Becky. Why is this encounter unique? How does it relate to manipulation and gaslighting? How do these behaviors impact Esperanza at the end? How is this story a prophetic tale for real life?
3. Another aspect of that story is how people of color might adopt whiteness in ways that, in the end, make us no less than Becky(s). Discuss the ways in which people of color, particularly women of color, adopt whiteness. Why is it different when people of color adopt whiteness? How is it the same?
4. In "When Mediocrity Fails to Shine" Becky is hell bent to join Sankofa. Describe the entitlement she feels to participate at AfroDiasporic University. Essentially, why does she feel she has a right to a space not designated for her? Describe the relationship she has with Dr. Washington. How does Becky's behavior ultimately negatively impact Dr. Washington? Do you see similar behaviors in your own environment? Describe.
5. How does this story relate to issues of manipulation and gaslighting? What are some aspects from the story to prove this? How have Becky(s) attempted to or have manipulated and gaslighted you or people around you? What impact does that have on you and others? Why are these manipulations and gaslighting strategies so detrimental to the hopes of racial justice? How are they expressions of whiteness?

6. In "Who is Dr. Farsa?" why is Alejandro so fearful? The story reveals much about how academia operates; how has a similar situation played out in your academic institution? Are there Becky(s) around you that lay claim to the cultures, languages, and identities of others? Are there Becky(s) who claim they are the experts for a particular racial group not of their own? How can this be problematic? In what ways can it be helpful? What must a white scholar do in order to ensure that whiteness, cultural appropriation, and/or cultural manipulation does not occur in their research? How do manipulations and gaslighting take place in this story? What are the impacts of such behaviors on communities of color?

7. If you are a white woman studying people of color, in what ways do you ensure that your work amplifies the voices of people of color and not of your own? How can you ensure that whiteness is not operating? What will you do to make sure that you are forever faithful to the discomforting work of racial justice? What makes you discomforted and why? What makes you comfortable about race and how can maintaining that comfort be problematic?

Conclusion

In some offbeat kind of way, it is almost mind-blowing how a simple term like Becky can have such an impact on our community. Whether in academia or popular society, the characterization of the Becky has taken us by storm. Though her mischief has been felt for years, the academic exploration of her characterization and how her whiteness impacts people of color have not been so readily articulated. Truth be told, by merely writing this book, some folks, contributing authors, and, admittedly, myself, are fearful of retaliation. That is, they were fearful to speak out about their experiences with white women because historically, doing so was never safe for people of color, particularly for women of color. Therefore, their fear is warranted. Their fear is real. This is a huge fact to be dealt with, one which we, as a society, cannot ignore. For if one feels fear to merely tell the truth, then what kind of environment are we living in and, for that matter, what are we willing to concede to in order to maintain an illusion of everything being copacetic? Who are we being copacetic for if some people are forced to live under a pretense of fear?

These are quandaries that bellow at the core of our human existence. I, for one, do not want, nor should I have to, live under the pretense of fear and nor should anyone else. Clearly, that is no life to live. In fact, I am keenly aware that in this epistemological political moment, many of us are living under this same emotional duress. It is almost as if we are living in a time that constantly triggers our posttraumatic experiences of being racialized in a racist society. As a society, we are seeing one group being banned from entering the country and another group being ripped apart from their families and locked up in concentration camps. We are witnessing Black churches burning, Black and Brown people being institutionally and systematically murdered by law enforcement, and women of color, particularly Black women, being beaten on the side of the road with not even a hint of sympathy. We are witnessing how white nationalists are taking to the streets, proudly displaying their hate as some twisted form of free speech, as if there is no world history to the impacts of such public white supremacist rhetoric. Nothing about these "modern" times are comforting to those who have marginalized, racialized identities. In fact, with triggering episodic events continuing to happen throughout our country, some folks buckle under the pressure and erroneously displace their anger for what is happening in our society onto the people most closest to them, a process that further divides us. To say that fear is present is an understatement. Plainly, one cannot feel safe in an unsafe space and anyone who asserts that such a fear is unwarranted is part of the problem.

So when we talk about safe spaces like universities, schools, or even faculty meetings, I scoff. It is not that I am being cynical, though, let's be real, anyone can be skeptical being that our history's track record ain't so bright. Instead, I am being realistic. I even wear a T-shirt that quotes James Baldwin. On the shirt it reads, "I don't believe what you say because I see what you do." This is a mantra for how people of color feel in a white supremacist society. Inasmuch as there were civil rights marches, repeals of race-based laws, and commitments to affirmative action policies, our history is nonetheless glittered by event after event of terror.

Similarly, just as education pontificates their commitment to social justice, equity, and diversity, it continues to operate in ways that force faculty and students of color to not only feel marginalized and unwelcomed but also experience discrimination, ostracism, and violence. And just because education is replete with a lot of "nice" white ladies does not mean education is absent of the same violence, terror, and oppression oftentimes found in a larger male-dominated society. In fact, since white women must cling onto whiteness more so than their white male counterparts for it is the only way to gain some semblance of power, the insidiousness of how this violence and terror manifest is particularly psychologically abusive. I cannot help but recall the movie *12 Years a Slave* to help explicate the vehemence these particular white women have for women of color, particularly Black women. In the movie, white Master Epps (played by actor Michael Fassbender) continually rapes his Black female slave, Patsey (played by actor Lupita Nyong'o). His wife, white Mistress Epps (played by actor Sarah Paulson) knows of this rape and in one scene, takes her anger out on Patsey by throwing a crystal whiskey decanter at her face. Screaming "sell her" and "You will remove that Black bitch from this property," Mistress Epps personifies the deep-rooted disgust she has not only for the power dynamics in patriarchy but also for the Black woman herself.

This hatred for women of color is repeated over and over again in media. From being mislabeled as nothing more than mistresses or home wreckers to crack mamas, women of color are constantly being characterized as someone who ruins the sanctity of white women's homes, as if women of color are going to come in, steal their white husbands, and ruin everything Becky has set up. As a university professor and a young-looking Filipina, I, too, cannot escape this vehemence. In fact, during my early years at the university, I had too many experiences with white female students where I felt the interaction eerily reminded me of a jealous girlfriend screaming at the other woman. I decided to test out my hunch by having them read a piece about Asian American female stereotypes. Espiritu (2001) describes how Asian women are either characterized by society as china dolls or dragon ladies, yet despite the characterization, they both are laden with sexual fetishes. The responses to the piece were eye-opening especially because as a teacher education course, many of the students were white women. Many divulged how they are aware of this stereotype and are disgusted in the ways *their* men utilize it. In fact, many said those exact words "our men" connoting a sense of ownership over white men; and by extension a sense of what belongs to them and their home. They talked about being angry at how "their" men engage in this sexual fetishizing of Asian American women. One divulged that her white male friend always openly shares how he wants to fuck Asian girls. According to hooks (2001), this is nothing more than eating the other. That much is known. Yet, more interesting to note, is how this white woman responds to his actions. Beyond the anger for white men who engage in this sexual fetish, there is a latent distancing toward Asian American women and by virtue of it all, disgust for them too. It is almost as if true love between whites and Asian American women cannot exist precisely because these white women believe that white men's fixations with Asian women are nothing more than exotic encounters. Additionally, by taking ownership of white men and showing disgust of their desires for Asian American women, these white women did not even realize they, too, had developed certain feelings about Asian American women themselves. The racial dynamics then become more complex when the issue of gender comes into play. For as this book explores how white women engage with people of color, there is a particular vehemence toward women of color, especially women of color who they might find a threat to what they perceive belongs to them. This is precisely the fearful context women of color must tip toe around. That is, because Becky(s) already perceives women of color as a threat, women of color live under fear, cautiously making sure they never upset her. But I digress.

So when my authors or the public comes to me saying they are fearful of retaliation, this fear is noteworthy—one that should be given full human consideration not belittled with statements like, "You have nothing to worry about." I am aware that retaliation is a common play out of the Becky behavior handbook but just like the fierce women of color before me, I will not succumb to that fear. As a racially just scholar activist, I know this is the task. I know that fear will always be present; for I am no stranger to the constant onslaught of racist and sexist hate mail, which negatively poisons the minds of administrators and folks around me. However, before I delve into what it takes to stand up to Beckys, I first explore how fear can be used as a manipulative ploy.

Now, I am aware that expressions of fear can be easily employed in ways that have no merit. Take for example how white women say they fear Black men. Yancy's (2008) thorough psychoanalytic analysis of the racial interpellation between a white woman and his Black body in an elevator provides a deep guide as to how this dynamics occurs. Calling the white women's projected sense of fear toward the Black male a phantasmagoria, he claims white women "suffer from a structured blindness, a sociopsychologically reinforcing opacity that obstructs the process of 'seeing' beyond falsehoods and various modes of whitely bodily comportment that continue to reinforce and sustain white hegemony and mythos" (p. 22). Yet instead of adopting the notion that white women are simply blind, Yancy goes on to assert that "the white woman is not simply influenced by racist practices, but she is the *vehicle* through which such practices get performed and sustained" (p. 22). Suffice it to say that white women who engage in these Becky-like behaviors are nonetheless active agents in the perpetuation of white supremacy. Applied differently, Becky(s) who claims to feel intimated or fearful of women of color is then suspect. For what exactly has transpired that thus justifies her claim to fear? Oftentimes when women of color merely assert their expertise, confidently disagree, or perform professorial duties, the fragile sensibilities of white women are triggered—enough for a Becky to claim she feels threatened.

In fact, I recently had two women of color seek me out for advice separately. However when listening to their stories, the two separate issues eerily became one overarching narrative: that to be confident, an expert, or even an equal is too much for white women to withstand. One Latina shared with me that during a regular office meeting, she respectfully disagreed with one of her young white women colleagues. Having finished the meeting, the Latina went off and continued to do work as usual. Later in the week, she received an email from her director stating that she needs to learn to be less aggressive. The Latina was dumbfounded, wondering how was she too aggressive in the first place. Turns out, after the meeting, the young white woman went to her older white woman director and cried to her about feeling attacked and intimidated by this particular Latina. Of course, both white women will not admit that they relied on an unsaid pretext of Latina stereotypes as feisty, angry, and aggressive. Instead of telling the young white woman to professionally discuss this matter directly with the Latina or even offering to mediate a discussion between both parties, the older white woman director took the side of the young white woman and without even discussing it with the Latina herself, went on to reprimand the Latina for her "alleged" behaviors.

Case two. Another Latina friend of mine, a professor, served on a master's thesis committee with two other white women professors. The student was Latina herself and used Critical Race Theory (CRT) to understand the experiences of Latinas in education. As such, the student deliberately employed theories of race to explicate her findings. During the oral defense, the chair, a white woman, commented on how the student should remove her analysis of race. My friend, as a researcher on Latinas in education and a CRT scholar, disagreed, claiming that to remove the analysis of race would render the findings useless. The student passed and my friend went on to do business as usual. Later that week, she received an email from the department chair, a white male professor, stating that she needed to behave more professionally. Shocked at this email, my colleague requested an immediate meeting with the chair. At the meeting, the chair revealed that the white woman professor came in crying about how she believed my friend treated her. Claiming that my friend acted unprofessionally and hinting at her being a racist, the white woman demanded something must be done to rectify this situation. After listening to this story, I could not help but think that the one who needs to act more professionally was the white woman herself. In fact, I joked, she was the one who was crying and tattle telling instead of having a professional conversation with my friend. Despite them being separate cases, the two stories are one in the same in that they reveal how white women can manipulate expressions of fear in ways that strategically position them above women of color. Clearly, they had no valid basis for their feelings of fear and entitlement. That is, their feelings are real but not warranted. Simply put, their fears stemmed from the fact that women of color shared equal power to express either their expertise or disagreement. And, that in and of itself, was too much for these white women. In fact, this is why so many white teachers say they love and have no problem with their K–12 students of color. They love them because they still have power over them just like Miss Ann had power over her slaves. That is why I always ask, will they have that same love when those same kids of color become their bosses of color? This dynamic becomes too overbearing for them because the power dynamics change. And this is a dangerous move because as they do this, unquestioned are their own motives, behaviors, and subscription to racial stereotypes. Instead, it forever positions the woman of color as the problem because the tenor of the world is based upon how copacetic white women feel.

Therefore, fear is complex depending on the social identities of the person who is expressing it interpellated by the social identities of the person who is causing it. Is it tangible or is it just sentimental? More often than not, for folks of color it is tangible, related to history whereas for white women, it is not. And this is where the Becky is so mind-blowing. That she can lay claim to a history or even a reality that is not of her own is a sad reality of how whiteness and gender operate. She can say she is fit to teach urban students of color when she has never had any substantial interactions with people of color. *Becky, please.* She can say she is an authority of position she never had any experience in truly undertaking. *Becky, please.* She can claim she is fearful when no immediate, direct or indirect, threat has ever been made. *Becky, please.*

Instead of allowing Becky(s) to engage in these behaviors unchecked it is high time we, as a society, put her on notice. As I mentioned above, I never became a racially just scholar activist to cower at the entitled behaviors of Becky(s). There have been too many folks, and in particular, women of color, before me who have struggled to get where we are now. They have made it possible for many others and me. As such, I refuse to dishonor their struggle by kowtowing to the demands of folks who are literally engaging in the behaviors that make our society so inhumane and unjust. Do not get me wrong. I also do not condone what I call vigilante social justice; for as a scholar, I think our society goes nowhere when we engage in shaming tactics that simply call for the unemployment of an individual racist person. Indeed, as a racially just educator, I adhere to a higher quality of life that is not dependent on tiny pyrrhic victories of so and so getting fired for being racist. Though I see the merit in those endeavors, it is not the ultimate goal of racial justice. If racial justice is about a larger systemic dismantling of white supremacy, the focus must be on the war not the tiny battles. Furthermore, as a scholar, I refuse to get caught up in mob mentality so often found in vigilante social justice. Instead, I am committed to sustaining the project of intellectual direction. For if I am to remain true as a teacher, then my goal is to educate society about racial justice beyond the momentary glory of a small victory. Meaning, in believing education can truly be transformative where I must be vigilant is in my teaching, even among the most racist of students. For in my commitment to racially just education, the hope is that education will transform them for the better.

There is a reason why the ivory tower is not called the ebony and ivory tower. The reputation stems directly from how they engage in this etiolated business. If I am to seek sustained change from the academy or in society, then I must remain steadfast in how I approach racism. Some call my scholarship brave. Others think my courage is straight *loca.* Regardless to how my scholarship or I am characterized, one fact remains, I am still here, just like the many other survivors of Becky behaviors. I, along with others, survive so that we continue to speak truth to power forever committing to a more racially humanizing world. And that is something no Becky can silence.

REFERENCES

Espiritu, Y. (2001). "Ideological Racism and Cultural Resistance: Constructing Our Own Image" in M. Andersen & P. Collins (Eds). *Race, Class, and Gender: An Anthology*. Belmont, CA: Wadsworth Thomson Learning. 191–200.

hooks, b. (2001). "Eating the Other: Desire and Resistance" M. Durham & D. Kellner (Eds). *Media and Cultural Studies: KeyWorks*. Malden, MA: Blackwell Publishing. 366–80.

Yancy, G. (2008). *Black Bodies, White Gazes: The Continuing Significance of Race*. Lanham, MD: Rowman & Littlefield.

Index

About the Contributors

Dr. **Kakali Bhattacharya** is a multiple award-winning professor at University of Florida. Housed in Research, Evaluation, and Measurement, she serves as a qualitative methodologist for the College of Education. For the last fifteen years, Dr. Bhattacharya has been exploring qualitative research through critical, de/colonial, creative, and contemplative perspectives. Grounded in the social foundation of higher education. Dr. Bhattacharya has explored the intersected nature of various structures of oppression from transnational and postcolonial feminist perspectives. She is the 2018 winner of AERA's *Mid-Career Scholar of Color Award* and the 2018 winner of AERA's *Mentoring Award* from Division G: Social Context of Education. Her co-authored text with Kent Gillen, *Power, Race, and Higher Education: A Cross-Cultural Parallel Narrative* has won a 2017 *Outstanding Publication Award* from AERA (SIG 168) and a *2018 Outstanding Book Award* from International Congress of Qualitative Research. In 2018, she was recognized as one of the top 25 women in higher education by Diverse magazine for her significant contribution to social justice work and efforts to de/colonize qualitative research. Additionally, she was one of the six distinguished scholars invited by the Association of Studies in Higher Education as a featured speaker for their 2018 *Inaugural Woke Methodology Series*. She routinely offers workshops, keynote speeches nationally and internationally. In addition to guest editing for leading journals in her field, she is the sole editor of Routledge Book Series entitled Futures of Data Analysis in Qualitative Research.

Dr. **Darryl Brice** was born and raised in Baltimore, Maryland. He attended Frostburg State University located in Frostburg, Maryland, where he received his BS in Political Science and Justice Studies. He received his MA and PhD in Sociology from Loyola University Chicago. Dr. Brice is currently an

Instructor of Sociology and Diversity and Globalism Studies at Highline College where he has taught since 2003. While teaching at Highline College he was awarded tenure in 2007. The next year, in 2008, Highline College recognized him as Faculty Member of the Year. In 2009 he was the recipient of the NISOD (National Institute for Staff and Development) Excellence Award. In addition, Darryl has appeared in Who's Who Among America's Teachers. More importantly, he is the father of two amazing children, Nia and Michael.

Derrick R. Brooms, PhD, is faculty in sociology and Africana Studies at the University of Cincinnati and serves as a youth worker. His research and activism focus on educational equity, race and racism, diversity and inequality, and identity. He is author of *Being Black, Being Male on Campus: Understanding and Confronting Black Male Collegiate Experiences* (SUNY, 2017), co-editor of *Living Racism: Through the Barrel of the Book* (Lexington Press, 2018), and co-author of *Empowering Men of Color on Campus: Building Student Community in Higher Education* (Rutgers, 2018).

Dr. **Nolan Cabrera** is a nationally-recognized expert in the areas of racism/ anti-racism on college campuses, Whiteness, and ethnic studies. He is currently an associate professor in the Center for the Study of Higher Education at the University of Arizona, and was the only academic featured in the MTV documentary *White People*. His new book, *White Guys on Campus,* is a deep exploration of White male racism, and occasional anti-racism, on college campuses – a text Jeff Chang (author of *We Gon' Be* Alright) described as "A timely, provocative, even hopeful book." Additionally, Dr. Cabrera was an expert witness in the Tucson Unified Mexican American Studies case (*Arce v. Douglas*), which is the highest-profile ethnic studies case in the country's history. He has given hundreds of lectures, keynote addresses, and trainings throughout the country on challenging racism/Whiteness, working through unconscious bias, creating inclusive college campuses, and the expansion of ethnic studies programs. Dr. Cabrera is an award-winning scholar whose numerous publications have appeared in some of the most prestigious journals in the fields of education and racial studies. He completed his graduate work at UCLA in Higher Education & Organizational Change and Dr. Cabrera earned his BA from Stanford University in Comparative Studies in Race and Ethnicity (Education focus). He is a former Director of a Boys & Girls Club in the San Francisco Bay Area, and is originally from McMinnville, Oregon.

shelby "xhey" dawkins-law evans-el is an Equity and Justice Scholar in the Higher Education Management program at the University of Pittsburgh. They are a graduate of the BA in Psychology and MA in Education: Culture,

Curriculum and Change programs at UNC Chapel Hill. They hold graduate certificates in Nonprofit Leadership and Qualitative Methodology from UNC-CH and are enrolled in the Gender, Women's, and Sexuality Studies certificate Pitt. Their research is grounded in Black feminist praxis, methodologies and epistemologies (Dillard, 2006; Evans-Winters, 2019; Hill Collins, 1990). They leverage qualitative inquiry, art and grant writing to reimagine and humanize higher education for multiply minoritized graduate students (MMGS). They are currently Co-Principal Investigator of 2 projects that together distribute resources and provide academic and wellness programs to build community for MMGS and students with hidden disabilities. Their work responds to a call for trickle-up high impact practices (TUHIPs) that recognize [whiteness] as a container by framing student leadership as an innovation space to brainstorm ways to shift institutional climate to be more loving toward the Othered among us (Stewart & Nicolazzo, 2018).

Dr. **Kelly E. Demers** is an associate professor in the Education Department at Saint Anselm College in Manchester, New Hampshire, where she teaches courses on multicultural perspectives, ESOL instruction, and arts integration. Her interests include the exploration of White teachers' beliefs and attitudes regarding students of color and the intersection of race and language. All of this research is conducted through a theoretical lens rooted in critical multicultural education, critical theory, critical pedagogy, and post-humanism. She received her doctorate in Curriculum and Instruction from Boston College, a Master of Education from Lesley University, and a Bachelor of Music from New England Conservatory. For seven years she was a public-school teacher in Somerville, Massachusetts.

Scott D. Farver, PhD, is currently a Clinical Assistant Professor at Michigan State University in the Department of Curriculum, Instruction, and Teacher Education. He teaches courses for future teachers that explore the relationships between power, opportunity, and oppression within social institutions. Dr. Farver uses critical lenses in his research to examine the ways whiteness is embodied within teachers and teaching, as well as how we might disrupt this whiteness. Dr. Farver is a former US Peace Corps volunteer and was a fifth grade teacher at a public high school near the Navajo Nation. He earned his PhD from Michigan State University.

Wyletta Gamble-Lomax, PhD, is currently assistant professor of Elementary Education at Coppin State University in the Department of Teaching and Learning. Dr. Gamble-Lomax received both a Bachelor of Science degree in Interdisciplinary Studies and a Master of Science degree in Elementary

Education from Old Dominion University; and a Doctor of Philosophy in Curriculum and Instruction with a focus in Minority and Urban Education from University of Maryland. Dr. Gamble-Lomax interests include Black feminism, culturally responsive pedagogy, mentoring, and family and community engagement. Dr. Gamble-Lomax desires to continue working with various stakeholders in education to provide equitable learning opportunities for our diverse student population.

Rebecca George joined Webster University as an Adjunct Counseling Faculty for the Columbia Metropolitan Campus in 2007. She became a Core Full time Faculty in 2015. Rebecca earned a Master of Science Degree in Rehabilitation Counseling from the SC State University in 2000 and earned her PhD in Counselor Education from the University of South Carolina in 2007. Rebecca is a Nationally Certified Counselor, a Licensed Professional Counselor Supervisor, as well as an Approved Clinical Supervisor Counselor. She has also worked as the Director of Family Life Intervention Program at Carolina Children's Home and taught Special Education in Columbia, South Carolina.

Melva R. Grant, PhD, (mgrant@odu.edu) is an associate professor of Mathematics Education in the Department of Teaching and Learning at Old Dominion University. Her post-tenure research is emergent for broadening participation in multiple spaces including STEM and the academy for inclusive social justice. She uses critical theoretical lenses that are at the intersection of Black feminism, epistemology, and identity. She intentionally and strategically allows this emerging scholarship to permeate every aspect of her work, including teaching and service.

Autumn Griffin is a PhD candidcate in Teaching and Learning, Policy and Leadership at the University of Maryland—College Park. Her research interests center on issues of multiple and digital literacies as they pertain to Black students. In particular, Autumn employs Black feminist and critical race theories to explore the literacies of Black girls both in and out of classrooms and hopes to use her research to influence policy related to literacy, race, and gender. Autumn hopes to amplify the voices of Black girls through her scholarship. Before returning to graduate school, Autumn was a teacher and teacher trainer. She has since served in multiple roles in education.

Kevin Lawrence Henry Jr., PhD, is a native of New Orleans, Louisiana, and a graduate of the University of Wisconsin-Madison (PhD) and Tulane University (BA). He is an assistant professor of Educational Policy Studies and Practice in the College of Education at the University of Arizona. His interdisciplinary scholarship and teaching are concerned with understanding how power and dominance shape and structure educational policies, practices, and reforms, as well as how those in education, often marginalized by race, gender, class, and/or sexuality resist and reconstitute educational fields to be more equitable, freeing, and humanizing. More concretely, his research focuses on the libidinal and political economies of education, racial capitalism and neoliberalism, charter schools and school choice policy, social stratification, and culturally relevant and restorative practices in education; it is informed by critical race theory, feminist theories, and queer of color critique.

Leta Hooper, EdD, is the assistant professor in the School of Education at Coppin State University. Dr. Hooper received a Bachelor of Arts degree in Elementary Education from Tuskegee University; a Master of Science Degree in Special Education with a concentration in Early Childhood from Johns Hopkins University; and a Doctor of Education Degree in Teacher Education and School Improvement from the University of Massachusetts Amherst. Dr. Hooper's research interests are teacher identity and development, biographical research on Black teachers, as well as Black feminism and critical pedagogy in education.

Justin P. Jiménez is a PhD Candidate in Education and Feminist Studies at the University of Minnesota, Twin Cities. His research interests concern neoliberal institutionality, white affects/emotional labor, and teacher education. Justin has served as a research and teaching fellow, working to overhaul reductive conceptions and metrics for understanding difference in teacher education. He is co-editor of a volume on queer affective literacies and is an inaugural fellow of the Research Advocacy in Critical Education (RACE) collaborative.

Korina Jocson, PhD, is an associate professor of education at the University of Massachusetts, Amherst. Central to her work are arts-informed sociocultural approaches that examine youth literacies and issues of equity among historically marginalized youth. She is the author of *Youth Poets: Empowering Literacies In and Out of Schools* and *Youth Media Matters: Participatory Cultures and Literacies in Education*, and editor of *Cultural Transformations: Youth and Pedagogies of Possibility*. Other publications include articles, chapters, essays, and poems. Currently, she serves as Editor-in-Chief of the *Equity & Excellence in Education Journal*. She received her BA in Ethnic Studies and PhD in Education at the University of California, Berkeley.

Justine Lee is a doctoral candidate in the Minority and Urban Education program within University of Maryland's Department of Teaching and Learning, Policy and Leadership. Prior to her role as a researcher, Justine was a public-school educator in New York City, where her work strengthened her commitment to issues of equity in access and outcome in education. Her research interests include exclusionary school discipline, school non-completion, and social studies and history education. Her goals as a researcher are to center the experiences of traditionally marginalized groups, to serve and advocate for these communities, and to contribute to humanizing narratives.

Luis Fernando Macías, PhD, is an assistant professor in Chicano and Latin American Studies at Fresno State University. His research focuses on the intersections of race and immigration status, particularly as it relates to immigrant youth's access to education. His work includes exploring the educational impact of parental deportations on U.S. citizen Latino children. Most recently, he has been examining the college admissions process for multi-racial DACA recipients. In addition to research, he has worked as a migrant student teacher and organized several educational summer camps for immigrant and refugee youth.

Eligio Martinez Jr. is a clinical assistant professor of Higher Education and Student Affairs at Claremont Graduate University's School of Educational Studies. He was previously a visiting faculty member at California State Polytechnic University, Pomona, and a postdoctoral scholar at the University of California, San Diego, where he served as Co-Principle Investigator for Project EXCEL, a study commissioned by the University of California Office of the President. Martinez is a P-20 scholar whose work focuses on understanding the experiences of boys and men of color across the educational pipeline. In particular, his research explores the stratification process that occurs for Chicano/Latino males beginning in middle school. His research interests include college access, community colleges, and boys and men of color. Martinez is a research affiliate for Project MALES at the University of Texas, Austin, and RISE for Boys and Men of Color through the Center for Race and Equity at the University of Southern California. Dr. Martinez is a native of Santa Ana, CA. He received his BA in History and Chicana and Chicano Studies from UCLA and his MEd and PhD in Educational Leadership and Policy Studies from the University of Washington, Seattle.

Paul Maxfield graduated from Kansas State University in 2018 with a PhD in counselor education and began teaching counseling at the University of

Florida in the Fall of 2019. In a previous academic life, he was an English literature major and avid monster-movie viewer.

Socorro Morales was raised in Fontana, CA. She earned her PhD from the University of Utah in Education, Culture, and Society. Her research agenda focuses on understanding and promoting educational equity for historically marginalized populations, specifically through the lenses of Critical Race Theory, Chicana feminisms, and Anzaldúa's Borderlands. In particular, she examines the educational experiences of Chicanx and Latinx youth, focusing on subjectivity, activism, and pedagogical practice. She is currently an assistant professor in the Department of Educational Leadership and Policy Studies at the University of Texas at San Antonio. Socorro has published both on Testimonio as a pedagogical tool with Latinx students, as well as on Chicana feminist approaches to working with and engaging Latinx elementary youth.

Geneva L. Sarcedo, not to be confused with her identical twin sister Genice M. Sarcedo-Magruder, is a PhD candidate, instructor, and academic advisor in the School of Education and Human Development at University of Colorado Denver. Her Master of Arts in educational leadership is from University of San Francisco. She earned her Bachelor of Science in human development and minor in education from University of California, Davis. She worked as an advisor for University of California, Davis and Berkeley, serving first-generation and low-income college students in the Educational Opportunity Program and Student Support Services. A first-generation college graduate from a low income background herself, her personal and professional experiences influence her research interests in student affairs, campus climate, undergraduate retention, critical race theory and whiteness in academic advising, and best and promising practices for working with first-generation and low income college students of color.

Dr. **Aubrey Scheopner Torres** is an associate professor in the Education Department at Saint Anselm College in Manchester, New Hampshire. She teaches literacy methods, children's literature, curriculum and assessment, and humanities. Her research interests include competency education, teacher retention, teacher preparation, and Catholic elementary and secondary schools. She received her doctorate in Curriculum and Instruction at Boston College and her Master's in Teaching and Bachelor's in Humanities from Seattle University. For three years she taught second grade at Our Lady of Guadalupe School in Seattle, Washington. Dr. Scheopner Torres' partner is Filipino and they have two biracial children.

Alexanderia Smith joined Webster University as the Counseling Program Coordinator for the Columbia Metropolitan Campus in 2009. She became the State Director for the Counseling Programs in South Carolina in 2013. Alexanderia earned a Master of Education Degree in Counseling from the University of Georgia in 2001 and earned her PhD in Counselor Education from the University of South Carolina in 2007. Alexanderia is a Nationally Certified Counselor, a Licensed Professional Counselor, as well as a Certified Addictions Counselor. She has also worked as the Director of Crisis Services at Sexual Trauma Services of the Midlands in Columbia, South Carolina.

Kara Mitchell Viesca, PhD, is an associate professor of Teaching, Learning and Teacher Education at the University of Nebraska-Lincoln. Her scholarship focuses on advancing equity in the policy and practice of educator development, particularly for teachers of multilingual learners. She began her career in education at Stanford University where she participated in the Stanford Teacher Education Program and became a middle school English as a Second Language, German and English Language Arts teacher. She taught in Virginia, California and China before earning her PhD at Boston College in 2010. She has been awarded over $4 million in federal funding for initiatives to support the professional learning of teachers of multilingual students and has published her research across varying academic outlets. She enjoys her family and friends, bike riding, walking her dogs, audiobooks, dance classes, sewing, do-it-yourself home improvement projects, playing the piano and violin, and simply spending time with her husband.

Erica Wallace is a PhD student in Educational Leadership and Cultural Foundations at the University of North Carolina at Greensboro and also serves as the Coordinator for Peer Mentoring & Engagement at the University of North Carolina at Chapel Hill. She earned her MEd in Counselor Education (Student Affairs emphasis) from Clemson University and her BA in Sociology from Davidson College. Rachel Kline currently works as a Resident Director at Loyola University Chicago. She earned her MS in Cultural Foundations of Education from Syracuse University with a certificate of advanced study in Women & Gender Studies, her MEd in Counselor Education (Student Affairs emphasis) from Clemson University, and her BA in Interpersonal Communication & Sociology from the University of Delaware. Their research interests include student development, social justice education, women's and gender studies, critical whiteness studies, and critical race theory.